CINCINNATI
BEER

CINCINNATI
BEER

MICHAEL D. MORGAN

AMERICAN PALATE

Published by American Palate
A Division of The History Press
Charleston, SC
www.historypress.com

Cover photo by Lindsay Meares.

First published 2019

Manufactured in the United States

ISBN 9781467140898

Library of Congress Control Number: 2018966264

This book is dedicated to one man with a questionable beer palate and to another whose taste in beer was unquestionably bad. Nevertheless, there are no two people I would rather walk into Milton's and have a drink with next Friday. To J.K. Smith and Dennis Suggs, as well as Carrie, Katie and everyone else who loved them.

Also to Bailey, the most tenacious and resilient spirit that I've ever known.

CONTENTS

Preface   9
Acknowledgements   13

River Water Ale   15
The Guy Who Was First and the Guy Who Wasn't   23
The First Great Brewery   27
Rats!   37
There Can Be Only One   39
Amour Pour Bière   51
Out of the Floodplain and Over the Rhine   53
Some Beer Bubbles Aren't Just in Your Head   58
Rise of the Beer Barons   71
Corn Juice, Rice and Other Poisons   80
Feud at Jackson Births Nashville's Biggest Brewery   95
The Second Generation Wrecks the Family Business   100
Why Somebody Had to Make a Law Against It   113
Dark Beers Make a Comeback and the Sheriff
        Gets into the Beer Business   133
Liquid Bread Lines   148
Reinventing Flavor   163
Some Beer Bubbles Aren't Just in Your Head 2.0   167
Urban Artifact Brews a 150-Year-Old Beer   190
Back to the Giant with the Axe   196

Select Bibliography   199
About the Author   205

PREFACE

I have had a front-row seat to the resurrection of Cincinnati's reputation as a beer town, and I have occasionally played a supporting role in the opus. This has created a complicated relationship between local beer history and me. In the words of the *Cincinnati Enquirer*, I have come to be known as the "top expert on Cincinnati beer history." This title has come with a lot of laughs, way too much to drink and a few scars.

My journey to "beer historian" began in 2005 when I volunteered to be part of a three-man marketing committee for the Brewery District, the friendliest, most disorganized and drunkest community organization I had ever encountered. The Brewery District's mission was to redevelop the northern half of Over-the-Rhine. Since we barely scraped together enough money to buy beer for the monthly meetings, this was an ambitious goal. The marketing committee was charged with changing the image of this troubled section of town—and to do it without any money or support from city government. If John Donaldson, Bryan Vielhauer and I felt intimidated by this seemingly impossible task, we just drank more beer until our attitudes improved. We observed that Cincinnatians repeatedly called for the wholesale demolition of the Brewery District because they only saw a dangerous, ramshackle area full of obsolete old industrial buildings. We couldn't change everything about the area's image at once, but it occurred to me that we could change at least one aspect of it almost immediately. We could use history to alter perceptions. Initially armed only with Robert J. Wimberg's 1989 book, *Cincinnati Breweries*, I began identifying which "old industrial buildings" were nineteenth-century breweries. The results of this work surprised me, and it even surprised many of the buildings' owners. Cincinnati, as it turned out, contains an unrivaled collection of nineteenth-century brewery buildings in its urban core.

Once we understood that our rotting hulks were a source of pride, an opportunity rather than an albatross, we asked ourselves how we could begin to share this information. Tours could be the answer, but the idea of tourism in northern Over-the-Rhine drew unapologetic criticism, mixed with a lot of laughter. Surely no one would pay money to tour abandoned buildings in a high-crime slum. By 2006, I had become the first executive director of the Brewery District Community Urban Redevelopment Corporation. I gambled everything that we had in the bank to organize the first Prohibition Resistance Tours in 2006. I scratched out a tour route on bar napkins at the Dunlap Café. Brewery District member John Back and I wrote tour scripts full of research, history, half-truths and some irresponsible speculation. Brewery District members volunteered their time to pull off the very first Cincinnati brewing heritage tours. These tours required a lot of refinement over the years, but the fact that they happened and that they made a little money for the nonprofit Brewery District was a victory.

Also in 2006, after a few too many pints at Arnold's Bar & Grill, bar owner and friend Ronda Breeden talked me into running a parade for the city's annual Bock Beer festival. My first parade resembled my first tours—sloppy and unprofessional—but it was successful because it saved the celebration from extinction. Afterward, I arbitrarily declared myself czar of the Bock Beer festival, gave it a consistent annual date, extended it to three days, lengthened the parade route and declared a permanent event hall. I also created a gender-neutral competition to crown an annual Sausage Queen. In the decade that I led this celebration of Over-the-Rhine and Cincinnati's brewing heritage, it grew from a few hundred attendees in 2006 to roughly thirty thousand by the time I ended my involvement in 2015.

Using my knowledge as both an attorney and a real estate agent, in 2009 I acquired a site for Christian Moerlein Brewing Company's production brewery in Over-the-Rhine, which eventually enabled the company to brew the city's most iconic beer brands in the neighborhood where they began. I also conceived of, obtained the licensing for and opened the Bier Garten at Findlay Market that year, in addition to releasing my first book, *Over-the-Rhine: When Beer Was King*. Through this unmapped journey, I succeeded in playing a role in what I set out to do in 2005: change the public's perception of Over-the-Rhine and help stop the destruction of the neighborhood. I also unintentionally became a local beer historian along the way.

For the past several years, I have had the privilege of serving as curator of Cincinnati's Brewing Heritage Trail, an ambitious, multimillion-dollar urban walking trail that will help bring the city's brewing history to life. After years of extensive research in that role, I thought that I knew most of what there was to know about the topic of local beer history, until I started writing this book in 2018. With the help of newly accessible, digitized public records and periodicals, I have been able to unearth a lot of new information and correct some widely believed misconceptions.

Beer touches on many aspects of the region's history, from the late 1700s until today. There are a lot of angles for telling Cincinnati's beer story—and far too many breweries to cover all of them. I have chosen to focus this book on the aspects that I think are most fascinating, which includes exploring how closely the brewing industry of the 2010s parallels the brewing industry of the mid-1800s. We are living in a time of unprecedented diversity in the choice of beers that we drink. Almost every neighborhood or suburban town has its own brewery, and large ones have many. This is great as a consumer, but it raises a lot of intriguing questions for those of us who sit on barstools and contemplate the big-picture questions surrounding the future of beer. Craft breweries started popping up in most major cities by the late 1980s, but they have only had a modest impact on the larger beer business. The explosive proliferation of nano-, micro- and regional craft breweries that we are witnessing in the 2000s bucks a consolidation trend in the industry that has been riding an irresistible current in the same direction for more than 150 years. Will the nature of the business change? Will Americans alter their relationship with their beer? Or will Big Beer, like a glowering giant leaning casually against the taproom wall, eventually step forward, swing its massive axe, still crusted with the dried blood of past generations, and viciously begin to slaughter our most beloved neighborhood breweries? Who knows? I don't, but history might hold some answers. At least it's worth consulting it. So, wrap your protective hand around a pint that you hold dear and let's start at the beginning.

ACKNOWLEDGEMENTS

T hanks to Amy Triplett Morgan for supporting and encouraging this book, as well as Jessica and Alex Jones, Julianna Carpenter, Bob Scott, Dan Phenicie, Drew Money, Kevin Feldman and other friends who contributed time, advice or otherwise helped push this over the finish line. Thanks to all the brewers who took the time to meet with me and tell their stories, including Kenny McNutt and Brady Duncan of Mad Tree, Bret Kollmann Baker and Scotty Hunter from Urban Artifact, Randy Schiltz of Wooden Cask Brewing, Dan Listermann and Jared Lewinski of Listermann Brewing and Mike Cromer of Barrel House fame. The images in this book would not have been possible without the help of Katrina Marshall, Christopher Smith and other stellar members of the staff at the Cincinnati and Hamilton County Public Library. Much of the research would not have been possible without the work of Jim Dempsey and other members of the Hamilton County Genealogical Society digitizing public records and making many accessible for the first time. The work, patience and support of John Rodrigue of The History Press has been essential. Also, thanks to Greg Hardman and the Christian Moerlein Brewing Company for info and consent to use images of our brewing past and present, as well as artists Brian Methe and Jim Effler. In addition, everyone interested in Greater Cincinnati's beer history, and particularly me, owe a debt to the research and work of Robert J. Wimberg and Timothy J. Holian, as well as people like "Beer Dave" Gausepohl, all of whom helped keep the torch of local beer history alive through some dark times.

RIVER WATER ALE

According to authors Henry and Kate Ford in their 1881 *History of Cincinnati, Ohio, with Illustrations and Biographical Sketches*: "In August [1811] the first in the long and costly list of Cincinnati breweries was established on the river bank, at the foot of Race street, by Mr. David Embree." Aside from correcting his first name—it was Davis—this became one of the most often repeated and well-accepted facts of Cincinnati brewing history for the next 130 years despite being absolutely, positively untrue. Davis Embree was a pioneer Cincinnati brewer, but he wasn't the first.

Rebecca Kennedy first stepped off her family's flatboat and onto the ground of the future city of Cincinnati on a frigid day in February 1789. She was a young girl at the time, a member of one of the first two families with children to disembark at this frontier settlement. It was called Losantaville. It was rugged, small and brutal, containing just three crude, dirt-floor cabins.

Life was hard. Hearing that the Kennedys had arrived with ample food stocks, a contingent of starving federal soldiers traveled upriver from their fort at North Bend, Ohio, and asked to buy some of Mr. Kennedy's flour. He refused to sell. When the armed soldiers said that they would take what they needed by force if Kennedy wouldn't negotiate, he pulled his rifle off the wall and backed them away in a standoff.

This doomed little colony might have vanished from the map entirely if the federal government hadn't began building Fort Washington the same year that the Kennedy family landed in town. To overcome the scarcity of food,

Davis Embree's Cincinnati Brewery was located where the drawing of a building appears on this map, between Elm and Race Streets, on the waterfront. *From the collection of the Public Library of Cincinnati and Hamilton County.*

the military hired "a noted hunter and Indian fighter" to supply the seventy men building the fort with meat. Fortified with an ample supply of buffalo, deer and bear felled in Kentucky, construction moved forward. Arthur St. Clair, governor of the Northwest Territory, visited the settlement and fort construction site in January 1790. During his visit, he officially changed the name of the place to Cincinnati. Several months later, more than 1,100 troops amassed in Fort Washington, and it quickly became the largest and most strategically important military base in the western territories. Pioneers did not always get along harmoniously with the soldiers, but the troops provided security from attacks. The troops' penchant for gambling and drink also provided business opportunities.

Joel Williams was one of the original founders of Cincinnati, one of the few people who arrived before Rebecca Kennedy's family. Like a lot of the city's first residents, Williams's ambition led him into a variety of entrepreneurial endeavors. This included owning one of the village's first taverns. Williams also probably opened the city's first brewery. Early records of Cincinnati are few and spotty, partly because the inhabitants were too busy trying to survive to jot down fun facts about who opened the first whatever and partly because some of the records that were kept were destroyed when Cincinnatians burned down their courthouse in a March 1884 riot. Fortunately, enough remains to at least permit responsible speculation.

In December 1798, Daniel Symmes bought two lots of land across the street from his home. Daniel's neighbor, William Henry Harrison, signed the deed as a witness. Exactly what happened next in the annals of Cincinnati brewing history gets fuzzy. Daniel Symmes had an impressive career. A graduate of Princeton College and an attorney by primary profession, he served a term on the Ohio Supreme Court (1805–8) and was one of Cincinnati's first mayors (1808–9.) He was also one of the founders of Ohio's first bank in 1803. Symmes's official biographies neglect to mention that he was also one of the first people in the state to have his property auctioned by the court to pay off creditors.

On March 4, 1817, the shared property of Daniel Symmes and tavern owner Joel Williams was sold at auction to satisfy a bad debt. The sale included the lots that Daniel Symmes had purchased in 1798, "[t]ogether with all the apparatus and utensils therein contained belonging to the Brewery" that sat on one of the parcels at the corner of Congress and Pike Streets.

This does nothing to clarify when Symmes and Williams built the brewery. Cincinnati's first city directory wasn't published until 1819. It contains a brief summary of the city's history, which notes that in 1805 the city only had 960 residents, most of the streets "were yet in a state of nature…impassable on account of the mud, stumps and roots," but that the village did boast two commercial breweries. Records also indicate that neither brewery existed in 1795. They are not named, and the fact that they were operating in 1805 does not mean that they weren't already in business for several years before. The first bank was founded in 1803. Daniel Symmes and Joel Williams borrowed money from it, and they may have pledged a brewery as collateral—speculation that is supported by the fact that they lost their brewery to satisfy a substantial debt. The Symmes & Williams brewery could have opened as early at 1798, but sometime between 1803 and 1805 seems more likely.

It is possible that James Dover opened the first brewery. This speculation is based on an 1806 advertisement that Dover published to let the public know that he was in the business of buying hops, barley and honey for his combination brewery and bakery on the corner of Sycamore and Lower Market Street. Clearly, Dover was making beer commercially for a while—or at least trying to—but it is unclear when he started or when he stopped. Dover didn't own the property at this location. His call for hops, barley and honey provides some indication of the kind of beer he was brewing. It was probably strong English ale. The honey would have added fermentable sugars, increasing the alcohol content. It may also have helped smooth out the flavor of a crude, harsh brew. Nobody understood what yeast was at the time. It was still the "magic" part of brewing, but the combination of a brewery and bakery suggests that he was probably using similar processes and the same yeast strain for baking bread and making beer. If Dover was running a brewery in 1806, it was out of business by 1813. It's possible that he was the city's first brewer, but if so, he didn't leave much of a legacy. The Symmes & Williams venture was a different story.

When Symmes and Williams's brewery was sold to satisfy creditors in 1817, it was purchased at auction by Joseph and Samuel Perry. The Perry brothers were businessmen, not brewers, so they hired an Irish immigrant named Patrick O'Reilly to run the plant. Between the Emerald Isle and Cincinnati, O'Reilly lived in Philadelphia long enough to marry "a great beauty" named Mary Ann. He moved to Cincinnati in 1814 to establish a new homestead, and his bride followed roughly a year later. Both Mr. and Mrs. O'Reilly helped shape their chosen hometown in several ways.

The Perry brothers' Congress Brewery also operated as the Patrick Reilly brewery by 1819. (O'Reilly appears to have "Americanized" his name for a while, dropping the "O" in his youth and then reclaiming it later.) The relationship between the Perrys and O'Reilly is curious. The brothers sold the Irishman an undivided one-half interest in 1824, just a few months before they lost the property at auction on a mortgage foreclosure. In a confusing set of transactions, O'Reilly emerged as the sole owner, but the Perry brothers retained a partnership interest. Both with and without the Perrys, O'Reilly operated one of the more notable ale breweries in the city until his death at the end of 1835, investing heavily in expansion during his tenure.

While Patrick O'Reilly was making the city's oldest brewery profitable, Mary Ann O'Reilly devoted herself to satisfying the town's spiritual needs. As a devout Catholic, she was disturbed to learn that Cincinnati lacked a Catholic church or even a congregation, so she established one. Mary Ann O'Reilly pulled together the city's six Catholics, including herself (and presumably Patrick), and convened the first Catholic services held in Cincinnati.

Unfortunately, Mary Ann O'Reilly's contributions to the city have been underappreciated. When the widow O'Reilly passed away in 1875, she was eighty-five years old. She died as both the oldest living Catholic in the city as well as Cincinnati's oldest living woman. As a result of this status, the inconvenient truth that a woman organized the first Catholic congregation in the city was briefly recalled, although from there the story of her impressive accomplishments as chronicled by the *Cincinnati Enquirer* trails off into a shameful and creepy preoccupation with her physical appearance. The reporter speculated that following Mr. O'Reilly's death, while she was still "in the prime of her womanhood," "she could have married again before the grass had grown green upon her dead husband's grave." She didn't. She remained Patrick's unmarried widow, which is how she became the first woman in Cincinnati to run a brewery.

In his will, Patrick O'Reilly entrusted his wife with broad power. He made her executrix of his estate and specifically left her "entire control" to "carry on the brewing business" for the benefit of their children, until the youngest of them reached the age of majority. Patrick left it up to Mary Ann's discretion to lease the business and let someone else manage it if she thought it was prudent to do so, but she was up for the challenge. After a few years, she even changed the name to Mrs. Mary Anne Reilly Brewery. She brought sons William and Francis into the fold, although that's when the business started to falter, and in 1847, she was forced to sell the brewery to satisfy creditors. It remained open, operating briefly under the ownership of Francis Fortman, a land speculator who would play a major role in shaping the city's brewing history, although not at this location. Fortman sold the business to partners Ferdinand Mueller and Christian Henry Gogreve in the spring of 1855. Mueller and Gogreve were representative of the German immigrants who were taking over local brewing in the 1850s. ("Congress Brewery" was commonly used throughout multiple ownerships.)

Ten years into their ownership, the business collapsed—literally. As Ferdinand Mueller stood in part of the brewery talking to the foreman about the malt stored in the upper floors of the building, he was alarmed by an ominous cracking. It sounded like timbers giving way. Mueller moved quickly into an adjoining building and implored the foreman and maltster to do the same. The foreman, who lived across the street with his wife and child, had worked for Mueller for eight years. The maltster was a recent German immigrant who had only been in the country six weeks. Both men shrugged off Mueller's panic, telling him that there was no danger. These were tragic last words. The timbers snapped. Roughly six thousand bushels of barley and two floors came crashing down on top of them, killing both instantly. The cause of the collapse was unclear, but it was the oldest operating brewery in the city. It also sat in a floodplain, which may have rendered it structurally compromised over its many years and multiple owners.

Mueller and Gogreve rebuilt and continued a successful partnership until Mueller's death in 1880. His sons, Oscar and Arthur, took his place, but it is difficult to understand how the brewery wasn't already obsolete. Business flagged. An attempt to sell the brewery fell through, and the business was insolvent by 1888. Attempts were made to auction it for the benefit of creditors, but no one offered a bid. The appraisal was reduced, and it was placed on the auction block three more times with the same result. The factors that had once made the location suited for brewing were no longer relevant. Proximity to river water was important in 1800, but it was a liability by 1889. The neighborhood surrounding the brewery had, in fact, become one of the least desirable in the city. Routine flooding made it a terrible place to live or own property. Real estate and rent were cheap, which attracted many of the city's poorest residents. Known as Bucktown, it grew increasingly seedy after the Civil War and was notorious for its crime, filth and violence, as well as being home to some of the city's sleaziest and most vicious dens of vice—a claim to fame that had a lot of competition in Gilded Age Cincinnati. So, Cincinnati's oldest brewery, and probably its first, died with a whimper. It was finally sold for about 60 percent of its appraised value, and beer was never made at this location again.

The fate of Joel Williams, Cincinnati's presumptive first brewer, was equally dismal. Williams is a tragic figure—Shakespearean, really, the rabbit who loses the race to the turtle. Cincinnati's original landowners conducted a lottery to spark development. Lottery winners received one "in-lot," in the planned core of Losantiville, and one "out-lot," a farmable parcel beyond the boundaries of proposed civilization. (All of these out-lots are now part of the urban core of downtown and Over-the-Rhine.) Williams was a winner. In addition to these lots, he acquired others while land in the savage settlement was still dirt cheap. Joel Williams's name litters the earliest deed records of Hamilton County. He owned large sections of the waterfront, the central business district and Over-the-Rhine. Nicholas Longworth followed the same business model, buying prime real estate cheaply at every opportunity.

From here, however, the fates of Williams and Longworth diverged. Joel Williams kept starting ill-advised business ventures and finding ways to screw up good ideas. He obtained a contract to supply General Anthony Wayne's army, the force that won a relentless, brutal battle against southwest Ohio's Native American tribes, putting an end to the constant, bloody skirmishes and attacks between natives and pioneers. This should have been a lucrative contract, but Williams somehow went in debt to the man who transported the supplies up the Miami River in pirogues and canoes. This was just one of the occasions when Williams turned an opportunity into a liability and offered to buy his way out of it by giving away land or selling it at a reduced rate.

A similar story was told about Williams when Nicholas Longworth died. In recalling Longworth's shrewdness, Williams—mostly forgotten by then—was recalled as a dupe. Longworth—who was a vintner, speculator and lawyer—was owed a legal fee for defending a horse thief. The thief offered to pay him in barter, offering up two used copper stills. Longworth accepted, but when he tried to collect the stills, he found them in the possession of Joel Williams. Williams's relationship to the horse thief is unclear, but he wasn't willing to part with the property, explaining to Longworth that he needed the stills to build a distillery somewhere in Butler County, Ohio. Williams offered Longworth thirty-three acres of land on Western Row Road, today Central Avenue and the west side of downtown Cincinnati. Longworth accepted. Williams kept the used stills, and Longworth got another huge chunk of prime land. When Longworth died in 1863, this piece of property was worth an estimated $3 million— roughly $50 million today. It is unclear whether Williams ever opened a distillery in Butler County. If so, it seems to have suffered the same fate as his brewery. Longworth died a multimillionaire, one of the richest men in America. Although they once held a comparable collection of assets, Williams died broke and irrelevant. In 1850, the *Cincinnati Enquirer* briefly recalled Williams as a forgotten pioneer with "scarcely a common slate to mark the resting place of his mortal remains." Davis Embree would erroneously be remembered as Cincinnati's first brewer, and Williams, who probably deserves that title, wouldn't be remembered at all.

The brewery that Symmes and Williams founded at the corner of Congress and Pike Street bore witness to an astounding amount of social change. Originally, it was surrounded by a sparse collection of log cabins dotted along a few narrow, muddy, rutted streets, one of which required a detour until the Kennedy family moved their house out of the middle of it. To the north lay a dense, almost impenetrable forest. In the intervening years, the center of government and commerce and the homes of the wealthiest citizens were all erected within a few blocks west. The courthouse and city buildings moved north, deep into the former Shawnee hunting grounds. Business boomed, aided by the advent of the steamboat, the War of 1812 and the birth of modern technology. By the time the first shots were fired in the American Civil War, the Congress Brewery sat within the second-largest manufacturing center in the nation. Cincinnati's first children had no fear that their offspring would lack playmates, as the population began to roughly double every decade, eventually growing to be the fifth-largest city in America. Steamboats had to jockey for dock space on the waterfront. Stevedores filled the multistory tenements that grew up shoulder to shoulder. Floods came and went, leaving either a little or a lot of destruction in their wake each time. Two or three taverns turned into roughly two thousand saloons.

Along the way, beer changed almost as much as the city around it. Francis Fortman, brief owner of the Congress Brewery, helped spearhead a revolution in local brewing techniques. The original population of Jersey-born Englishmen was joined by large waves of Irish and German immigrants in the mid-1800s. As this occurred, there was a sea change in American culture. Tastes in beer changed, and this was accompanied by tectonic shifts in how beer was made. Whether or not Cincinnati—or the broader world—got better or worse during the life span of the Congress Brewery will remain an unanswerable philosophical debate. The question of whether beer improved is much easier to answer. Yes, it did.

THE GUY WHO WAS FIRST
AND THE GUY WHO WASN'T

Regardless of who opened the first brewery in the city of Cincinnati—whether it was Joel Williams, James Dover or someone else—the first brewery in the immediate area was founded by James Smith in Newport, Kentucky. Smith was brewing in Newport by 1798 on a plot of land in the northwest corner of town, near the confluence of the Licking and Ohio Rivers. In 1803, Fort Washington was disassembled in Cincinnati and replaced by the Newport Barracks, situated a short stumbling distance between Smith's brewery and the Ohio River.

James Smith was English, and he made ales. Not much more is known. Even in the primitive days, Newport was much smaller than the settlement across the river, and recordkeeping was scant. Smith died in the spring of 1807, leaving his wife, Sarah, some real estate and "two barrels containing beer, Tubs and barrels in Brue house [*sic*], Steel mault [*sic*] mill &co." Unlike Mary Ann O'Reilly, Sarah Smith did, in fact, marry again before the grass had grown green on her dead husband's grave. She was involved in some undefined form of scandalous behavior within a month of James's death and was remarried to David Downard fewer than ninety days after the funeral. Downard solicited barley and hops "to be delivered at the Brew House in Newport" in 1808, although it is unclear how long the brewery remained in business. By 1840, Cincinnati had grown formidable as a western city, but Newport was only home to one thousand inhabitants. It wasn't deemed worthy of inclusion in early directories, and David and Sarah Downard appear to have closed shop during their lifetimes without selling the business. He died in 1856, and she followed in 1863. Both lived to roughly the age of seventy-eight, a rare feat at the time and proof that Licking River ale wasn't toxic.

Although Davis Embree wasn't Cincinnati's first brewer, he may have been the first to export Cincinnati ale. He's also a fascinating character. Davis and his brother, Jesse, were born in Pennsylvania. They moved to Cincinnati to get into land speculation, which could be very profitable in the city's infancy. They also explored several other business ventures. In the summer of 1811, Davis bought land on the south side of Water Street, between Vine and Race. Water Street got its name honestly. The Ohio River was the southern boundary of the property. This was important to Embree's business in two ways. It provided an ample supply of water for brewing and easy boat dock access. By 1812, he was brewing English-style ale. Davis and Jesse Embree were partners in all their business ventures, but Davis oversaw the brewery. Jesse and Davis also owned a steamboat. The Embrees didn't venture far from the obvious when choosing names. The brewery was christened Cincinnati Brewery, and the steamboat was named *Cincinnati*. If the brothers owned a dog, it was probably named "Cincinnati Dog."

As anyone who bought a house between roughly 2004 and 2007 knows, real estate bubbles can bite with razor-sharp teeth. The Embree brothers

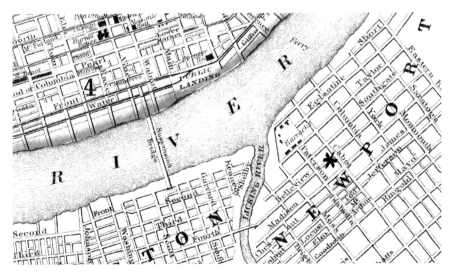

James Smith founded the region's first brewery in Newport, Kentucky, circa 1798. It was located somewhere around the intersection of Southgate and Isabella Streets on this map, southeast of the mouth of the Licking River. *From the collection of the Public Library of Cincinnati and Hamilton County.*

got a taste of this, indicating in letters back home to Pennsylvania that they found themselves upside down for a while. The brewery continued to grow, but Davis felt compelled to recruit a partner. In the summer of 1813, he sold half of the business and the real estate that it sat on to Benjamin Warner, a "Bookseller and Stationer of the City of Philadelphia." By at least 1816, Embree's Cincinnati Brewery was shipping "superior quality" porter to Nashville in both barrels and bottles, probably loading it out of the back of the brewery onto the Embree's steamboat to make the voyage.

Davis Embree sold his remaining half of the business to Benjamin Warner in 1821 and started another career. He replaced his brother as captain of the *Cincinnati*, although the ship was wrecked and lost by May 1825. River traffic was largely unregulated at the time. Greed and irresponsibility ran rampant. Ships weren't properly maintained, and even when they were, captains often enjoyed racing one another, a sport that periodically resulted in boiler explosions. When this happened, inadequate egress and a complete lack of lifeboats or floatation devices contributed to passengers and crew either burning alive or drowning within sight of the shore. As Davis Embree continued a long career on the river, he became a vocal and prominent advocate of substantive federal regulation of riverboat traffic. His work contributed to the passage of groundbreaking steamboat safety legislation in 1852. As reward for this work, President Millard Fillmore appointed Embree to the position of supervising inspector of steamboats in the district encompassing the Mississippi River. Embree held the position through the Franklin Pierce administration but fell on the wrong side of President Buchanan and was sacked in 1858. Stationed in St. Louis, Embree was described as "honest, faithful and competent" at his job, and he appears to have handled safety infractions and the inspection of steamboat accidents with noble professionalism. After his days on the rivers came to an end, Embree returned to Cincinnati for a while and then moved to Clark County, Ohio, where he and his wife, Lydia, lived for the remainder of their lives.

Embree's Cincinnati Brewery remained in business after his departure. It was purchased by a man named Samuel Longstreath in 1823, although it continued to operate under either Embree's name or Cincinnati Brewery until 1825. Between 1825 and 1829, it was called the Wood & Metcalf Brewery, and then it was named after its next owner, Dr. William Price, who periodically used the name Cincinnati Brewery as well. Price, a physician and land speculator, probably knew Davis Embree. Both were Pennsylvania Quakers from adjoining counties, probably part of the same regional Quaker

Cincinnati brewers started shipping to southern markets early in the city's history. By 1816, Davis Embree was shipping ale on the steamboat *Cincinnati*, which he owned with his brother, Jesse. *From the collection of the Public Library of Cincinnati and Hamilton County.*

congregation, and roughly the same age. Price presided over the brewery that Embree founded for several years, continuing to operate under his name and partial ownership until its closure in 1838. Although small by later standards, Embree's Cincinnati Brewery was substantial, containing a malt house, brewhouse, a mill house, a cooper shed and an office. It continued to open and expand export markets. By 1824, steamboats were carrying dozens of barrels of Cincinnati Porter downriver, delivering shipments of thirty to fifty barrels of ale to Nashville buyers on a single trip.

Other breweries popped up in Cincinnati in the 1810s, some more successful than others. William Floyd is believed to have operated a brewery on Fifth Street between 1813 and 1817. During this time, he was also leasing a 160-acre farm. Although Floyd ran his own ad seeking hops and barley, he may have also been growing his own raw ingredients. Ads seeking hops and barley suggest that the region's earliest breweries faced a chicken-and-egg dilemma. The Ohio River Valley contains rich farmland, but the climate is not ideal for growing either hops or barley, so there would have been no reason to cultivate these crops until breweries produced a demand. By 1819, a "hop gardener" was operating on Elm Street, just north of the city's first potter's field (today, north of Music Hall). The desperation for raw ingredients waned as more breweries sprang up in the 1820s and more farmers recognized the opportunity that this created. The large breweries that emerged after the Civil War also began investing in their own farms as a way of ensuring the supply and quality of their raw ingredients.

THE FIRST GREAT BREWERY

The first brewery to make Cincinnati synonymous with great beer was a happy accident. In the summer of 1831, business partners William Chorly and Cornelius Scott leased a plot of land at the southeast corner of Sycamore Street and Jail Alley (now Michael Bany Way). As the name implies, Jail Alley was adjacent to the county jail. Chorly and Scott leased the land from Hamilton County for eight years. The terms of the lease made it "renewable forever," but the Chorly & Scott Brewery didn't make it to forever. In fact, the Chorly & Scott Brewery didn't even manage to open. The work dragged on and they went into debt, couldn't pay their bills and were sued by contractors and creditors in 1833. Two years after starting the project, the brewery was described as "partly built." The court ordered the unfinished business on leased land sold at auction.

An "engine finisher" named John Walker was one of Chorly and Scott's biggest creditors. He wasn't a brewer, but buying the incomplete brewery and finishing the project seemed to be his best shot at recouping his money, so he placed the winning bid and the John Walker Brewery opened in 1834. A Scottish immigrant, Walker started brewing the ales of his homeland, and he was surprisingly good at it for an accidental brewer. In the following years, Walker expanded the "frame shanty" into a formidable business. By the time of his death, Walker's Ale had become a household name, not just in Cincinnati but throughout the southern and western states, and downriver markets looked to the Queen City as a source of the highest-quality ales.

In the summer of 1853, John Walker fell. Some sources say that he lost his footing getting out of his carriage, and others say that he was injured while repairing something at the brewery. But there is agreement that it was a fluke and a relatively minor accident. Walker was diagnosed with a fractured leg and was prescribed a few weeks of bed rest while it healed. Instead, something about either the injury or the treatment induced an attack of "constipation and ulceration of the bowels," and Walker lost his life to an undefined internal ailment. He died a successful, wealthy businessman, but he was remembered more for his amiable character, integrity, generosity and "delightful social qualities."

Although Walker and his wife, Marion, were childless, they treated nieces and nephews like their own children and some of their employees like family. Walker instructed his executors to personally operate his brewery for seven years. At the end of this period, he wanted the estate wrapped up and permanent ownership of the brewery transferred to the children of his three siblings.

Seven years later, the will created problems. As the various Walker siblings and offspring procreated—with some dying young, passing their share of the inheritance to multiple children—the number of heirs inheriting equal shares of the business ballooned to nineteen. By mid-April 1861, the Walker family had become embroiled in a civil war that had nothing to do with the shots fired at Fort Sumter. The court finally resolved the protracted dispute by ordering the property sold. The long period of executor management and estate litigation could have destroyed the Walker Brewery, but it didn't. Brothers James, Andrew, William and Archibald Walker, all nephews of the brewery's founder, purchased the business at auction, formed a four-way equal partnership and grew the business.

By the time of John Walker's death, the county jail beside Walker's brewery was obsolete. As the city had grown to become one of the largest in the nation and began to experience the infancy of modern urban crime, Hamilton County still relied on a brick building with just "fourteen rooms for prisoners, and a yard enclosed with a high brick wall" for its jail. It wasn't secure, suffered from overcrowding and was inadequate in every way. In 1858, in addition to prisoners, the "rickety old institution" with fourteen cells also housed "thirteen lunatics." Cincinnati, however, has a long, consistent history of excessive municipal handwringing. Citizens, politicians and newspaper editors pontificated over where to build the new jail. Once this was resolved, they argued about the cost and design. Then, after the new jail was completed, they wrestled over what to do with the old one for several additional years. Finally, when the last prisoners were transferred to the new facility in June 1862, the Walker brothers wasted no time making an offer to buy the adjacent property. Their offer was accepted, and a significant expansion of the J. Walker Brewing Company ensued.

Walker Brewery defied the odds at almost every opportunity. Its founder was thrust into the business by financial necessity but produced a beer so good that Walker's Ale usurped the market on English-, Scottish- and Irish-style ales. When Walker died, Cincinnati—and the rest of America—was undergoing a revolution in beer styles, technology and tastes, a wave of social and market change that would render the city's earliest breweries obsolete. Nevertheless, Walker Brewery thrived under the management of estate executors, survived a probate dispute and grew under the leadership of four brothers, who somehow escaped the sibling rivalries that often doom these arrangements. All the while, Walker stayed true to its roots and brewed nothing other than Scottish- and English-style ales and porters, beers that were rapidly falling out of favor in a city bursting at the seams with German immigrants who tossed back steins of light, amber lagers. Also, at a time when bottled beer was generally considered impractical, Walker employees hand-bottled, corked, packed and shipped roughly 2 million bottles of beer per year. The Walkers probably enjoyed some luck, but there were other reasons for the brewery's unlikely success. Water was one of the first and most important parts of the formula.

Water constitutes roughly 90 to 95 percent of beer, which is why we can be certain that the city's first breweries made terrible beer. It wasn't panned at the time. In 1815, the beer and ales produced in Cincinnati were considered "at least equal to that of the Atlantic states." That may have been true, but it would not have appeased a modern palate. Breweries either drew water directly from the Ohio River or other tributaries, from a municipal supply that piped unfiltered Ohio River water from reservoirs directly into businesses and homes or from private wells. As early as the mid-1800s, large amounts of raw sewage was being drained into the river above the municipal pumping stations. Clearly, city water was not ideal for brewing—or even for human consumption. Walker had a better source of beer's primary ingredient. The Walker Brewery had an artesian well. This benefited the business in two ways. Most obviously, and most importantly, it laid the foundation for good ales. A reporter for the *Cincinnati Gazette* who toured the brewery discovered that a drink of Walker's "cool, pure and invigorating" well water produced "a genuine surprise party to the stomach of unfortunate individuals accustomed to the wretched liquid drawn for city consumption from the channel of the muddy Ohio." By contrast, most of the city's brewers were relegated to using the "wretched liquid" that flowed from municipal water lines.

The Walker Brewery also gained a competitive edge by embracing and even inventing new technology, all while remaining loyal to the standards of integrity that allowed John Walker to build respect for his brand. Beer has four primary ingredients: water, malt, hops and yeast. These ingredients are added sequentially in the brewing process, and the J. Walker Brewing Company demonstrated both integrity and ingenuity in each step along the road from raw ingredients to nationally renowned ales. Malt starts as grain, typically barley. Even in the mid-1800s, some of Cincinnati's barley was shipped in from Canada and western states, but a lot of it was grown locally. Barley varied as a result of regional origin, the specific farm that it was grown on and other factors, although multiple sources of the crop were typically mixed together in regional grain elevators. The Walker brothers avoided buying mixed grain, insisting on selecting the best crops and buying barley by the bag. This was expensive, but it ensured quality.

The next step in the brewing process is to convert barley grain into malt. Modern breweries buy their malt in pelletized form from commercial maltsters. The maltsters use sterile conditions, expensive equipment and automation to produce a consistent product. In the 1800s, breweries— particularly the midsize to large ones—typically made their own malt, and the process involved a lot of physical labor. Barley begins its journey to becoming malt by being steeped in water. Moist, warm grain is then laid out in a thin layer on a malt room floor until it begins to germinate. As this process occurs, it is important to circulate it to ensure that the same grain doesn't remain on the top or bottom during the entire process, as this will result in temperature differences that cause the same room full of grain seeds to germinate at different rates. Today, a machine does this. In the nineteenth century, the job was done by men with rakes. Once the grain has sprouted the correct amount to produce malt, it is removed from the malt room floor. Removing it too soon or letting it germinate too long will ruin the batch, so when the Walkers made malt, their maltsters slept in a room adjacent to the malt floor, and they were responsible for raking, watching and monitoring it twenty-four hours a day until it was transferred to the kilns. There it was heated (kilned) and dried, producing malt. In most breweries, the kilning process took between fifty to sixty hours, but Walker used a patented ventilation system that cut this time in half.

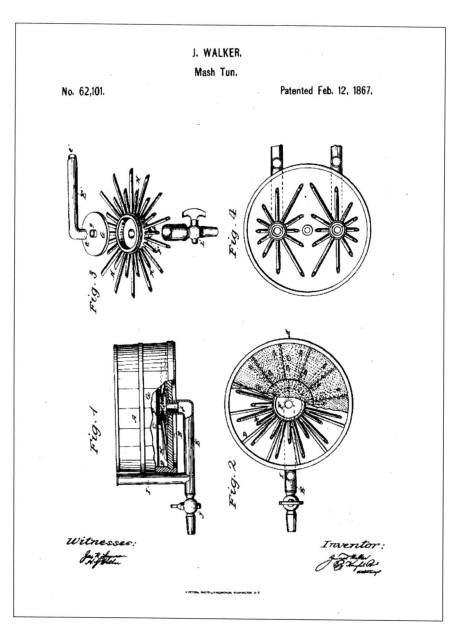

On February 12, 1867, James Walker was granted a patent for a new type of mash tun. At the time, mash tuns (a tank where water is mixed with malt to produce wort) were just wooden vats. Walker's version used copper pipes and a strainer that could be raised and lowered. This allowed the brewer to fill the tank with hot water from the bottom and to better separate solid grain particles from the liquid wort. The moving parts boiled the malt more evenly, and they could be disassembled after use to more thoroughly clean both the mechanisms and the tank. *U.S. Patent no. 62,101.*

After the malt was thoroughly dried, it was stored until used in a batch of ale. Walker's select grain was then mixed with its "pure, cool and invigorating" water in two vessels designed and patented by James Walker. The unique tanks were an improvement on traditional equipment. After malt and water were mixed to produce the sugary liquid known as "wort," perforated copper plates in Walker's patented mash tun separated the liquid from the used malt (called "spent grain"). The wort was then transferred to a brew kettle, where it was boiled with hops. Here, Walker's patented equipment allowed more even boiling.

J. Walker Brewing Company's commitment to quality and innovation extended to the hops that it imported from New York State and England. Observing that just a few decayed hop flowers could "spoil an entire brew," James Walker found a way to address the problem. He discovered that "old or damaged hops could be completely cured" by immersing the hops in water heated to one hundred degrees Fahrenheit. Although his device for soaking hops in warm water was rudimentary, it was deemed innovative enough to be granted a U.S. patent.

Yeast are living, single-celled microorganisms, and as any lobster will tell you, living things are typically averse to being dropped into boiling temperatures, so after wort is boiled with hops, it needs to be cooled before adding the yeast. In modern breweries, this occurs when the liquid passes through a hose from the brew kettle into equipment that rapidly chills it en route to the fermenting tank. In the nineteenth century, the process was a little more complicated. Bored forty feet below a cellar floor, Walker's well produced water that was both tasty and perpetually chilled. This provided an additional benefit because the brewery did not need to rely on ice to create cold water. Hot wort was moved into shallow troughs. Here the liquid was cooled using a combination of fans and copper coils that circulated cold well water under the troughs. Once cooled by this geothermal process, the wort was pumped into fermenting tanks, pitched with yeast and aged into ale. To ensure correct and even fermentation temperatures, tanks were surrounded by pipes that contained either cool or steam-heated water as a means of climate control.

Walker brewed with two 60-barrel tanks, producing roughly 120 barrels of ale at a time (approximately 3,720 gallons). A "very considerable portion" of this ale was exported to southern and southwestern states, largely in bottles. Walker's atypical success shipping bottled beer is attributable to quality, high standards and invention. Until 1890, federal tax law required beer to be barreled before it was bottled, so the brewery kegged it, bunged it and then moved it to a bottling room. Then 16 barrels of beer were lined up side by side and tilted. All were tapped simultaneously and allowed to flow from spigots while young boys scurried underneath them, filling 2 bottles at a time and quickly exchanging full bottles for empties. Next, one man corked up to 250 bottles a day, using a machine to set the cork and a mallet to drive it flush. Once again, a James Walker invention improved the product. Before the advent of pasteurization, live yeast caused natural carbonation to continue increasing after the beer had been bottled. This could drive the corks out far enough to let in air and spoil the beer. The common remedy for this problem was to place a wire over the cork and fasten it to the neck of the bottle, but there was a flaw in this method. The cork could still move and the wire simply cut into it, rendering the solution ineffective. Walker addressed this by inventing a bottle cap, or what he alternatively called a bottle "saddle," that kept the cork in place and locked air out more effectively.

Walker may also have been the first brewery in Cincinnati to produce an India pale ale. IPAs were born when the East India Company started looking for a beer that could remain fresh during the long, hot journey from England to India. George Hodgson's brewery in east London answered the call by brewing a beer with an unusually high hop content, because hops have a natural preservative effect. Hodgson, however, had a dispute with the company, and East India approached the Samuel Allsopp brewery in 1822 to ask if it could reproduce Hodgson's East India pale ale. It couldn't, not exactly. Burton-on-Trent, the town where Allsopp was located, was renowned for its beer thanks to the unique mineral content in the region's water. The mineral content in the water paired well with the high-hopped beer, and Allsopp's "India pale ale" grew in popularity beyond westerners living in British India. Attempts of rival breweries to slander the beer backfired. Allsopp's responded to claims that the crisp, bitter flavor of its IPA was attributed to strychnine with a public relations campaign featuring physicians. Not only were English beer drinkers dispossessed of the idea that IPA was poisonous, they began to believe that it was especially healthy. This helped propel and spread the popularity of IPAs and pale ales in England by the mid-1800s.

J. Walker Brewing Company was best known for its Scotch ale. However, James Walker traveled across England and Scotland in 1867 learning about new styles and brewing techniques from some of the world's best brewers, including Younger's of Edinburgh and Samuel Allsopp's of Burton-on-Trent. Visiting Allsopp's Brewery doesn't constitute proof that

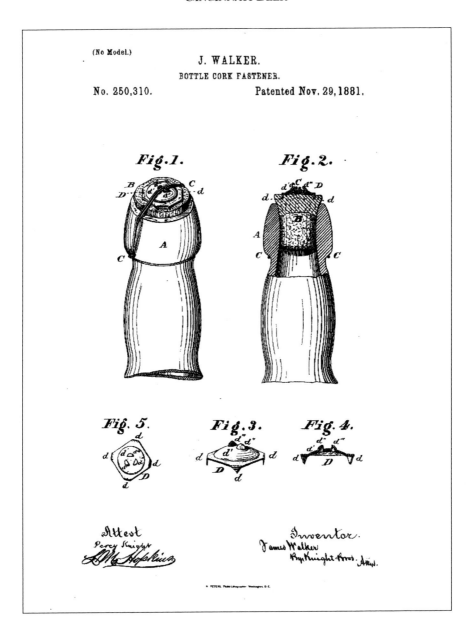

(No Model.)

J. WALKER.

BOTTLE CORK FASTENER.

No. 250,310.   Patented Nov. 29, 1881.

Fig. 1.   Fig. 2.

Fig. 5.   Fig. 3.   Fig. 4.

Attest
Percy Knight

Inventor.
James Walker
By Knight Bros. Atty.

James Walker's 1881 patented bottle cap, or "saddle," fixed the problem of wires cutting into beer bottle corks by placing a square, spurred plate between the cork and the wire. Walker preferred to use metal, and he noted that the name of the brewery or its beer could be stamped into the cap. *U.S. Patent no. 250,310.*

Walker brewed Cincinnati IPA in the 1860s, but there are several pieces of circumstantial evidence that support the idea. Walker's business model required brewing beers that would remain fresh on long journeys to hot, southern states, and the company put a great deal of thought and effort into the taste and quality of its hops. Its artesian well water was important to the brewery's continued popularity into the lager era, and it may have possessed a mineral content that produced a drinkable IPA. Walker's Brewery also cask-conditioned its stronger ales, meaning that it transferred fermented beers into wooden casks with live yeast strains. This acted as a secondary fermentation, resulting in more natural carbonation and higher alcohol content. This process was consistent at the time with producing porters, Scottish ales and IPAs.

Quality and innovation allowed J. Walker Brewing Company to prosper generations beyond the days of Davis Embree and Patrick O'Reilly, decades after the lager revolution dominated Zinzinnati's taste in bier, but nothing lasts forever. The original era of the brewery and its steadfast reliance on Scottish- and English-style ales ended in November 1878 when the Walker brothers went separate ways.

James and Andrew Walker remained stubbornly faithful to Scottish and English ales, a conviction that should be respected, but that ultimately did not prove profitable. William and Archibald Walker took a different path, trading some of their principles for prosperity. They bought their brothers' share of the business and brought in new partners, Conrad Shultz and Peter Andrew. The J. Walker Brewing Company continued to make ales, but it also began to brew German-style lagers. In 1883, the Walker brothers sold their remaining interest in the company to Shultz and Andrew, who subsequently remodeled and refitted the brewery, unceremoniously removing James Walker's patented mash tuns and other inventions and replacing everything with "new vessels of the best material and latest design."

J. Walker Brewing remained a successful enterprise for another few decades, until the heirs of Conrad Shultz and Peter Andrew started ripping it apart through litigation in 1910. The business founded by an accidental brewer never failed on its own. It had to be bludgeoned to death by greed. All its real estate, stock, equipment, wagons and everything else that constituted the oldest brewery in the city had to be auctioned off in pieces. Alms & Doepke Department store bought most of the land. Walker ales had been synonymous with quality for so long that the business's brand name was still valuable enough to spark a bidding war between the Crown

Brewing Company and the Hudepohl Brewing Company. Hudepohl won, paying $1,600 (roughly the equivalent of $43,000 today) for the rights to use the name.

William and Archibald Walker conceded the death of the ale market, packed up and left Cincinnati, but they didn't leave the beer business. These two Walker brothers moved south and cemented their place in the history of American beer.

RATS!

Fred Huber, a carpenter from Cumminsville (now the neighborhood of Northside), came into the city to raise a little hell. After drinking his way through Over-the-Rhine, Huber ferreted out a free place to sleep, stumbling into an unused and "partially wrecked" building in the rear of J. Walker Brewing Company. Erroneously believing that he had found a safe place to crash, Huber dove headlong into the black depths of a drunken slumber. He probably started to snore with aplomb, as something drew the attention of a police officer walking his beat, leading him to enter this dilapidated building to investigate. That's when a public intoxication arrest might have saved Fred Huber's life. As the officer entered, a veritable army of well-developed rats scampered away, although not before they had chewed off part of the carpenter's right thumb. Huber was taken to the hospital on the way to the drunk tank, and the *Cincinnati Enquirer* considered him lucky that "the vicious little creatures, which fairly swarm about the locality of the brewery…did not attack his eyes and face."

Rats were not an indication that the Walker Brewery was unhygienic. It had a rat problem for the same reason that all breweries struggle with rodents. Several things attracted rats to breweries in the nineteenth century. Beer was paramount. Floors were covered with drain pans and spilled beer, enough that colonies of rats lived on it. Men who worked in the cellar of the Lion Brewery even became amateur ethologists, observing that the old rats "that have roamed about the brewery for several years indulge with moderation," while the "young and verdant rats from other neighborhoods go on a tear as soon as they come into the brewery." Unlike many of its competitors, Lion didn't employ a cat because brewery management feared that a cat "might indulge in beer and make friends with the rats, which are friendly and fearless when they are half seas over" (aka drunk). Instead, the brewers at Lion used intoxication against the vermin. Sometimes the watchman claimed to find about a dozen of them so drunk that they would lay on their backs, kick up their legs and squeal with hilarity. That made them easy to kill.

Grain was a secondary attraction. Since most large breweries made their malt, they stored grain before converting it to malt and then stored dried malt before using it in a brew; they also filled tubs with spent malt grain at the end of brew days. At every stage in the process, grain attracted rodents. Barley malt is nutritious, and the combination of grain and beer allowed Cincinnati's distillery and brewery rats to grow fat and up to eighteen inches in length, dragging tails an additional foot long and as thick as a man's thumb and sporting "teeth like a saw."

Modern breweries and modern health codes reduce the threat of rats and mice in a variety of ways. Open wooden vats have been replaced with sterilized, stainless steel tanks. Pans of spilled beer don't lie around a modern brewery, and health codes require various forms of pest control. It's safe to assume that you can pass out drunk in a back corner of any of the city's breweries without having one of your appendages gnawed off by rats, but as long as beer contains malt, breweries have to be constantly vigilant against rodents. Traps work, but only after the enemy has breached the perimeter. That's why many craft breweries utilize the source of rodent control that dates to ancient Egypt: cats. They're fluffy, friendly, funny, stealthy, perennial killing machines. More importantly, rodents learn to avoid a cat's domain altogether, which makes them more effective than traps. The next time you see a cat in your local brewery, raise a pint in honor. He or she is protecting the malt. And if you're one of those people whose personal insecurities lead you to harbor some irrational hatred of cats, then may rats with razor-sharp teeth chew off your thumb while you sleep.

THERE CAN BE ONLY ONE

There is an old saying: "The pioneers take the arrows and the settlers take the land." It's a truism that summarizes the fate of a lot of visionaries, people who see the future, break down walls and only have scars as a reward for the prosperity and honor bestowed on those who meander up from behind. Charles Louis Fleischmann may be one of the people who suffered this fate in the history of Cincinnati beer. After German-style lagers devastated the ale trade and dominated both the local and national beer markets, at least a half dozen brewers were credited with brewing the first lager in Greater Cincinnati, but there can be only one first, and that man was definitely Charles Louis Fleischmann—unless it was Francis Fortman…or Peter Noll…or somebody else.

The German-language publication *Der Deutsche Pionier* posthumously recalled the life and times of Cincinnati brewer George Herancourt. As part of the reminiscence, the article noted:

> *In 1834 Charles Louis Fleischmann became the first brewer to brew lager beers in Cincinnati with his brewery being located on Main, between 9th and Court streets. In the following year, Fleischmann built a storage cellar on the corner of Main and 12th streets. However, Fleischmann didn't continue brewing lager beer as he went to Washington a couple of years later, where he got a job in the patent office. A few other people tried brewing lager in the breweries between 4th and 5th Streets on Central Avenue, but they were not successful. Then, in 1846, Fortmann and Münzenberger*

tried brewing lager in the old Fleischmann brewery on the corner of Main and 12th street which they continued for two years without any real success. Then in 1850 came Peter Noll, who brewed lager in smaller quantities in the location on the west side of Vine Street, between 13th and 14th Streets. Noll had the first success, and turned his brewery over into the hands of Bauer and Class who continued to brew lager beer in that location. This caused Herancourt to start the brewing of lager in larger quantities. As a result, in 1851, he completed the construction of a large stone beer cellar on the side of the hill opposite his brewery. This enabled Herancourt to be the first brewer to offer lager beer in the summertime. The summer brew became very popular and Herancourt, who was the first brewer to deliver beer in the summer in such a large amount, quickly became a rich man.

Some of this appears to be either true or partly true, some of it is incorrect and other aspects of the history remain fuzzy. The idea that anybody was brewing lagers in Cincinnati in 1834 is presumed inaccurate. Yeast has always been in beer. It gives it flavor and carbonation, and most importantly, by feeding on sugars in malt, it is what makes beer alcoholic. However, for the vast majority of human history, brewers did not understand what yeast was. They introduced it into a batch of beer by transferring some of the old beer to the new. Before that, they reused the same uncleaned fermenting vessels; in the Belgian tradition, brewers "spontaneously" captured a new batch of yeast that floated through the air and dropped into exposed vats. All these techniques for introducing yeast were more of an art than a science. Yeast was "the ghost in the beer." It was "magic." Lager beers are made with lager yeast, a strain of brewing yeast that requires temperatures under roughly forty-two degrees Fahrenheit to ferment. Lagers have probably been around for centuries. German brewers began "lagering" certain types of brews hundreds of years ago, meaning that they aged and finished the beers by storing them in caves and naturally chilled environments for months. This produced cold-fermented beers by the 1400s, although brewers of this era did not understand the nature of yeast or how to consistently reproduce batches of cold-fermented beers.

It was not until the 1830s that Germans started to understand that yeast are living microorganisms. Once they possessed a basic understanding of yeast, they began to understand how to manipulate, control and reproduce different strains, and the "magic" part of brewing began its journey into a science. This was the most important development in beer production since the discovery of hops around AD 1000. Harnessing the knowledge that different yeast strains either thrive or go dormant in different temperatures, brewers were able to change and develop styles, producing lighter beers, including golden lagers that were lower in alcohol content, crisper, lighter bodied and more refreshing.

By the time Pilsner Urquel brewed the first pilsner in 1842, German-style lagers were a completely different animal from whatever sludge James Dover was brewing with Ohio River water and honey in 1806. The world's oldest alcoholic beverage was reborn, sparking a revolution in brewing techniques, consumer tastes and consumer demand. According to traditionally accepted history, the first lager was not brewed in the United States until 1840, when an immigrant named John Wagner brought lager yeast from Bavaria, brewed a batch of beer in his kitchen and aged it in his basement. Wagner then shared his lager yeast strain with two friends who became the first people to produce American lager on a commercial scale at the Engel & Wolf Brewery outside Philadelphia in 1844. Some scholars question this history and believe that lager yeast may have been showing up on American shores at different locations in the mid- to late 1830s. However, nobody who has looked at the issue seriously has suggested that anyone possessed lager yeast in inland Cincinnati as early as 1834. Until there is a solid reason to rewrite broader American beer history, this date is wrong. Fleischmann, however, was up to something.

Charles Louis Fleischmann and his partner, Camille Agniel, entered a long-term lease on a piece of undeveloped land at the southwest corner of Main and Twelfth Streets in 1834. One year later, a contractor had to file a mechanic's lien against them to collect an unpaid bill. Among other things, the contractor erected on this lot "stone walls in or out of the ground." This implies that the brewery that was built at Twelfth and Main originally extended below ground, and a later description confirms that it had a cellar fourteen feet high and one hundred feet long that was used for lagering beer. This may mean that Agniel and Fleischmann were aging their beer in cool temperatures for longer periods than other brewers, and they may have been producing a more palatable beverage as a result. Naming the business Bavarian Brewery further suggests that Agniel and Fleischmann were inspired by German traditions and techniques.

Fleischmann left the brewing business and was living in Washington, D.C., by the fall of 1837, leaving Agniel with power of attorney to dispose of the property, which he did before moving out of town himself. The Bavarian Brewery passed briefly through the hands of two different owners, who also lost money running it.

Portsmouth Brewing Company's lagering cellars were built to age ale circa 1843. Due to the age, they are only one story deep and probably reflect what beer cellars looked like in Cincinnati's oldest breweries. *Author's collection.*

Francis Fortman and Conrad Munzenberger purchased the Bavarian Brewery in 1844. Fortman and Munzenberger filed a copy of their partnership agreement with the County Recorder. The agreement contains a lot of standard provisions, along with some intriguingly odd ones. Fortman, who owned a saloon and hotel on Front Street, put up most of the capital, and Munzenberger brought knowledge—valuable knowledge. Both partners agreed "not to teach said business of brewing nor any part thereof to any other person or persons," although the clause was clearly aimed at Munzenberger, an immigrant from the Alsace region of France. In the event that the partnership dissolved before its stated six-year term, yet "after said Fortman had learned said business of brewing," Fortman agreed to pay Munzenberger "the sum of Three thousand dollars as a compensation for the instructions in the business of brewing." In 1844, the same year that the Engel & Wolf allegedly brewed lager for the first time commercially in the United States, Cincinnati's breweries were still pretty crude, and some of the most successful brewers in town, like John Walker, appear to have been self-taught. That renders it curious that Fortman was willing to pay Munzenberg $3,000 for his brewing knowledge—roughly the equivalent of $100,000 today. That's valuable wisdom, and Fortman intended to take advantage of it in the Bavarian Brewery building, including the lagering cellars that had been constructed by Agniel and Fleischmann a decade earlier.

In 1850, Fortman bought the O'Reilly Brewery and owned it for five years. He was using the brewery as additional brewing space, but he wasn't satisfied with it in its present condition. Fortman petitioned the city council for the right to construct lagering cellars that would extend five feet beyond his building under the street. The council denied the request, but Fortman went ahead with construction as planned. Roughly a day or two before the stealthy underground work was completed, one of the members of the council who denied the petition happened to be in the area and caught wind of the illegal work. As a result, Fortman's stone-arched cellar under the street was filled in by the city. By the time Fortman sold the brewery to German brewers Ferdinand Mueller and Christian Gogreve several years later, it is unclear what, if anything, Fortman had done to modify the brewery, but Fortman was clearly on a quest to strap a saddle on the future of beer—a future that required specialized knowledge and beer cellars.

Some sources—most notably his own son—claim that Peter Noll brewed the first lager beer in Cincinnati. Noll has an interesting claim. Noll immigrated to the United States from Bavaria in 1839 or 1840, around the same time that John Wagner smuggled the legendary first American lager yeast strain from the same kingdom. Noll traveled with Andrew Brehm, the man who would construct most of the lagering cellars in Cincinnati. Most importantly, before moving to Cincinnati with the dream of becoming a wealthy brewer, Noll worked at the Engel & Wolf Brewery in Philadelphia. This would have provided him the opportunity to procure (steal) lager yeast from the one brewery in the nation that was known to possess it in the early 1840s. He leased a twenty-five-by-one-hundred-foot property on Vine Street in 1849, began construction, obtained a tavern license from the city council and opened the Cincinnati Brewery (reviving the named used by Davis Embree) and the Peter Noll Coffee House sometime in 1850. ("Coffee house" was the preferred euphemism for a bar at the time.)

For a brief, glorious moment, Peter Noll was probably brewing and serving lager beer on Vine Street. Then he went broke. By 1852, he was in debt and in court. He could not fulfill his five-year lease. Everything that Noll built became the property of the landowner, who entered a lease with new tenants. They slapped their own names onto the Bauer & Class Brewery, and Peter Noll moved to Louisville. Bauer & Class didn't fare much better. They made the business work for a while but started slipping underwater, and the "Brewery and Coffee House" was sold at auction to satisfy creditors in 1855. This early nanobrewery with a taproom had access to proper lagering cellars—meaning cellars that were thirty to forty feet deep—and appears to have been making lagers. The reason for the failure is unclear. It may have simply been too small to remain competitive as new breweries began popping up all over town in the mid-1850s.

Part of the problem of identifying the first person to brew lager in Cincinnati is the fundamental ignorance of brewing that is conveyed by the people who chronicled and otherwise wrote about it in the 1800s. The technical difference between lager and ale is simple. They use different yeast strains. Both types of yeast combine with sugars that come from the malt in beer to ferment, the process that makes beer alcoholic. Ale yeasts do this primarily at the top of the fermenting vessel, and they thrive at around room temperature, whereas lager yeast dance the tango at cooler temperatures and most of the fermentation occurs in the bottom of the fermenting tank. When beer was fermented in open wooden vats, fermentation was easier to watch. Both lager and ale yeast did the same thing, but lager yeast may have been stronger than the typical ale yeasts in use, possibly resulting in more visible carbonation.

This is speculative, but something caused writers and historians who didn't understand the basic science behind brewing to refer to lagers as "fermented beer," inaccurately implying that ale, by contrast, didn't ferment. They also distinguished ales from lagers by how dark or light they were in color and by whether they contained a high or low percentage of alcohol. One writer explained, inaccurately: "[A]le signifies a kind of beer distinguished chiefly by its strength and the quantity of saccharine matter remaining undecomposed." Ales that were popular at the time apparently contained roughly 6 to 8 percent alcohol by volume (although it may have been measured differently than that number is calculated today). The problem is that both light and dark malt can be used in both lagers and ales. Porters are black and pilsners are straw colored, which gives credence to this misunderstanding, but a pale ale and amber lager can look alike.

After the collapse of Peter Noll's Cincinnati Brewery, he purchased the City Brewery in Louisville. Bavarian-born Noll ran up against the city's Sunday closing laws several times. On one occasion, when he was arrested for selling "malt, fermented, spiritous, vinous, or intoxicating drinks" on the Sabbath, a *Louisville Daily Courier* reporter displayed an astounding ignorance of lager beer. He predicted that the prosecutor would have a hard time convicting Noll because lager beer is "neither malt, vinous, spirituous, or intoxicating, but a weak decoction of hops and molasses, in a cistern of water." Regardless of whether Noll's beer was tasty or terrible, this is not how he made it. All of this makes pinpointing the first lager difficult because it makes any light-colored, refreshing beer susceptible to being christened "a lager," even though what people were enjoying at the Bavarian Brewery in 1834 was almost certainly an ale brewed with a pale malt and enough hops to make it crisp rather than sweet.

In adjudicating the merits of Agniel and Fleischmann, Fortman and Munzenberger or Peter Noll's claim to the crown of first lager beer brewer in Cincinnati, pioneer brewers Pierre Jonte and Friedrich Billiods may provide some clarity—or at least some additional complexity. Jonte and Billiods were cousins. Like Francis Fortman's skilled brewing partner, Munzenberger, they came to Cincinnati from the Alsace region of France. In 1829, they bought property across the street from the future site of the John Walker Brewery on Sycamore Street. This may mean that Jonte and Billiods also enjoyed access to a good source of clean artesian water. Sources differ on when they opened, but they were probably brewing no later than 1832.

The partnership didn't last long. Jonte and Billiods went their separate ways in 1835. Jonte retained the brewery on Sycamore Street, and Billiods moved to the outskirts of town. On a site that would later become the northwest corner of McMicken Avenue and Vine Street, Billiods founded the Lafayette Brewery, named in honor of the Marquis de Lafayette. Only a few things are known about Billiods's beer, but these scant pieces of information are useful. He utilized spring water piped in from the hillside above him, meaning that he had a source of clean, clear water. A stone-arched lagering cellar roughly the same dimensions as the one built by Agniel and Fleischmann and then used by Fortman and Munzenberger still rests under the brewery building today, and Billiods temporarily partnered with another Alsatian named John Kauffman (the older one, not his nephew who would later own the John Kauffman Brewery). We're also told that both Jonte and Billiods "brewed in the Strasbourger style" and principally employed "Swiss and French Alsatians." It is unclear what any of this means, but it suggests that the connection to Alsace was important to the evolution of Cincinnati beer and that early departures from English ales were inspired by brewing innovations in Strasbourg, France, which sits on the Rhine River, bordering Germany.

Although Jonte and Billiods started business making ales, the beers that Jonte and Billiods, Agniel and Fleischmann and Fortman and Munzenberger made may have all had common elements. They may have all been lighter in color and body and used more hops than traditional, strong ales. Choice of hops as well as access to clear water with a desirable mineral content may have affected their color and clarity, making them radically different beers from what Cincinnatians were used to in the 1830s and early '40s—but not actually lagers. Alternatively, the version of history that has been endorsed by *American Breweries II* is that Fortman and Munzenberger were doing something distinct from Billiods and Jonte and that they brewed the first lager in Cincinnati in 1844. It's a viable claim, although it seems unlikely that anyone will ever be able to either verify or refute it.

If the muddled nature of explaining beer production renders the identification of the first lager in the city difficult, the transient and occasionally sketchy nature of some of its pioneer brewers doesn't help. Both Agniel and Fleischmann left Cincinnati after apparently building the city's first lagering cellar on Main Street. Munzenberger broke off his partnership with Fleischmann and then vanished from local public records (assisted by multiple spellings of his last name), and Peter Noll followed up his financial failure in Cincinnati—where he may have utilized stolen yeast to brew the first true lager in town—with a troubled second act in Louisville. Noll operated a lager brewery and two saloons there, one attached to his brewery on Sixth Street, between Main and Water Streets, and another on Third Street, also in downtown Louisville. He seems to have done fine, but true financial success eluded him. He sold the brewery, and the new owners reverted to the production of "XX & XXX Ale, Pale, Amber, Cream, Champagne, and Stock Ale" by early 1866.

Noll returned to Cincinnati by 1870 and opened another saloon. Briefly, between 1872 and 1873, he ran another brewery on Vine Street, just a few doors north of his previous location. During this period, he was acknowledged at a ceremony for "being the manufacturer of the first glass of lager beer made in [Cincinnati]." This, of course, doesn't prove that the claim is true. Noll's sons made their own contributions to beer and chronicling its history. Son Albert P. Noll retained an affiliation with the City Brewery in Louisville and was part of a group of owners that formed the Louisiana Brewing Company, which built the first brewery in New Orleans in 1884. Son Charles P. Noll worked for the E. Becker Brewing Company of Lancaster, Ohio, and defended his father's title as the first man to brew lager in Cincinnati when the *Enquirer* bestowed the honor on George Herancourt. Both men were dead by then. Noll moved back to Philadelphia and died in 1887. If he smuggled the first lager yeast from Philly to Cincy, nothing in either town commemorates the connection or disproves it.

Even George M. Herancourt, the man credited with becoming the first to brew lager on a large scale—and the man whom some celebrate as the first local "beer baron"—is shrouded in some contradictions. Herancourt was born in the Rhineland-Palatinate region (now part of Germany), along the border with France in 1807. His father was a successful farmer, and he grew up affluent. In the spring of 1830, using family money, Herancourt migrated to the United States, landing in New York and traveling to Philadelphia, where he worked as a brewer. He then traveled around the country for a while, working briefly as a brewer in Wheeling, Virginia (later West Virginia), and Lexington, Kentucky, before then landing in Columbus, Ohio. He became a partner in a small brewery in 1834 that grew into the City Brewery in Columbus by 1836.

It's around this time that contradictory accounts make Herancourt's biography a little fuzzy. The City Brewery was successful, but it is unclear how much Herancourt contributed to that success. Although he certainly had knowledge by this time, he seems to have possessed an active disdain for brewing, possibly because it was hard work. He left management of the brewery up to his partner and focused his attentions on a combination sporting goods and jewelry store. He married his brewing partner's sister-in-law in 1840, which gave him access and legal control to her modest estate. The couple had a daughter named Louisa, but Mrs. Herancourt died soon after childbirth. George gave Louisa to a trustee who raised her for the next four years. This wasn't particularly unusual at the time, but aspects of the arrangement were uniquely convenient to the "entrepreneur" Herancourt. According to a glowing, posthumous biographical sketch of George M. Herancourt, following his wife's death, he "decided to let his sporting goods company be managed by others." According to his daughter, he drove the business into the ground. Stalked by creditors, he took the money that he had—just a few hundred dollars more than he had acquired through marriage—and placed it in trust with his brewing partner for the purported benefit of his daughter. This shielded his assets from debt collectors. It was less of a gift than the law intended, though, and Herancourt continued to access the funds in "his daughter's" estate.

Herancourt remarried and moved to Cincinnati as the head and general agent of the Ohio Mutual Fire and Life Insurance Company in 1846. He left this vocation in 1848, the year before the company went bankrupt. Herancourt abrogated himself of any responsibility for the failure, which had caused "many thousands of Germans who had used their meager savings to buy insurance" to lose their money. He placed the blame on a

Herancourt Brewery workers forming a "Jolly Bunch." With one mug, a puppy, a sign painter who didn't plan out enough space for the word *Time* and a few dozen kegs of beer, these guys brought their own twist to a party. *From the collection of the Public Library of Cincinnati and Hamilton County.*

cholera epidemic and "the total incompetence of the new officers." This may have been accurate, but people seemed to have had a way of losing money around George M. Herancourt. During this time, his most successful venture was the ownership interest that he retained in the City Brewery, a business that was run by someone else and that he drew dividends from by using his daughter as a means of laundering money.

Herancourt's second wife, Barbara, had several children and an estate of her own. Daughter Louisa came as well, but this child of his first marriage never quite fit into the family fold. Apparently using some of his new wife's money, George and Barbara Herancourt bought a small brewery in what is now the neighborhood of South Fairmount in 1850. The brewery had been built by a man named Yengling around 1841 and fell briefly dormant after his death. (Some sources say that Barbara Herancourt was Yengling's widow and that Herancourt was operating her inherited brewery in 1847.) Along with the brewery, Herancourt purchased a few adjacent lands and the perpetual right to use a stone-walled ditch that channeled water from the Mill Creek to the brewery.

Herancourt constructed lagering tunnels into the steep hillside north of the South Fairmount Valley and, by consistent accounts, was running Greater Cincinnati's first commercial-scale lager brewery by 1851. It was originally called the Philadelphia Brewery, reflecting Herancourt's ongoing connections to the city that likely served as the source of his lager yeast. Apparently using water straight from Mill Creek, the Herancourt Brewery is credited with brewing the city's first pilsner, a crisp, clear beer "recommended by leading physicians." By the time of Herancourt's death in 1880, his brewery had grown and physically expanded consistently over the years, reaching an annual production capacity of seventy-five thousand barrels. It evolved and utilized the newest equipment and techniques, but Herancourt's sons and the brewery that they ran continued to show pride in the city's first extensive lagering cellars.

Even though it was soon eclipsed by the beer behemoths of the late 1800s, the Herancourt Brewery remained in operation until Prohibition. Herancourt died an extremely wealthy man, worth an estimated $1 million. His obituary spoke glowingly of his "three daughters and five sons." Both the obit head count and the dead man's will neglected to mention Louisa. After using her for multiple transfers of his interests in the City Brewery in Columbus to retain a steady income, skirt creditors and reap at least one windfall profit, George Herancourt denied the only child of his first marriage any part of his sizeable fortune. It wasn't a healthy relationship. She sued him in 1876, settled that dispute and then filed a second lawsuit against the estate after his death. Louisa alleged, in part, that her stepmother and the children from her prior marriage, along with the children of George Herancourt's second marriage to Barbara, had conspired against her, convincing her father to sign a Last Will and Testament shortly before his death, when he was in great pain and "under the influence" of painkillers. Her stepbrother Louis attempted to separate the family dispute from the brewery that he ran. Nevertheless, it isn't good for a brand if the name on the bottle evokes the image of greedy scoundrels stealing from family members, and the Herancourt heirs settled the lawsuit a few months later.

When the Herancourt Brewery opened in 1851, it was the first to produce lager beer on a commercial scale. It originally drew its brewing water straight from the Mill Creek. Although it is mostly remembered as a product of the 1970s, Herancourt produced a "light" beer before Prohibition. *From the collection of the Public Library of Cincinnati and Hamilton County, courtesy of Carl Grohs.*

There is an additional contender for the claim of first lager brewer in Cincinnati. Some people have credited William Fey with the accomplishment, but there is little to support the claim. Fey's brewery is best known for spreading a cholera epidemic in 1849. The charge wasn't true, but a reputation for killing people doesn't help sell beer. William Fey's Sycamore Hill brewery was short-lived, and if he was making lager at that location, no remnants of lagering cellars have been discovered or discussed in the intervening years. Fey left the occupation of brewing for a while. He eventually returned to the trade as one of the owners of the Lafayette Brewery in the 1860s. When he did so, he doesn't appear to have made any grandiose claims about brewing the city's first lager.

Many things can be said about the eclectic group of men who vie for the title of first to brew lager in Greater Cincinnati. Individually, they may be characterized as transients, scoundrels and occasionally misguided, but collectively they were all men of vision and grit—men who understood that the brewing industry was on the cusp of a revolution and who wanted to ride the wave of lager into a prosperous future. With the aid of other people's capital, Herancourt succeeded, but the rest of the lager pioneers mostly took the arrows, clearing the way for the settlers who would become Cincinnati's beer barons.

AMOUR POUR BIÈRE

Two French immigrants named Friedrich Billiods and Peter (Pierre) Jonte were part of a brief, transitional period in local brewing, bridging a gap between the early, heavy ales brewed with river water and the lager beer era. Billiods left the partnership and the brewery that they built together in 1835 and founded the Lafayette Brewery. Jonte continued to operate the original brewery until selling it, along with all the equipment and stock on hand, to David Ray and Christian Boss in 1855. These German-born owners would transform it into a much larger lager brewery. Boss would later incorporate it as the Gambrinus Stock Brewing Company, and it would continue in business as a successful midsize brewery into Prohibition.

It is unclear how and where he focused his attentions, but Jonte ran two breweries for a while. He founded the Covington Brewery on Scott Street in Covington, Kentucky, in 1837 and operated it for several years. Under different ownership, this brewery was also in business until Prohibition. Little is known about Jonte despite significant contributions to local brewing, and he apparently moved back to France after selling both breweries.

Friedrich Billiods left more of a personal legacy. The Frenchman constructed his brewery on land that he held under a ninety-nine-year lease. One aspect of the lease proved to be a critical element of the brewery's success. The landowner agreed to lay water pipes from a spring that was located roughly a quarter mile north of Billiods's lot and to provide as much spring water as Billiods needed for the brewery. Starting with a clean, fresh water supply, the beer was apparently good and became popular. Geography also didn't hurt. In the early years, the Lafayette Brewery was located in the Northern Liberties, an area north of Liberty Street and beyond the original city limits. The Northern Liberties was sparsely populated in the 1830s, but that made Lafayette an oasis for the hundreds of people in the surrounding area, as well as people traveling on the Hamilton Road, which was a primary artery.

Billiods's first brewery was a wood-frame structure located in a grove of trees. Originally, his business focused on taproom sales. Customers came to the brewery with their own steins. The steins were weighed and then filled until they weighed one pound more than their empty weight. A pound of beer cost three cents, and bibbers enjoyed enough of them to make Billiods a wealthy man. When the brewery was destroyed by fire in 1847, he built a new, much larger facility at a cost of $110,000 (around $3,400,000 today.) At the time of its construction, it was the pinnacle of modern brewing, including its single-chamber, basement-level lagering cellar. Business started to focus more on keg sales, and Billiods became one of the first brewers in the city to employ the tied-house system, supplying his own beer to saloons that he leased to operators in properties that he owned on and near Vine Street.

Tenacity was clearly part of Billiods's success, and although this trait can be seen in the consistent growth of his business, it is best displayed in his romantic life. He fell in love with a German girl. His affections clearly had nothing to do with her conversation skills because she couldn't speak either English or French, and he couldn't speak German. Nevertheless, "he managed somehow to make her understand that he wanted to marry her, and she made him understand that she was willing." Together, they had eight daughters.

OUT OF THE FLOODPLAIN AND OVER THE RHINE

It would be nice to confidently identify the first brewer of lager in Greater Cincinnati, mostly for the benefit of a city full of taprooms with trivia nights, but unless solid evidence emerges to support the claim that Agniel and Fleischmann were brewing it years before lager yeast was used in Philadelphia, it doesn't really matter. The broader story is that multiple Cincinnatians foresaw a radical change in brewing and were striving to become part of it. As this occurred, the principal concentration of the city's breweries moved out of the floodplain and over the Rhine. The change in beer was happening in conjunction with radical shifts in broader society.

Attee & Lofthouse Brewery illustrates the combined evolution of both the city and its beverage of choice. On the south side of Fourth Street, between John and Smith Streets, an area that was paved out of existence during the construction of I-75, William Attee founded the brewery in 1829, soon bringing in William Lofthouse as a partner. They were Englishmen who brewed traditional ales under the trade name Eagle Brewery, a name that Lofthouse retained after Attee's early death. Cincinnati was in the midst of rapid growth when the Eagle Brewery kegged its first ale. By 1820, the Spartan, bloody frontier that awaited the settlement's first residents had grown into a prosperous western trading center with a population of more than ten thousand.

A decade later, the completion of the Miami & Erie Canal had dramatically boosted Cincinnati's trading economy, linking the steamboats on its riverfront docks with the Great Lakes and all the farmland in between. The town was rising from the site of felled forests "too quickly for people to have any system or plan about it." Muddy streets "encumbered with debris" were unpaved and lacked street signs. Multistory tenements and industrial buildings sat beside cottages with thatched roofs, and none of them was numbered. The sounds of construction perpetually filled the air.

As the city grew, its ethnic composition changed. Although one of the first two families with children to settle in Losantiville in the 1790s was German, the early residents of the city were predominately native-born New Englanders, and Britons constituted the largest immigrant group. This had changed dramatically by 1840, when roughly 28 percent of the city's population was German-born. This had broad implications. Most immigrants were young and single, and men outnumbered women. German immigrants increased the city's Catholic population and gave rise and circulation to its first German-language newspaper. By 1850, Cincinnati had become a diversified population of more than 100,000 residents. It was the fifth-largest city in the United States and the second-largest manufacturing center in the nation. For the seven decades preceding the Civil War, no other American city rivaled Cincinnati's growth. It was the nation's first great boomtown, catapulted rapidly from a dangerous backwater to "the Paris of America." It embodied American ingenuity, industry and optimism. And it was thirsty.

As the population exploded, aided largely by immigration from Germanic states, everything about the city changed, but one of the most obvious changes was the way it relaxed after work. Taverns were replaced by "saloons," places where a city full of young men gathered at a chest-high piece of furniture called "a bar" and drank shots of liquor and pints of beer, and few things changed as much as the beer that they drank. A flood of Germanic immigrants created a city full of consumers who demanded German-style beers, and by 1850, this meant light-bodied lagers. Fortunately, some of their fellow Germans knew how to brew the beer that they longed for, and others who didn't possess this knowledge were eager to learn.

Around 1850, Germanic immigrants William Schaller and John Schiff purchased the Attee & Lofthouse Eagle Brewery. Eagle was successful on a small scale, exporting at least as far south as Nashville, but it was only producing three thousand barrels of beer annually when the Germans bought it. Historic sources suggest that Eagle tried to produce lager but failed, probably because the brewery lacked proper infrastructure. Making beers that needed to be fermented at chilly temperatures and then aged for months in a cold environment required lagering cellars. Basements simply weren't adequate. This made it difficult to convert ale manufactories into lager breweries, so Eagle's new owners hatched a more ambitious plan.

In 1854, William Schaller and John Schiff purchased land on the bend of the Miami & Erie Canal at Plum Street and began construction of the new Eagle Brewery. The site held several benefits over the original location. First, sitting on the south side of the canal made it easy to load barrels of beer onto canalboats, where they could be part of the export trade to northern towns and suburbs, or hitch a short ride to the riverfront, where the Schaller & Schiff brand made its way to markets in Louisville, Nashville and Memphis.

As the city filled with German immigrants, the highest concentration of this demographic moved to the sparsely populated land north of the canal. The area grew quickly, and it developed a Germanic identity. Originally known as the German Quarter, the area north of the canal developed a distinctly European feel. German was the predominant language spoken in this half of town, and thousands of residents here relied on German-language newspapers for their news, conducted business in the German tongue, attended German church services and preserved old-world customs—like drinking copious amounts of lager beer. The area north of the canal became so uniquely German that Cincinnatians nicknamed the section of the Miami & Erie Canal that ran through downtown "the Rhine" and referred to excursions over the canal bridges and into the German Quarter as going "over the Rhine," a phrase that eventually morphed into the neighborhood's formal name. Saloons blessed and infested almost every part of Cincinnati in the mid-nineteenth century, but Over-the-Rhine had a particularly high concentration of drinkeries and was home to most of the city's largest beer halls and beer gardens. This was an added advantage to Schaller and Schiff's location on "the Rhine." The new Eagle Brewery would be literally surrounded by hundreds of public houses full of potential customers. Most importantly, however, this vacant plot of land on soft, sandy soil was a blank slate, the perfect place to construct a modern lager brewery from the bottom up.

February 1848 witnessed one of France's several revolutions deposing a head of state—King Louis Philippe on this occasion. Successful revolts across Europe, but particularly in France, sparked insurrections across German states. Scared of far worse consequences—like losing their heads or being forced to work for a living—frightened German monarchs readily acceded sweeping liberal reforms. German territories were combined as a unified Germany, a doctrine of fundamental rights was adopted and most men in this new nation were given the right to vote. A bloodless coup delivered moderate, rational results, but it was all short-lived. Once the "former" conservative ruling elite realized that the new government—

Schaller & Schiff's new Eagle Brewery (both the light and dark structures on the left side of the etching) was constructed on Plum and South Canal Streets at a bend in the Miami & Erie Canal in 1854. The domed building behind it is the Unitarian church (demolished), the building with the twin spires farthest back is the Plum Street Temple and the steeple farthest to the right is the top of St. Peter in Chains Cathedral. *From the collection of the Public Library of Cincinnati and Hamilton County.*

composed chiefly of professors, lawyers, journalists and other professional intellectuals—lacked the muscle to enforce any of the legislation or decrees that it passed, the previous government structure regained control in a counterrevolution. Many skilled and talented German professionals found themselves disillusioned. Some were blacklisted or watched reinstated rulers seize their property in retaliation for supporting the revolution and its temporary democratic government. With hope for a better German future crushed, scores of the best and brightest Germans, collectively referred to as "Forty-Eighters," set sail for the United States. This would have a profound, practical impact on Cincinnati beer.

Joseph Goettle was an eminent architect and a "Forty-Eighter." He found a new home within Cincinnati's German community, and his work on Schaller and Schiff's new Eagle Brewery earned him widespread prominence and acclaim. Goettle designed the extensive lagering cellars at the Eagle Brewery to use ventilation systems in a way that allowed warm and cool air to "be turned on at pleasure, for the purpose of keeping the beer in the proper condition." This system of ventilation shafts and dampers was probably a far cry from the convenience of a modern thermostat, but it constituted radical improvement in brewery design, permitting lager beer production to be less dependent on the seasons. Through a combination of depth, natural insulation, ventilation and ice, Goettle designed extensive cellars that could hold beer at relatively constant temperatures for months. Enjoying both success in its own right as well as the flattery of imitation, Goettle's brewery cellar design was quickly "adopted by all the leading breweries in the West."

German immigration also supplied Cincinnati with the practical knowledge and skill to implement Goettle's architectural plans. Andrew Brehm came to the United States with Peter Noll and, at least according to legend, built the city's first proper lagering cellar in 1849 on Vine Street. Brehm, a skilled and celebrated stonemason, was a fixture in the city's brewing community. He owned interests in breweries himself, including real estate partnerships with famed local brewers Christian Moerlein and John Kauffman. Following the construction of Schaller and Schiff's Eagle Brewery in 1855, the city, particularly Over-the-Rhine and the areas adjacent to it, started filling with deep, multistory lagering cellars. All of them either used or were inspired by Joseph Goettle's design, and Andrew Brehm managed construction of every notable lagering cellar in the city until his death in 1873.

SOME BEER BUBBLES
AREN'T JUST IN YOUR HEAD

L ager changed the beer industry in virtually every way. It changed consumers' tastes and expectations. Drinkers began demanding lighter-colored and lighter-bodied beers, and they began to expect a degree of consistency in their brands, a feat that is more difficult with lighter beers than heavy ales. The Eagle Brewery excelled at consistent quality, earning its lagers a nickname, "Old Reliable." Eagle also claimed to be the first brewery in town to bottle lager for export. The Walker Brewing Company had been exporting bottled ale for years, but reaching the South with a fresh lager was more challenging. In the years before pasteurization (1864) and the crown bottle cap (1892), lagers needed to be kept at cool temperatures to remain fresh. Natural carbonation in the beer dissipated through corks, and automated bottle manufacturing wasn't possible until the early 1900s. Producing, filling and corking bottles was expensive before brewery workers placed beers into rigid wooden crates that stevedores loaded and unloaded several times on boat trips to Nashville or New Orleans.

Even if Eagle's claim to be the first brewery in Cincinnati to export lager is true, it wasn't alone for long. As perilous as bottling lagers was, it was still one of the few ways to get this coveted new beverage into southern markets, where the climate made lager production impractical. Multiple breweries throughout the city were bottling lager by the start of the Civil War. Even the relatively small F.&J.A. Linck Brewery had a semi-independent bottling company, named Pioneer Stone Bottling. Pioneer claimed to manufacture "the choicest kinds of ale, porter and lager-beer," including a cream ale that was a particular favorite among "medical gentlemen who usually recommend it to their patients." Regardless of how much doctors loved it, Pioneer didn't make the beer. Linck Brewery made it and Pioneer bottled it, although most breweries used separate companies to bottle their beers. There was an independent value and skill to the service, especially if a bottling company managed to seal and retain carbonation effectively.

We can assume that some breweries bottled for one basic reason: they had to. Herancourt and Schaller were early leaders in the lager beer market, but they soon found themselves in a crowded field. In 1850, just as the pioneers of lager were scrambling to brew the city's first taste of this revolutionary wonder drink, Greater Cincinnati had about sixteen breweries. The introduction and popularity of lager beer sparked a gold rush mentality, and this number climbed rapidly. By 1855, the number of regional breweries had more than doubled. Among the roughly thirty-four breweries were some hangers-on from the first generation. French Alsatians, Friedrich Billiods and Peter (Pierre) Jonte were still operating the Lafayette Brewery on McMicken and the Jonte Brewery on Sycamore. Francis (Frantz) Fortman was keeping O'Reilly's old Congress Brewery alive and racking up code violations by trying to expand its lagering space under a city right-of-way. The Washington Brewery, opened by Conrad Schultz, a native of Strasbourg, France, in 1834 near the riverfront, remained in operation with a predominantly German staff. David Harries was running the brewery on Sycamore near Fourth that originally opened as William Metcalf's Brewery in 1829, and the Walker Brewery continued to be regaled for its Scottish ales. In the years to come, all these breweries would need to either adapt to a new environment or die—some were already in the process of one or the other. Heralded as "one of the most extensive establishments in the West" in 1840, the Washington Brewery, for example, survived the Civil War but then succumbed to the future.

Founded in 1825, the Eagle Brewery was technically a legacy institution by 1855, but Schaller and Schiff were changing more than its location. Everything about the business model and its product was reinvented. Schaller and Schiff would continue to use the original location as an extension of their brewing operations for a while, but the facility was already obsolete. A German named George Schmelzer reportedly ran a tiny brewery on Hamilton Road (now McMicken) on the outskirts of town as early as 1829, but it did not graduate into a formidable business until Forty-Eighters Meinrad and Fridolin Kleiner purchased it in 1854, changed the name to Jackson Brewery and began radical expansions that including carving lagering cellars into the adjacent hillside. (Several sources credit Schmelzer with opening his brewery in 1829, but he didn't purchase the land that it sat on until 1845.) Similarly, although Peter Jonte's Strasbourg-style ales were part of a transition in the local beer scene, the original brewery was dwarfed by expansions built by German immigrant Christian Boss, who added lagering cellars and changed the name to Gambrinus Stock Brewery.

Accurately counting the number of breweries in this era is difficult. Areas that are now considered inner-city neighborhoods like Fairmount, Clifton and Walnut Hills were all well beyond city limits in the 1850s, which means that they were often left out of city directories. If they remained in business long enough or were otherwise memorable for some reason, they leave traces of their existence. However, many of the aspiring lager beer millionaires who flooded the Ohio River Valley with new breweries in the mid-1800s were infinitely forgettable. In a phenomenon that repeats itself in modern times, there are a score of fetal ghosts and stillborns. Today, this lowest layer of the Darwinian brewery pile pops up occasionally on Internet lists with scheduled opening dates that come and go without ever pouring a pint. In the 1800s, these apparitions of crushed dreams make brief, inexplicable appearances in city directories or land records. Barney Pelser, Christian Weaver, Francis Stouffer and Thomas Webb all advertised their breweries in

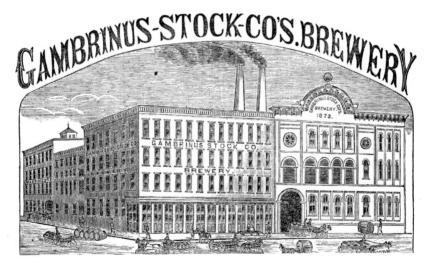

Alsatian brewing pioneer Peter Jonte's brewery on the east side of Sycamore and Twelfth Street grew precipitously after it was purchased by David Ray and Christian Boss in 1855. Boss converted it to lager production and renamed it the Gambrinus Stock Brewery.

1855, but they had all vanished by 1856 and it is unclear how many of them actually brewed a batch of beer.

Breweries that died in infancy constitute a second category. Frank Weber (north Main Street), George Schmeid (McMicken) and Henry Meyer (Twelfth and Elm) each operated a brewery for roughly one glorious year between 1859 and 1860. Marhoffer and Webben's Western Brewery struggled on Western Row Road (Central Avenue today) between 1855 and 1856. Payne & Gold's Brewery around South Fairmount was in business between 1859 and 1862, and although Peter Noll may have been the first man in Greater Cincinnati to brew a true lager, he began work on his brewery in the summer of 1849 and had become insolvent and moved to Louisville by the summer of 1852. Jacob Bauer and Charles Class took over the lease. They retained the Cincinnati Brewery name and had the benefit of inheriting the infrastructure that Noll built but nevertheless had lost the combined brewery and saloon by the fall of 1855.

Some breweries lived into early childhood. Strueve & Conradi's Brewery survived briefly between 1858 and 1863 on Hamilton Avenue (today McMicken, near Mohawk Place). Paul Andress (or "Endress") appears to be a great example of a man who got caught up in the hallucinatory effects of brewery fever. He owned a standard-sized parcel of land on Hamilton Avenue (McMicken), just west of Walnut Street. He purchased it in 1844 but didn't begin to convert the property into a small brewery until 1851—the dawn of the lager gold rush. The following year, he purchased the adjacent lot and appears to have dramatically expanded operations. More than 150 years before 100 percent loan-to-value mortgages helped collapse the global economy, one helped collapse Paul Andress. He loaded up on debt to finance his dream, borrowing against every dollar that he had paid for the combined real estate, including a second mortgage at 10 percent interest (at a time when 6 percent was standard). Overleveraged and facing fierce and rapidly growing competition, Andress lost everything to creditors in 1857. A fellow German named George Schmidt purchased the brewery that Andress built, reopened it and went out of business by the spring of 1861.

Paul Andress appears to have done nothing to shape the future of beer. It is unclear what he brewed, and after George Schmidt failed at the location, the next owner deemed the property better suited to another use. All traces of the Andress Brewery were subsequently erased from the earth. It is easy to write Andress off as a failure and a fool or to assume that his beer was mediocre to bad, but that would bypass an important lesson from this period in history. Andress came from Bavaria. Just making the trip took moxie. He was a cooper, a skilled trade that probably gave him some insight into the brewery business, and he may have worked in breweries. He was roughly thirty-eight years old when he convinced investors to lend him the capital that he needed to get off the ground. People believed in him, and this belief wasn't necessarily misplaced.

Andress was no fetal ghost. He opened his brewery and was successful enough to stay in business for more than five years. The Paul Andress Brewery opened at roughly the same time as George Herancourt's Brewery. His timing was good, but whereas Herancourt had the benefit of family money and a daughter whom he utilized in a financial shell game, Andress was shouldered with oppressively large mortgage payments. If Andress made lager, he was probably only able to produce it in the winter months, and he was not big enough to remain competitive in a changing market. He might have brewed a good product, but it was not one that could survive an unhealthy amount of competition. Regardless of who he was—a hardworking visionary who would be remembered as a wealthy beer baron if he had only had enough capital to start with, a con man who gambled with other people's money and lost or a decent brewer who simply couldn't survive in a saturated beer market—Paul Andress has his equivalents in the modern craft beer business.

Other brewers in the 1850s floundered for a variety of reasons but built infrastructure that lived on to spawn subsequent, prosperous empires. Andrew Sommer and Jacob Fuchs opened the St. Louis Brewery on Hamilton Road (McMicken) a few blocks west of Main Street in 1853 or 1854. Initially small, Sommer and Fuchs purchased multiple adjacent properties and expanded the brewery consistently through the 1850s. It was a successful venture, but Jacob Fuchs was essential to the operation and Sommer and Fuch's widow struggled after Jacob's unexpected death in 1859. Market disruptions caused by the Civil War exacerbated problems, and the first iteration of the brewery shut down in 1863. It struggled under a few brief, successive owners after the war but didn't really get back on track as an ongoing business until it was purchased by brothers Friedrich and Heinrich Schmidt in the mid-1870s. As Schmidt Brothers Brewery, and subsequently as the Crown Brewing Company, the facility would remain open as a midsize brewery until it was clubbed to death by Prohibition in 1925.

Gottfried Koehler made several unintentional contributions to the growth and development of the city's brewing industry. Somewhere around 1850 or 1851, Koehler opened the Buckeye Brewery, aptly named for its location on Buckeye Street (East Clifton today). Like his near neighbor, Paul

Andress, Koehler already owned the property, which he had converted from a cooperage shop into a brewery during the lager gold rush of the 1850s. Gottfried brought his brother, Henry, into the business. Together they formed Gottfried Koehler & Company and expanded their Buckeye Brewery, both in volume and physical size, gobbling up nearby land, erecting a malt house south of the brewery on Hamilton Avenue (where the Hudepohl Bottling Plant building sits today), shipping their product to southern markets and building a vibrant business throughout the 1850s and '60s.

Although Gottfried Koehler founded the brewery alone, the death of his brother in 1868 began an unravelling process. Two years later, the brewery was insolvent. It was offered for sale at auction in its totality, including two malt houses and a large "first-class brewery in complete running order," down to supplies of hops, malt, work horses, beer wagons and "1,200 barrels lager-beer" on hand. Unfortunately, the real estate and the individual parts of the brewery were eventually sold piecemeal. Building lager cellars was expensive—so expensive, in fact, that the need for them produced interesting bedfellows. A loose partnership between Andrew Brehm, the lager beer cellar and masonry contractor, and rival brewers Christian Moerlein and John Kauffman purchased the former Koehler Brewery property together. Andrew Brehm also purchased the malt house south of the brewery.

Brehm leased and then sold the Koehler malt house to Albert Schwill & Company, which operated a malt business. Unlike today, most large and moderate-size breweries purchased raw barley and used it to produce their own malt. Moerlein and Kauffman, for example, already had their own facilities for making malt. But Albert Schwill & Company was one of the companies that built its business on supplying smaller breweries and otherwise filling gaps in the market. Koehler's Buckeye Brewery was formidable for its day, but it was dwarfed by the empires that the space helped birth and nurture. Moerlein and Brehm eventually sold their portion of the facility to the John Kauffman Brewery. Moerlein then grew into the largest brewery in Ohio, while Kauffman became renowned for a pilsner that it aged in the former Koehler cellars.

Technology eventually rendered the need for these cellars less important, and the Kauffman Brewing Company sold the facility to Louis Hudepohl II and George Kotte. They revived the name Buckeye Brewery for a while before the plant became regionally famous as the Hudepohl Brewing Company. Hudepohl bought the malt house property back from Albert Schwill & Company, which moved down the street, and then opened an additional facility in Chicago, growing into the largest malt company in the nation. All of this was more than just the serendipitous fate of several parcels of real estate. Between the emergence of lager beer in Cincinnati around 1850 and the common availability of artificial ice machines and commercial refrigeration units by the 1880s, multistory stone lagering cellars were essential for making the beer that drove the market, and they were expensive to build. Malt houses were more diverse in their construction, but the ones built in the traditional fashion also employed difficult feats in masonry design.

Access to lagering cellars became an important component of a successful brewery, but they didn't guarantee success. Frank and Joseph A. Linck proved it. The brothers were raised above a tavern that sat at the modern site of Grant Park in Over-the-Rhine. Their father's tavern was in the sparsely populated outskirts of town when they were boys, but the area was growing crowded when they purchased the land from family members, extended their holdings and opened a brewery in 1855. F.&J.A. Linck Brewery had a malt house and lagering cellars that were inexplicably located several blocks west of its brewhouse, on Race Street near Findlay Market.

F.&J.A. Linck had an ominous debut. Francis (Frank) Linck, who may have suffered from an inability to focus his attention, both opened a brewery and ran for a seat on Cincinnati's city council in the same year. That spring election of 1855 was particularly tumultuous for everyone involved. Anti-immigrant nativists stormed the polls in German American neighborhoods, including the Eleventh Ward, the one that Linck was running to represent. The polling location was just down the street from the brewery, between its brewhouse and its malt house and lagering cellars. Frank Linck, along with his brother, Joseph, and brewery employees, got caught up in a vicious street battle that was waged on McMicken Avenue. A brewer at Linck, George Reeder (or "Roder"), was stabbed in the melee and succumbed to his wounds. After the dust settled on three days of urban warfare, Linck was elected to represent the Eleventh Ward for a two-year term on the city council.

Frank Linck's political career was unspectacular, and his brewery didn't do much better. It collapsed under the weight of massive debt by 1860. The malt house and the lagering cellars below it were separated from the main brewhouse, but both locations were subsumed by more successful breweries that fed on the F.&J.A. Linck corpse. A decade after its demise, the John Kauffman Brewery purchased the McMicken Avenue brewery, just north of its own facility, and oversaw its conversion to a malt house. Kauffman then subsequently sold it to Christian Boss, president of the Gambrinus Stock Brewing Company. Boss operated the malt house until sometime around the turn of the century, eventually selling it to the City of Cincinnati in 1911 so that it could demolish all that remained of the F.&J.A. Linck brewhouse and create Grant Park.

The Linck cellars on Race Street had a more interesting fate. In 1863, the owner leased the "Malt House and Lager Beer Vaults" to a rock star list of local brewers who were all acting in concert: Christian Moerlein (Christian Moerlein Brewing Company); Conrad Windisch (Windisch & Muhlhauser Brewing Company); Meinrad and Fredolin Kleiner (Jackson Brewing Company); George Eichenlaub, Rudolph Rheinhold and John Kauffman (John Kauffman Brewing Company); Michael Beck and Leonard Bauer (Beck & Bauer Brewery); George Klotter and F.S. Sohn (George Klotter Brewery, later Bellevue Brewing Company and Mohawk Brewery); Gottfried and John Koehler (Buckeye Brewery); and Joseph Schaller (Schaller & Gerke Brewery). All, individually and through their respective businesses, leased and shared the former Linck cellars for a period of ten years.

This open-top, wooden tank is a typical pre-Prohibition fermenting vessel. It has two spigots. After beer fermented for roughly two weeks, foam would form at the top and physical sediments would settle at the bottom. Clear, fermented beer would be transferred to aging barrels from the top spigot. Then yeast and sediment would be removed from the lower spigot. After undergoing a cleaning process, the yeast was reused in the next batch of beer. *Photo by the author, www.queencityhistory.com.*

This list of names—the most successful brewers in the city—implies profound, albeit unclear aspects of the Cincinnati beer business during the Civil War. First, it suggests several things about the broader economy. The war temporarily froze trade with the South, Cincinnati's primary beer export market. Some of these ports were occupied by the Union army and reopened by 1863, including Memphis and Nashville. Presumably this was good for business, although there was still disruption in the labor force and the supply of raw building materials. These combined forces may explain why so many of the city's biggest beer competitors were willing to work together for their individual and mutual benefit. This laundry list of German immigrants also conveys a sense of community that existed within the pre-Prohibition beer industry.

Lager made beer more popular than it had ever been before in American history. This drove an expansion of the industry. However, beer taste did not immediately become monolithic. The lager revolution was really more of an evolution. Even the new startup breweries, like F.&J.A. Linck, included ales in their repertoire, and Moerlein & Dillman, the precursor to the behemoth Christian Moerlein Brewing Company, brewed nothing but ales between 1853 and 1855. Rooted in a long, proud and successful tradition, the John Walker Brewery was able to remain afloat until 1878, but after that it reflected a new reality. There was a split in the brewery: brothers William and Archibald retained their ownership, while brothers James and Andrew left. With new partners, William and Archibald added lager to Walker's stable of brews, and this kept the business profitable into the 1900s.

James and Andrew Walker remained stubbornly faithful to Scottish and English ales. In June 1879, they opened the Champion Brewery on the far west side of downtown (an address that was eventually subsumed by the rail yards west of I-75). James and Andrew tried to carve out a niche in the market. They only produced porter and ale with focused distribution. Champion ales could be found in several of the largest and most prestigious hotels in the city, places where out-of-town guests might share the Walkers' enthusiasm for Scotch ale, as well as in independently owned saloons and groceries, places that weren't controlled by the larger German breweries. They also emphasized the health benefits of their beer, targeting "physicians and everybody interested in pure, healthy malt liquors." Champion guaranteed that its beers were free of isinglass, or "Fish Sounds," meaning that they did not use the dried swim bladders of fish, an ingredient used to clarify beer for mostly aesthetic reasons. (Isinglass is still used in modern brewing to give consumers a clear pint of beer.)

James and Andrew Walker were not taking any shortcuts in flavor, filtration or clarity. Unfortunately, almost nobody cared. Like many modern craft brewers, James and Andrew made the mistake of being too smart for the average consumer. Given the choice between pure, bold English- and Scottish-style ales versus crisp, clear German-style lagers and pilsners full of dried fish guts, Cincinnatians voted overwhelmingly in favor of fish guts. The Champion Brewery lasted less than two years. By March 1881, it had been offered for auction to satisfy creditors. When it didn't sell, a subsequent auction notice pointed out that it could "be changed into a Lager Beer Brewery at small expense." After several failed attempts to sell it as a brewery, the property was broken up and sold piecemeal. The inventive James Walker, holder of multiple U.S. patents, became an insurance salesman. Andrew Walker continued to list his vocation as brewer in city directories, but it is unclear where he worked, if at all.

At least some of the city's famous lager breweries continued to produce ales and porters up to the impending days of Prohibition, but the failed Champion Brewery suggests that a commercial brewery could no longer function in Greater Cincinnati by the 1870s without making lagers, and this had probably been true for a while. The Henry Meyer Ale Brewery opened at the southwest corner of Twelfth and Elm Street in 1859 and was out of business by 1860. Paul Andress may have struggled with an inability to produce the beer that the public clamored for or an inability to produce it year-round.

William and Archibald Walker saw the writing on the wall. Not only did they compromise the original mission of the John Walker Brewery in 1878, but they also experienced something akin to a full religious conversion a few years later. In 1883, they sold the rest of their interest in the Cincinnati brewery, packed up and started over. Cincinnati was saturated with lager breweries by this time, but the southern market that the Walkers knew so well was still a land of untapped opportunity. Three months after divesting themselves of ownership in the Walker Brewery, William and Archibald announced their new partnership with John Burkhart, owner and proprietor of the Nashville Brewing Company. The brewery had been around since 1859, but Nashville and most of the South still relied heavily on beer imported from the North, namely Cincinnati, Milwaukee and Pittsburgh. Beers made by Cincinnati's Hauck and Lion breweries were as popular as local brands, so the Walkers invested in expansion, and men who made their reputation producing classic ales

The Old Brewery as it was, before rebuilt.

Brothers William and Archibald sold their remaining interest in the J. Walker Brewery in 1883 and purchased the Nashville Brewery. The brewery was founded by German owners in 1859 to brew ales, but the Scottish Walker brothers converted it to lager production. *Tennessee State Library and Archives.*

started making crisp pilsners for hot Tennessee summers. They also brewed Nashville's only locally made bock beer every spring. It was a wise move. As one of the few lager beer makers in the south, Nashville Brewing Company did well, and the renegade Scotsmen made a killing selling German-style brews.

Life was harder in Cincinnati. The approximately thirty-four breweries in Greater Cincinnati in 1855 only counts breweries in what constitutes modern Cincinnati, Covington and Newport. Hamilton, Ohio, and Aurora, Indiana, gave birth to formidable beer empires, and breweries of various size popped up through the Ohio River Valley. Maysville, Kentucky, much more famous for its role in the birth of bourbon, maintained Joerger Jacob's brewery for decades, as well as Martin Nicholas's Brewery, in the mid-1870s, although the town relied heavily on brew imported from Cincinnati. Small Ripley, Ohio, was home to two breweries in the mid-1800s. Farther downriver, Ironton and Portsmouth both supported several notable local breweries.

Discussing Greater Cincinnati beer history requires a lot of repetitious reference to debt, insolvency and business failure—at least to do it honestly. History is written by and about the winners, so there is a natural tendency to focus on famous brands and the beer barons of the region's past, men who rose from poverty and adversity to wealth and social prominence. This is part of the story, an important part. There are lessons to be learned from the brewers who built empires while others quickly lost their life savings, but it is a mistake to assume that these outcomes were inevitable. As clear as they are in hindsight, the right choices are much harder to recognize in the fog of the present.

It is reassuring to assume that winners and losers deserve their fate, but that isn't a good way to learn from history. The truth is more complicated, and exploring the realities of beer in the nineteenth century has never been more prescient. There are a lot of fun, cheery stories in the region's brewing past, but one of the most consistent themes is tragedy. Williams and Symmes, who probably opened the first brewery in the city, lost it to debt. Davis Embree suffered financial embarrassments, and the James Smith Brewery in Newport, a monopoly when it was built, faded away without fanfare. Patrick O'Reilly only made the Congress Brewery successful after the Perry brothers went insolvent like their predecessors, and Mary Ann O'Reilly eventually lost it to creditors. John Walker built a great brewery, but that story started as happenstance. He only entered the profession because the men who envisioned and began the business lost all of it to debt, and Walker's heirs experienced mixed destinies. The two brothers who rolled best with changing times prospered, but the two brothers who took a more romantic lesser path had to watch everything except their integrity sold at auction. The Walker Brewery itself enjoyed a long life, but it was ripped apart in a courtroom in the early 1900s. Agniel and Fleischmann fell into debt and moved away, and Peter Noll fled from creditors to Louisville. Paul Andress and the F.&J.A. Linck Brewery simply didn't sell enough beer to cover costs. Partnerships like Sommer & Fuchs and the Koehler brothers hummed along quite happily until one of the partners forgot the financial perils of dropping dead at a young age. Lists of "breweries" throughout the second half of the nineteenth century are littered with smothered ambitions.

Several of the brewing facilities that were born in the 1850s and grew into formidable brands during the Gilded Age had to pass through multiple owners and at least one bankruptcy (or the nineteenth-century equivalent) in their journeys to becoming the Foss-Schneider Brewing Company, Schaller's

Main Street Brewery, Crown Brewing Company or the Hudepohl Brewing Company. There were, of course, exceptions. Christian Moerlein, Conrad Windisch, John Kauffman and Frederick Bruckmann, for example, would all open breweries in this decade, follow a relatively consistent trajectory upward, and end their lives as wealthy beer barons, presiding over brewing empires that bore their names.

RISE OF THE BEER BARONS

C hristian Moerlein is the archetypal beer baron. He was born in a medieval "castle" in northern Bavaria, although the large home was humbler than it sounds. His father was a blacksmith. His uncle was a brewer, and Moerlein apprenticed in both trades. At the age of twenty-three, he bid his family farewell and set off on foot for America with a small amount of money and a bag of tools. After walking three hundred miles, he boarded a ship and spent fifty-eight arduous days at sea to reach Baltimore, arriving on American soil sick, broke and friendless, and he couldn't speak English. Once in the United States, he traveled west, working short stints at jobs along the way, including some time as a brewer in Portsmouth, Ohio. Moerlein arrived in Cincinnati in the spring of 1842, working as a laborer until he could afford to open his own blacksmith shop.

Moerlein's business did well, but there was more adversity in store. He married a young woman named Sophia Adams in 1843, and the couple had three children. Six years into their marriage, Sophia and the couple's daughter died during a cholera epidemic. Several years later, cholera also took one of Moerlein's remaining sons.

He remarried in 1849, sold his blacksmith business in 1853 and used the profits to open a small brewery with a partner named Adam Dillmann. Even with the sale of the shop and modest beginnings, the partners still had to borrow part of their startup capital. Moerlein and Dillmann sold their first ale on March 1, 1854, and business started to grow. Then Dillmann died unexpectedly the following year. Moerlein had the good fortune to find a new partner, Conrad Windisch, a fellow Bavarian immigrant with an impressive résumé.

Windisch began working in his father's brewery at the age of thirteen and immigrated to the United States during the revolutionary turbulence of 1848. Windisch's journey to Cincinnati was even more Dickensian than Moerlein's. His trip across the Atlantic was grueling, lasting three months. Arriving on February 1, 1849, Windisch took a coach to Pittsburgh, but the winter was unusually harsh and the overland trip from New York was almost as harrowing as the one he had taken from Europe. He failed to find financially satisfying employment in Pittsburgh, Chicago or St. Louis before getting a job at the Herancourt Brewery.

After working for a while in Cincinnati's first large-scale lager brewery, Conrad Windisch was hired as the brewmaster at the Koehler brothers' Buckeye Brewery. He held this respected and lucrative position for three years. Then the death of Adam Dillmann provided the opportunity to become a business owner. Windisch brought a modest inheritance and a wealth of knowledge to the partnership. Moerlein and Windisch began to brew lagers in the winter of 1855, and the partners were on a trajectory to riches. Within four years, annual production rose from 2,000 barrels to 4,000 and kept climbing. By 1866, after acquiring additional properties and continual expansion, the Moerlein & Windisch Brewery was producing 26,500 barrels of beer per year. Although it would soon become modest in the rapidly industrializing brewing industry, this volume of production made Moerlein & Windisch one of the largest breweries in the country. The partners then had a difference of opinion about the future. Windisch had more conservative growth plans, so Moerlein bought his partner's share of the business for $130,000 (roughly $3 million today) and invested in the construction of a much larger brewery across the street, with three stories of underground lagering cellars. In the fall of 1868, the new brewhouse was christened. Moerlein razed his modest, wood-frame house as well as his original brewery and constructed a titanic malt house on the site, capable of converting 300,000 bushels of barley into malt annually.

The Christian Moerlein Brewing Company continued its breakneck growth, and Moerlein's family was critical to the brewery's success. Barbara and Christian Moerlein had nine kids together. Including John, the only child to survive from his first marriage, Moerlein had seven children who lived to adulthood. All played some role in the business, and all four sons worked in its management. Son George, in fact, came to be called the "soul of the company." George was placed in charge of representing the brewery at the

Brothers Gottfried and John Koehler built the Buckeye Brewery in the early 1850s. It was successful but closed in 1870 after the untimely death of both brothers. Competitors Christian Moerlein and John Kauffman shared the facility for its lagering cellars between 1870 and 1873. John Kauffman then used it exclusively as an extension of his Vine Street Brewery until Louis Hudepohl II and George Kotte began brewing there in 1885, reviving the Buckeye name. *From the collection of the Public Library of Cincinnati and Hamilton County.*

1876 Centennial Exposition in Philadelphia. As a gregarious showman, he was the perfect man for the job. George oversaw construction of an expo display that featured life-size statues of historic figures and pyramids of Moerlein beer bottles. It all rotated around on an elevated platform— kitschy by modern standards but jaw-dropping in 1876. The display drew a lot of attention from both exposition attendees and the press, and George Moerlein used the opportunity to make the Moerlein Brewery a nationally recognized brand. Also known for stunts like riding horses into Over-the-Rhine bars, George had an innate understanding of marketing that helped propel the business to new heights.

By 1878, the Christian Moerlein Brewing Company was producing 100,000 barrels per year—twice what it produced before the Centennial Exposition. It doubled production during the 1880s. Then, in just five years, the brewery more than doubled production again, growing from 225,000 barrels to 500,000 barrels between 1890 and 1895. Thanks largely to the vision and ambition of George Moerlein, the company was exporting to cities that included Boston, New York, Philadelphia, Pittsburgh, Baltimore, Buffalo, Nashville, New Orleans and Mobile in the United States by the

1870s, and Moerlein brews were being served in Brazil, the East Indies, Cuba, Central America, South America, Mexico, the West Indian Islands and Australia by the early 1880s. As the nineteenth century came to an end, Moerlein had become the largest brewery in the state of Ohio and one of the five biggest breweries in the United States.

There were several reasons for Christian Moerlein's success. Grit and tenacity top the list. With the help of Conrad Windisch, he built an early reputation for quality lagers, and he enjoyed the luck of good timing, establishing his place in the field early in the lager gold rush. During the brewery's history, the German population in Cincinnati would rise from 20 percent of 115,000 people to 58 percent of a population of roughly 300,000. Moerlein was always cognizant of new opportunities in the market. He never got trapped under the weight of loans or debt, but he grew the company aggressively and invested wisely in new technologies. The Moerlein Brewery was an early adopter of artificial refrigeration, installing one of the first cooling systems in the United States in 1874. Although the equipment was expensive, it paid off. In the following years, the company upgraded and expanded its cooling systems, eventually employing three "gigantic cooling machines" manufactured by the Arctic Ice Machine Company, a Cincinnati business. The machines pumped compressed ammonia through miles of serpentine pipe. Running twenty-four hours a day, the system kept lagering cellars and above-ground stockhouse rooms at a constant, uniform, frigid temperature. Cooling more than 800,000 square feet of space, it was the second-largest refrigeration system in the country.

Investment in this technology benefited the brewery in a variety of critical ways. It saved $60,000 to $70,000 per year in fluctuating ice costs. Although the machines were huge, they saved space compared to ice, which effectively increased the brewery's production capacity. Artificial refrigeration also ushered in an era of better, more consistent beer. Moerlein replaced old wooden vats with new, cylindrical, twenty-two-foot-high tanks. Whereas ice cooled the wooden vats at irregular temperatures, resulting in inconsistent fermentation, refrigeration cooled the new equipment evenly. This decreased fermentation time from sixteen to eighteen days down to twelve to thirteen days, and constant temperatures allowed beer to be stored longer without spoiling. Eliminating ice, which often came from sources as bacteria-laden as the Miami & Erie Canal, also eliminated common sources of contamination and humidity, which reduced rot and corrosion of equipment.

Christian Moerlein also raised children he could rely on to help build the family empire. After George Moerlein's untimely death in 1891, Christian's

Christian Moerlein Brewing Company began using this image in the late 1800s. It was resurrected in modified form when Hudepohl revived the brand. *Author's collection.*

eldest son, John, took over the position of vice-president. When Christian passed away at the age of seventy-nine, John ascended to the helm. In addition to continuing to operate one of the nation's most respected breweries, John Moerlein deserves credit for knowing when to get out of the business, preventing Prohibition from bankrupting the company, a fate that befell many of the city's breweries in the 1920s.

Moerlein's former partner, Conrad Windisch, also enjoyed a prosperous future. In partnership with Gottlieb Muhlhauser, he built and served as president of the Windisch-Muhlhauser Brewery, also known as the Lion Brewery. At the time of Windisch's death in 1887, Lion was one of the

In 1870, George Wiedemann left his position as brewmaster at the Kauffman Brewery to become John Butscher's partner in the Jefferson Street Brewery in Newport, Kentucky. He bought Butscher out in 1878, expanded, changed the name and constructed the brewery pictured above in 1888. Rising from poverty, by the time of Wiedemann's death in 1890, he had grown his business into the largest brewery south of the Ohio River and east of the Mississippi. *From the collection of the Public Library of Cincinnati and Hamilton County.*

largest and most respected breweries in the city, specializing in amber-colored lagers made exclusively from hops and barley imported from California.

Historian Don Heinrich Tolzmann has noted that the biographical sketches of most of Cincinnati's beer barons "closely resemble one another." This is partly due to actual commonalities. With just a few notable exceptions, virtually all these men arrived in the United States broke and unfamiliar with the language or the culture. They worked hard, made a good product, grew their businesses and became very wealthy examples of "self-made men." As a generalization, this is an accurate portrayal. These beer barons did, in fact, exemplify the full realization of the American Dream as it existed during the Industrial Age (and before Congress started limiting immigration). Men like Christian Moerlein, who seems to have been a generally decent person in addition to a shrewd and dogged businessman, are entitled to the respect of history. However, the biographical sketches that we are left with for the men who reached the status of beer baron are also a whitewash. Moerlein and the boys deserved respect, but they could also afford to have their lives airbrushed for print, and this does a disservice to history.

Even Moerlein, who appears to have been one of the most venerated beer barons, leaves a record of some morally questionable behavior. He is

Bavarian immigrant Conrad Windisch (1825–1887) worked at the Herancourt Brewery and served as brewmaster at Koehler's Buckeye Brewery before partnering with Christian Moerlein in 1854. *Author's collection.*

remembered as a diligent public servant for his three-year term on the Water-Works Board of Trustees. His tenure in this position appears to have been beneficial to the city, although he was also accused of using his influence to save roughly $2,000 in water charges at his brewery. Moerlein was also capable of being cruel and vindictive.

The death of George Moerlein was clearly devastating to his family, as well as the community at large. Although he had suffered from inflammatory rheumatism for the previous fifteen years, George was only thirty-nine when he died from pneumonia. He had traveled to parts of Europe and the American West in search of healing environments and received the best medical care that the nineteenth century had to offer. He passed away at home, surrounded by his family. His death was foreseen, but his gregarious nature, broad personal popularity and indomitable spirit left a gash in the city's social fabric. The mayor, members of city and county government and all the region's notable brewers were among the roughly ten thousand mourners who attended his funeral. So many floral tributes were given in his honor that flower shops within a three-hundred-mile radius were needed to make floral arrangements.

George and Carrie Werner Moerlein were married in 1885, and George died less than a month shy of their sixth wedding anniversary. Her loss must have been devastating, but she had little time to mourn before she was embroiled in bitter litigation with her wealthy father-in-law. Not long before his death, Christian and George had reached an agreement that provided George with money he needed to fund the Georgia Granite Company, a business that George owned outside Atlanta (from which most of the granite that paved Cincinnati streets was quarried). George sold his father eighty shares of Christian Moerlein Brewing Company stock, retaining ownership of seventy shares. Following George's death, Moerlein claimed that the remaining shares were supposed to be distributed among George's brothers, partly because George and Carrie did not have any children. George died intestate, and the beer baron had no clear legal basis for his claim. Carrie Moerlein refused to relinquish the roughly $200,000 worth of stock, which constituted a large portion of the estate. Moerlein responded by suing his son's estate, making vague claims that George had borrowed unrecorded sums of money from the brewery's business account and that, although he did not object to these alleged loans at the time, he now wanted them repaid. The litigation was protracted and nasty. When the case was finally settled in 1892, Carrie Moerlein reportedly agreed to sell the stock to her father-in-law that she had legally inherited for around half of its value. There were, of course, two sides to the story, but Moerlein's treatment of his grieving daughter-in-law was decidedly less than chivalrous.

This does not despoil Moerlein's general character or detract from his accomplishments, but it illustrates the fact that Cincinnati's beer barons were more complicated and more flawed than their saintly, two-dimensional biographies reflect. Their philanthropy was recalled in generalized, repetitive ways, whereas any role that they played in crushing justified demands from workers are either overlooked or lionized as "shrewd." In most cases this appears to only neglect the ugly parts of an otherwise true story or to slant events with a transparent bias, but occasionally it leaves a false perception. Beer barons could beat their wives or abandon their children and still be recalled as warm, loving men of family. How a man handles being charged with murder, taking William Schaller as one example, seems to define his character more than the size of the check that he writes to an orphanage. Cincinnati's beer barons shared commonalities, but they were more dissimilar than their official, sanitized stories reveal. Unfortunately, the whitewashed biographies of these men further the popular narrative that anybody who simply works hard enough can get rich in America, and this is such an oversimplified cliché that there is little to learn from it. Beatification of dead rich guys is dangerous because it suggests that success or failure is preordained.

While some breweries floundered, failed or struggled during the mid-1800s, a time when new breweries seemed to pop up almost monthly, others found a path to precipitous growth and extraordinary wealth. The ones

When John Hauck arrived in Cincinnati in 1852, he worked for his uncle, George Herancourt. He then married Friedrich Billiods's daughter, Katherine, and worked as brewmaster at his father-in-law's Lafayette Brewery before building his own brewery in 1863–64. Hauck maintained the highest standards of production and earned a reputation for stellar beer. By the mid-1890s, the John Hauck Brewing Company was the second largest in the city, producing 300,000 barrels of beer annually. *From the collection of the Public Library of Cincinnati and Hamilton County.*

that succeeded seem to have had a few things in common: strong, smart, decisive, driven leadership; competent management teams; a consistent reputation for good beer; a willingness to grow and change with the market and technological advances without sacrificing quality; aggressive growth without excessive debt; and luck. Of course, starting out with a fat bank account never hurt. One of George Moerlein's endearing qualities was his honest appreciation of the power of money. Not long before he died, a lifelong friend asked him, "George, you are sick. Would you exchange places with all your wealth with a poor man and have perfect health?" George straightened himself up in bed and replied, "No, sir. I enjoy my wealth."

CORN JUICE, RICE AND OTHER POISONS

As beer became big business, and as lager moved rapidly from a novelty to the norm, breweries began searching for ways to distinguish themselves from their competition. Tag lines and the larval stages of modern marketing campaigns began their evolution around the 1870s. Sometimes, like in the case of the John Kauffman Brewery Company, the rhetoric was tied to an actual difference in the beer.

At the age of fifteen, traveling alone, John Kauffman left his home in the Alsace region of France and immigrated to the United States. His uncle, also named John Kauffman, gave him a job at his Franklin Brewery, located just northeast of downtown Cincinnati. Starting as a laborer in 1845, the teenage Kauffman learned malt production and then rose quickly to the rank of brewery foreman. The elder John Kauffman briefly entered a partnership with fellow Alsatian Friedrich Billiods, and his beer likely shared the same Strasbourg influences. Unfortunately and unexpectedly, the older Kauffman died not long after the younger Kauffman started his meteoric rise through the brewery hierarchy. His rise was a little too quick for his aunt. She had a falling out with her teenage nephew. She replaced him as brewery supervisor, and he left Franklin to work at two other suburban breweries for the next few years.

Kauffman returned to the family's Franklin Brewery with partners and a purchase offer in 1856. He bought the business with Rudolph Rheinboldt and George Eichenlaub, both older men with notable business experience. Eichenlaub, who had run a brewery in Walnut Hills, also became Kauffman's father-in-law when he married Maria Ann (Mary) Eichenlaub. Taking the name John Kauffman & Company Brewery in homage to the elder, deceased Kauffman, the three men operated the Franklin plant for just a few years before they began constructing a new, extensive lager brewery on Vine Street.

After a twenty-five-year career as a successful brick mason, land speculator and brewer, Bavarian-born Eichenlaub was a wealthy man even before the John Kauffman & Company Brewery began its expansive growth. When Eichenlaub died in 1870, he willed the vast majority of his estate to his only child, Maria Ann Kauffman. The Kauffmans lived in a stately mansion across the street from the brewery, and they had enough money to purchase Rudolph Rheinboldt's share of the business when he retired in 1877. This placed John Kauffman and his family in complete control of one of the city's largest and most respected breweries. Kauffman was also regarded as the elder statesman of Cincinnati brewers. Having started his career at age fifteen, he had been in the business for thirty-two years when he assumed full dominion of the brewery. Kauffman used the opportunity to transform his product and brand.

Kauffman intended to make better beer than his competitors. He started by acquiring information from some of the world's most respected brewmasters and by searching the globe for the best raw ingredients. He sent one of his brewers on a two-year tour of European breweries and dispatched one of his four sons, Michael, on a shorter but similar journey. Son Charley Kauffman developed a highly refined palate (for the era) and was admired for his abilities to "tell a sack of malt that is in the least degree tainted" by smell. Knowledge, however, was insufficient to replicate the most renowned European lagers. Kauffman also needed the right barley and hops.

Some hops were grown in the Greater Cincinnati region at this time. Today, this practice is being revived by the recent advent of several Ohio and Kentucky hop farms. However, hops are a difficult and risky crop. They are a vining plant, which requires building fields of infrastructure. Soil heavily influences their taste and aromatic properties, and many varieties of the plant will only survive in climates with narrow temperature fluctuations. All of this means that acquiring hops in the late 1800s wasn't radically different than today. Although hops are grown throughout the world, modern craft breweries in the United States draw most of their hops from the states of Oregon and Washington. In the 1870s and 1880s, the states were different, but the principle was the same. Most U.S. hops were grown in New York, in a region between Albany and Syracuse. Due to cool temperatures and a plethora of German farmers, Wisconsin was also a notable hop producer. California, the Washington Territory (before Washington became a state) and

Oregon were all emerging but much smaller markets. A lot of the hops grown in California were exported to China, Japan, Mexico, the Sandwich Islands, South America and Australia. Most of the hops used by late-nineteenth-century Cincinnati breweries probably came from New York, supplemented with some from Wisconsin, some grown locally and a small amount from the Northwest. It wasn't necessary to import European hops. By the early 1880s, North America was producing about 20 million pounds of hops annually and only using 18 million pounds. It exported the difference to hot climates that were inhospitable to hop cultivation, but it also shipped some of this crop to England and other parts of Europe. Even Germany, the world's largest hop producer and the snobbiest hop consumer, used some U.S. hops.

Despite hop production spreading to various parts of the globe, hops grown in certain regions continued to enjoy a much better reputation than others. Hops from Bohemia, then part of Austrian territory (today part of the Czech Republic), were most coveted, particularly for making the lightest, crispest pilsners. Hops from the Saaz region of Bohemia were particularly praised and correspondingly expensive. If, however, you wanted to make a truly world-class pilsner, you made it with the best ingredients. Kauffman began importing Bohemian malt and "Sanzer Langot" hops, which appears to have been a "noble" hop variety from Saaz, Bohemia.

Importing ingredients from Austria when most local brewers were satisfied with the hops that could be purchased from Syracuse demonstrated a true commitment to brewing a superior beer, and Kauffman extended this philosophy to the process of finishing his beer. Although modified in practice by technical advancements, most of the modern brewing process looks like it did in the late 1800s, except for fermentation and aging. Microscopes and advances in chemical science dramatically improved the understanding of yeast and fermentation in the mid-1800s, but the science of beer still mingled some scientific uncertainty with a little brewing voodoo. By the late 1830s, scientists generally agreed that yeast could be acquired from multiple sources, including floating through the air, and that live yeast were necessary to ferment beer. By the mid-1800s, science was able to explain the effect of different yeast strains on beer, and brewers were able to look at the physical properties of yeast under a microscope and observe physical differences between yeast that would ferment at between 54.5 and 77 degrees Fahrenheit ("ale yeast") versus strains that fermented at between 39.2 to 42.8 degrees Fahrenheit ("lager yeast"). Scientists recognized that fermentation produces CO_2, and beer drinkers knew that the amount of carbonation in a beer affected its flavor and the enjoyment of drinking it. Brewers also understood that bacteria would cause a beer to sour. By the early 1880s, however, scientists were still debating how much oxygen yeast needed to produce different amounts of fermentation, resulting in the desired amount of alcohol and carbonation. Many people argued that ample exposure to oxygen was necessary for making good beer. As a result, fermenting tanks were open at the top, despite the obvious risks of contamination—especially if there were rats sitting on the rim of the vat getting fat and sloppy drunk.

Although the process of pasteurization was well understood, yeast in the beer were kept alive after it was kegged to provide the consumer with a fresh, carbonated product. As an 1882 brewing manual explained: "Fermentation is not concluded in the fermenting-cellars, it continues in the storing barrel, in the transport cask, and even in the beer, when, filled in glasses, it is placed before the consumer." Fermentation remained the trickiest and least understood aspect of brewing, the part of the process where "the brewer most frequently suffers shipwreck." Although some fermenting vessels in the late 1800s were made entirely of glass or enameled cast iron, most fermentation vats were made of oak, round and staved like a barrel. The wood affected the flavor of the beer, and it was difficult to keep sanitary.

To make lager, fermenting cellars needed to be cool, generally below forty degrees. They needed to be well ventilated but also clean and as bacteria-free as possible because the beer fermented in open vats for roughly ten to fourteen days. Fermented beer was then piped into barrels and moved to a lagering cellar, where it would be stored on ice for months. During this time, it continued to ferment to a lesser degree before it was kegged and released to consumers.

Even though lager was only produced during the winter until the late 1800s, a productive brewery required massive amounts of cellar space to age lager, and the specifications for lagering cellars were no less demanding than they were for fermenting cellars. Cold temperatures helped slow fermentation, which caused the beer to retain carbon dioxide, prevented it from spoiling and decreased the chance of the most common forms of bacterial and fungal infections. Good lagering cellars needed to be a uniform temperature year-round, optimally between thirty-four and thirty-six degrees Fahrenheit. Conventional wisdom held that the closer the beer was kept to freezing, the better it aged and the better it tasted. Before the introduction of cooling systems that used pipes filled with ammonia, these temperatures had to be maintained by ice, which required lagering cellars to be well insulated. They also needed to remain clean and dry despite containing at least a year's worth of ice at a time. Ventilation shafts were used to allow cold air to permeate the cellars during winter months and were sealed during the summer.

Breweries distinguished between "young beer" and "stock beer." They could both be lagers, but "young beer" was made with less malt and hops and often cheaper ingredients. It was also aged for a lot less time, which is what made it "young." Only the best malt and hops were used for producing stock beer, and both were used more plentifully. While "young" beers were often stored for as little as two weeks, "stock" beers were often aged for six months or more.

In April 1882, Kauffman began building anticipation for its newest brew in advance of its release. This is common in modern marketing but was very unusual for the time. Finally, on May 10, 1882, the John Kauffman Brewing Company's Bohemian was "drawn direct from their immense arched cellars," where it was kept at near-freezing temperature until it was delivered directly to the consumer. Ads explained that any "brewer can brew a dark heavy beer, but the art of brewing a pale, mild and pleasing beer, with the aromatic hop flavor and containing the same strength as the choicest dark beer, requires the most select barley, malt and finest hops that the earth produces." Kauffman's Bohemian was not just intended to be a good local beer. It was brewed to compete with the best beers in the world. Kauffman trotted out European diplomats and professors who declared this brew superior to European competitors and assured consumers that they had "overcome the alleged superiority of imported beer." There was no longer any reason "whatever to drink beer that [had] undergone a sea voyage."

Although it would constitute an illegal monopolistic practice in later generations, Greater Cincinnati brewers of this era entered agreements to sell their beer at a mutually agreed-on price. This was intended to prevent any brewery from gaining an advantage in the market by selling its beer for less, which could start a downward price spiral, so Kauffman didn't take much flack when he told the public that he would be charging twenty-five cents more for a keg of his beer than his competitors. Kauffman's Bohemian was more expensive than other beers because it was worth it.

Reporting a capacity of about 100,000 barrels per year, Kauffman was one of the largest breweries in the city by the early 1880s. Although most of its business was local, the brewery also shipped its beer throughout the United States, particularly to southern markets. Bohemian played no small role in the brewery's growth. Following the release of this highly hyped brew, sales of all Greater Cincinnati breweries combined fell 3,128 barrels between 1882 and '83, while Kauffman's sales increased 12,112

John Kauffman was French Alsatian. He immigrated to Cincinnati at the age of fifteen and began his career in brewing in 1845. At the time of his death in 1886, Kauffman was just fifty-five but was considered the city's "elder statesman of brewing." Under his leadership, the Kauffman Brewery grew to a 100,000-barrel capacity, and Kauffman's lagers were highly praised. *From the collection of the Public Library of Cincinnati and Hamilton County.*

barrels in the same period. Kauffman's better beer strategy worked, but this came with its own hazards. Kauffman physically distinguished its draft beer by painting the bottoms of the kegs green, a mark that was visible to bar patrons when saloons used draft systems that sat on top of the bar. As the sales of Kauffman's Bohemian rose, the brewery discovered that some shysters were selling an inferior product by falsely labeling it with the Kauffman name and that a Milwaukee brewery was hocking "Milwaukee Corn Beer" from kegs with the bottom deceptively painted green like Kauffman's. Kauffman Brewing Company ran ads informing the public of these encroachments on its brand.

"Milwaukee Corn Beer" was a special kind of insult, one that encompassed a lot of vitriol in just a few choice words. *Reinheitsgebot* is the world's oldest food purity law, adopted in Bavaria in 1516 and later incorporated into the national laws of Germany when it became a unified state in 1871. *Reinheitsgebot* restricts the contents in beer to water, barley malt, yeast and hops. The law forbids the use of any additional or alternative ingredients known as "adjuncts." *Reinheitsgebot* has never been the law in the United States, but following it was considered a code of honor among Cincinnati's German-born brewers, and the drinking public—especially the large German element of it—regarded deviations from *Reinheitsgebot* with grave suspicion, assuming that even if adjuncts weren't harmful, they still produced an inferior beer. This was particularly true of rice and corn. By the late 1800s, consumers were driving a market for very light-colored, clear, crisp beers, and some large American brewers began to understand that supplementing barley malt with ground rice or corn was a sure route to a lighter-bodied brew. Eventually, breweries like Anheuser-Busch would come out of the adjunct closet. Anheuser, in fact, was declared the best malt beverage in the world at the 1878 Paris Exhibition, and the judges attributed its particularly appealing flavor to the use of rice. However, in Cincinnati in the late 1800s, brewers still avoided using rice or corn, and they sometimes denied it when they broke this unwritten contract with the public.

"Imported" beer referred to beer from anywhere outside the Greater Cincinnati Region (in the 1870s and 1880s), whether that was Germany or St. Louis. Attacking foreign breweries located in strange and backward places like Milwaukee was fair game, and although certain local brewers probably cringed anytime one of their competitors did it, Kauffman remained within the bounds of gentlemanly competition by accusing unspecified foreigners from Wisconsin of using corn in their infinitely inferior beer. In his quest to distinguish his brand among the competition, George Weber took this a step farther. Weber stepped out of line and sparked a beer war.

Meinrad and Fridolin Kleiner were heirs to a distinguished brewing empire. Their great-great-grandfather learned to brew in a German monastery in the late 1600s, and the Kleiner family's brewery grew for roughly the next 150 years, making successive generations of Kleiners quite wealthy. If Meinrad and Fridolin Kleiner had stayed out of politics, they would have had comfortable futures. Instead, they used their wealth and influence to support the Revolution of 1848. After the counterrevolution restored the previous power structure, the Kleiner brothers found themselves on the wrong side of the law. The family's brewery and personal assets were seized and confiscated by the government. As social pariahs stripped of their livelihood and wealth, the Kleiner brothers became "Forty-Eighters," immigrating to the United States in search of both economic opportunity and democratic ideologies. Meinrad came first, landing in New Orleans virtually penniless and working his way to Cincinnati, where he was a waiter in a beer garden. Fridolin eventually joined him, and in 1854, they purchased a small brewery at the north end of Elm Street in Over-the-Rhine. Although they were starting their financial lives over from scratch, the Kleiners possessed generations' worth of accumulated brewing knowledge. They made good beer, and in the following years, they expanded the little shack of a brewery.

Immediately following the Civil War, the Kleiner brothers began extensive expansion of their Jackson Brewery, named after Andrew Jackson. As Americans, the Kleiners remained political. They supported the Union during the war but were otherwise ardent, populist Democrats. Work done to the brewery in the late 1860s constituted much more than remodeling and expansion. The Kleiners purchased multiple surrounding parcels, dug lagering tunnels into the adjacent hillside and constructed an entirely new, august brewery lording over the city below it. Jackson Brewery did brisk business both locally and in the export market. Writing in the summer of 1869, a New Orleanian observed that beer gardens and saloons had grown "almost as thick" in parts of New Orleans as they were in Cincinnati and that Cincinnati beer brands like Kleiner's were almost as prevalent in the Crescent City as in its northern cousin.

The original, regal era of the Jackson Brewery came to an abrupt end when Fridolin Kleiner died in 1869, and Meinrad followed him to the grave in 1873. The business appears to have been highly reliant on the Kleiner brothers' personal knowledge, and so the heirs decided to sell the brewery to George Weber. Weber had no background in the brewing business, but he was a smart, ambitious and wildly successful businessman—or so he appeared.

George Weber started his career in the hotel business as a bellboy. He worked his way up the ladder in a quintessential story of American success. After years of proficient hotel management, Weber bought the Galt House Hotel, one of the city's larger and more respected establishments. He initiated extensive remodeling. Several years into Weber's ownership, Galt House ads audaciously claimed that the hotel had "reached a perfection probably unprecedented in the hotel business in the West." Although the "perfection" claim is suspect, the hotel was profitable and enjoyed a good reputation. According to Weber, it also netted him a princely profit when he decided to sell it and enter the brewing business.

It is here that George Weber's financial history starts to become as controversial as Donald Trump's. At different times, Weber claimed that he made profits of $100,000, $300,000 or $900,000 from the sale of the Galt House. Aside from the extraordinary gap between the low and high ends of this claim—the modern equivalent of between approximately $2 million and $17 million—it's possible that after paying off creditors and the cost of renovations, in which "no pains nor expense [were] spared in enlarging and improving," Weber may have only broken even on his sale of the hotel. He utilized boastful claims of his wealth, however, to buy a brewery on credit.

Weber claimed that he put $100,000 cash down and financed the remainder of the $385,000 that he paid for the Jackson Brewery. Some people were skeptical about this claim, and for good reason—he was lying. Weber actually paid $280,000 for the brewery. Undoubtedly buoyed by the inflated stories of his success and the significant capital that Weber was apparently holding to ensure the brewery's profitable transition in ownership, Meinrad and Fridolin Kleiner's heirs sold him the brewery and surrounding real estate entirely on credit. He executed a purchase mortgage to the Kleiner heirs and gave them $1 in cash to render the transaction legally binding.

Although Weber claimed to be a millionaire, he had a cash flow problem almost immediately after he started operating the Jackson Brewery. Under the Kleiner brothers' ownership, there were months when Jackson had a higher volume of production and higher sales than any other brewery in the city. During the month of April 1869, when Jackson lager was flooding New Orleans beer gardens and theaters, the Kleiners brewed 4,020 barrels of beer, almost twice the output of the Christian Moerlein Brewery that month. There were, however, inherent problems with the facility. Like every lagering cellar in the city, the tunnels below Jackson were designed to be chilled with ice. Beginning in the 1870s, large breweries like Moerlein began using new forms of mechanical refrigeration. These systems paid for themselves quickly, but they required large capital investments. In the late 1870s, Weber was still tied to the fluctuating price of ice. Also, as large as the Jackson Brewery was, Weber was not making his own malt. Buying from maltsters allowed him to purchase malt as needed, which could decrease some of his massive overhead, but it had the disadvantage of making the Jackson Brewery subject to fluctuating retail malt prices in a way that other large breweries that produced their own malt were not.

Weber needed to increase his profits to remain solvent. Every brewery in Cincinnati, Covington and Newport belonged to the Brewers' Association. Among other things, this organization established a uniform price for a keg of beer in Cincinnati, as well as other standard industry protocol. Other cities and regions throughout the country had similar organizations, but Cincinnati's was envied by brewers throughout the United States for its cohesion and effectiveness, despite periodic squabbles and tantrums. Later eras would look on this type of price control with disdain, and it would eventually be deemed a monopolistic business practice. At the time, some people considered it unseemly, but it wasn't illegal. Weber, the new kid on the block with a dearth of brewing experience, was initially an enthusiastic member of the Brewers' Association. Shortly after he entered the industry, he asked his fellow brewers to raise the price of beer from ten dollars per keg to twelve. The matter was taken under advisement and held over for a future meeting. Weber was desperate. He needed the increase to balance the red and black columns on his accounting ledgers. He repeatedly visited several of the city's largest firms, urging them to support the increase, but his fellow brewers thought that the spike was too high. They eventually split the difference and raised the price to eleven dollars per keg. This cleaved a fissure between the hotelier and his fellow brewers, a divide that would fill with toxin in the months ahead.

In December 1874, less than eight months after Weber took over ownership, the Jackson Brewery sought court protection from creditors. The brewery was broke. Weber vehemently denied that it was his fault. He blamed the rest of the city's brewers, claiming that a conspiracy to harm his credit had rendered it impossible for him to purchase raw ingredients. Cincinnati brewers flatly denied this allegation, pointing out that inefficiencies in Weber's operation caused him to use twice as much ice as his competitors and that he could net an addition seventy-five cents per barrel if he simply started producing his own malt. Management at Jackson denied the claims of other brewers. Weber's spokesman said that they were producing more beer than any other brewery in the city, and he insisted that Weber had, in fact, invested

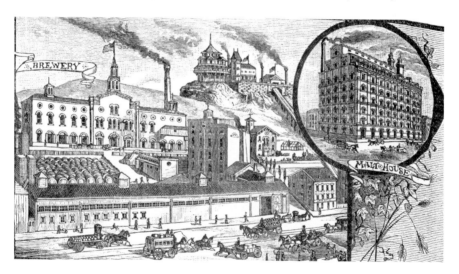

This is the Jackson Brewery as it appeared at the head of Elm Street in the late 1800s. The malt house depicted in the circle was located at Twelfth and Clay Streets. On July 4, 1887, fireworks caused the malt house to burst into flames. The fire spread quickly. The building was lost, and two men were killed in the conflagration. (The Bellevue House at the top of the Elm Street Incline Plane is behind the brewery.) *Author's collection.*

$100,000 of his own money into the purchase of the brewery. Land records clearly refuted this, but Weber embraced the idea that "alternative facts" can overcome reality if you repeat them frequently enough. The bickering grew even more childish and self-defeating.

Weber accused a collection of other brewers, principally Christian Moerlein, of trying to raise enough money to lure away his brewmaster, William Gerst. Moerlein denied this, countering that Weber had, in fact, tried to hire *his* brewmaster.

Then Weber started airing dirty laundry. He claimed to be the only brewer in the city who had correctly and honestly reported his use of cornmeal in federal tax filings. He, however, had only used it twice. For Weber, using corn was just a regrettable, youthful indiscretion. It was wrong. He knew it was wrong, and he had laid off the corn immediately, not even providing himself the opportunity to make it a habit. By contrast, Weber claimed that many of the city's other largest and most respected brewers were using corn on a regular basis but were lying about it because they didn't want the consumer to know that they were brewing inferior beers.

The allegation was true, and before they tasted the backlash, several of Cincinnati's most prominent brewers came out of the silo and openly confessed to occasional corn use. During recent spikes in the cost of barley, supplementing barley malt with cornmeal saved money. Corn was not employed, however, to simply cut costs. Christian Moerlein, Conrad Windisch, Gottlieb Muhlhauser and George Sohn were just several of the city's beer barons who explained that substituting 25 percent of the barley malt used in a batch of beer with cornmeal not only saved money but also produced a better beer. Corn helped increase the alcohol content and made a more flavorful brew. Customers preferred it, which is why eight to ten of the largest breweries in Cincinnati, and roughly 50 percent of breweries nationwide, were using corn. According to his rival brewers, Weber didn't abandon his corn use out of principal. He just "could not master the process." Although the brewers assured the public that there was "no injurious effects" from using cornmeal, this innovation in industrial brewing was not popular with consumers, and Cincinnati brewers would eventually backpedal, relying on the short memories of the public when they would categorically deny ever using corn in the near future.

Insolvency was the best thing that happened to the Jackson Brewery since George Weber took the reins. The business's assets far exceeded its debts, and its beer still enjoyed a good reputation and a healthy export market. Liquidating the brewery would have been foolish, so the court appointed receivers, trusted third parties who would run the brewery on behalf of both Weber and his creditors until the creditors were satisfied and the business was back in the black. (This state law process was roughly equivalent to Chapter 13 bankruptcy under modern federal law, in which debts are renegotiated, restructured and paid under court supervision.)

The court appointed businessmen Alex Starbuck and Jacob Pfau to act as receivers, granting them broad authority to manage the brewery, make tactical decisions and satisfy creditors. Under Starbuck and Pfau's leadership, production increased during 1876 by roughly eleven thousand barrels, surpassing Christian Moerlein as the fastest-growing brand in the city. The following year was even better—production increased by an additional twelve thousand barrels. Jackson's management attributed its increased market share entirely to its product, touting its lager as the "genuine, unadulterated article, made from the very choicest barley-malt." Although these claims could easily be viewed as a continued dig at breweries like Moerlein, Windisch-Muhlhauser and Sohn, who had admitted to brewing with cornmeal, Jackson stayed on the right side of business etiquette by avoiding any direct comparison or criticisms to other local breweries.

Outside agitators helped spark the "Beer War." America lacked any meaningful regulation over the ingredients used in beer. Temperance advocates used this lack of common-sense regulation to fearmonger, warning Cincinnatians that their local breweries were probably poisoning them. George Weber's Jackson Brewery saw an opportunity. The company published a lengthy ad disguised as news, hiding behind several layers of hearsay to warn "that Cincinnati lager-beer is no longer pure, but adulterated with molasses, sugar of starch and the poisonous colchicum." (Colchicum is a beautiful but poisonous flower.) The faux news story also suggested that some breweries used *Cocculus indicus* and *Nux vomica*, homeopathic remedies that could be deadly, particularly the latter, which is a source of strychnine. This was, of course, alarming news. How could the average, hardworking beer drinker avoid "guzzling some narcotic poison or damaging medicine"? Fortunately, the answer was simple: "The managers of Weber's Brewery, in adhering to the use of barley malt and hops, despite the unfair competition of adulterators, have relied on the good taste and intelligence of the public, whom they believe will sustain the honest brewer of pure lager." In other words, if you wanted a poison-free lager, you had to drink Jackson. Weber even went a step further. He offered a $5,000 reward "to any one who shall detect the use of any poisonous drugs in the Weber Beer, or who can prove the use of any corn, rice or other cheapening article in its manufacture."

Advertising the purity or even superiority of your beer was one thing. Implying that every brewery in town other than Jackson was poisoning people was another. That, in fact, was an act of war. The response was immediate and indignant. A collection of the city's premier brewers jointly published a reply to the Jackson Brewery, accusing it of giving "countenance and support to the Temperance movement." The city's brewers defended the quality of local brews, assuring the public that "no dangerous or poisonous substances, preparations or ingredients are employed by us in the manufacture of beer, but that, on the contrary, we brew our beer from barley, hops and malt." George M. Herancourt also felt compelled to publish his own ad, offering a $10,000 reward to anyone who could "find any impurity or adulteration or any poisonous ingredients whatsoever in the Lager or Pilsener [*sic*] Beer manufactured by [the Herancourt Brewery]."

The trap was set and sprung, and the predator sadistically circled his prey. Weber, Pfau and Starbuck innocently reassured their competitors and beer drinkers throughout the region that the Jackson Brewery had not made any allegations against Cincinnati brewers. Temperance quacks had slandered *all* Cincinnati beer. Jackson had responded only in its own defense because the brewery lacked sufficient knowledge to speak on behalf of fellow Cincinnati brewers. After obfuscating the fact that Jackson was responding to accusations that Jackson itself was responsible for disseminating, the brewery bared its fangs and offered its competitors some brotherly love. Weber pointed out that in their defense of their beer, Cincinnati's other breweries were extremely guarded in their language. They claimed to brew "from barley, hops and malt" but failed to say that they brewed exclusively with these ingredients and left the public wondering whether or not these breweries were conceding to the use of "corn, rice, grape sugar and other cheapening articles." Weber offered to help defend Cincinnati beer generally. He invited his fellow brewers to join him in signing a pledge to the public that would state:

> *We, the undersigned, Brewers of Cincinnati, hereby declare that all the beer manufactured in our establishments is pure and unadulterated by any drugs of any kind; that it is made exclusively from barley malt and hops, and that no corn, rice, grape, sugar, or other cheapening article is used in its manufacture. In attestation of the truth of this statement each of us agrees to deposit $5,000.*

If any brewer who signed the pledge were discovered breaking it, the guilty brewery would lose its $5,000 as a donation to the city's various orphan asylums. Weber offered to open his own doors at any time, without advance notice, to "any chemist desiring to elect a sample specimen for analysis." Checkmate. Weber's competitors continued to cry foul at his approach, but they stated that since "discussion in regard to the management and extent of any special branch of business is of no advantage to the persons engaged in the same," the brewers would "henceforth take no longer part in this controversy." Weber and the Jackson Brewery won the battle. In May 1878, Pfau and Starbuck published a "Proclamation of Peace and Good Will" on behalf of Weber and the brewery.

The Beer War wasn't really over, although the battle lines shifted. September 1878 brought controversy in both Milwaukee and Chicago when brewers who reported exclusive use of barley malt were caught liberally using corn and rice. This provided the *Cincinnati Enquirer* with an opportunity and "a solemn duty" to stir the Beer War back to blood in Cincinnati. Based on investigative reporting, the paper reached a firm conclusion: "Cincinnati beer is pure barley beer—some of it is, some of it isn't." Weber stood behind his beer, but he declined to comment on other breweries. George Moerlein, son of beer baron Christian Moerlein, explained that although they used to use rice in a pilsner, and that there was nothing wrong with using corn, they now used only barley. John Kauffman said that he only made barley beer and never used corn or rice. Both Moerlein and Kauffman said that although corn had been used in the past, no Cincinnati brewer continued to use it. Speaking on the condition of strict anonymity, a fourth brewer disputed this, telling the reporter that "corn-meal is used in this city to mix with barley in the making of beer, and that it is used pretty extensively."

The *Enquirer* lamented that although Cincinnati beer drinkers wanted "conclusive evidence that all the streams that flow into all the vats in all the great lager cellars in this great lager city are pure barley beer," there was simply no way to know. Drinkers, they concluded, would have to be content with the knowledge that they had probably "been unjust to corn and rice," which might actually "be very innocent" ingredients. That was one approach, but the Jackson Brewery had a different idea. It used the occasion of this renewed corn controversy to double its pure beer reward to $10,000 for anyone who could find "poisonous drugs…corn, rice or other cheapening article" in its beer. Wisely, however, it chose foils from among the foreigners rather than the locals, advising "Cincinnati beer connoisseurs who have gone astray after Milwaukee beer" that government records prove that "Corn and

This Jung Brewing Company ad depicts the superiority of *Reinheitsgebot* lagers over beers brewed with adjuncts. The goat representing a pure, barley-malt bock lager is winning a decisive victory over St. Louis rice products that prance along behind and Milwaukee-style corn beer, which is so inferior that it can't even stay upright. *From the collection of the Public Library of Cincinnati and Hamilton County.*

Rice are extensively used in the beer manufactured in that city." Jackson also won some converts to its side of the battlements. Foss & Schneider's Queen City Brewery ran an ad matching Jackson's $10,000 reward for "any one who may detect any Corn or Rice in the beer manufactured at our Brewery." This is also when John Kauffman felt compelled to run an ad advising the public that a manufacturer of "Milwaukee Corn Beer" was trying to pass off its inferior product as pure, barley-malt Kauffman lagers and pilsners by painting the bottoms of the kegs green.

Ultimately, although it was a nasty public squabble, Weber's Beer War furthered Cincinnati's reputation for quality, all-malt beer as opposed to Milwaukee's corn swill. Although Anheuser-Busch in St. Louis used rice, even it piled on when company vice-president August A. Busch said, "We do not now, nor have we ever, used corn in the production of any of our beers, and we have always contended that first-class beer cannot be made by using corn as a substitute for barley malt."

FEUD AT JACKSON BIRTHS
NASHVILLE'S BIGGEST BREWERY

Chaos was the order of the day at the Jackson Brewery under George Weber's tenure. Feuds with other brewers and creditors got nasty, but the ugliest fight was over control of the brewery itself, and this battle had an unpredictable side effect. It indirectly changed the landscape of the beer business in the South.

By February 1878, Jacob Pfau and Alexander Starbuck, the men assigned to manage the Jackson Brewery on behalf of George Weber's creditors, had run the business for more than two years, longer than George Weber managed to stay at the helm. Pfau and Starbuck performed their task well. Business improved, debts were being paid off and the long-term health of the brewery looked good. Pfau and Starbuck had made these strides even while they stood aligned with Weber in the Beer War. In short, they were good at the job, which is why their contract to continue managing the business was extended by the creditors and the court for another year, but not everyone was happy with that decision. Ginned up by George Weber himself, some creditors alleged that Pfau and Starbuck were milking their position, prolonging debt repayments in order to retain control of the brewery. This contingent wanted to replace Pfau and Starbuck with a mildly shady character and close friend of Weber's, a man named Leo Brigel.

Other creditors, most notably the Kleiner heirs who were still owed the bulk of the sales price of the brewery itself, objected to replacing honest brokers with Brigel, a man who might prove to be no more than Weber's puppet. A nasty squabble started at a creditor's meeting, spread into the courtroom and then escalated to physical confrontation. The litigation became so complex that it led to conflicting orders from different courts. One order replaced Pfau and Starbuck with Brigel, putting him in command of the brewery, while the other order issued an injunction against Brigel that barred him from taking possession of the brewery.

Pfau and Starbuck responded to this state of indecision by posting guards, sentries and a battalion of police around the building, justifying their militarism with a valid court order. This wasn't sustainable, and Brigel laughed off the idea of gaining control of the brewery by force. Pfau and Starbuck eventually lowered their guard, which is when Brigel, backed by the sheriff and armed with his own valid court order, took control of the brewery one morning when Pfau and Starbuck were out of the office. Brigel immediately restored George Weber's neutered authority, and together, they fired thirty-five workers who remained loyal to Pfau and Starbuck.

Brewery foreman William Gerst became Pfau and Starbuck's inside man, instructed to "hold the brewery at all hazards." While the 35 sacked employees and more than 12 other men prepared to storm the brewery, Gerst mounted a revolt. He armed his Pfau-Starbuck loyalists with revolvers, rifles and red-hot pokers pulled from engine room boilers. Brigel and Weber needed the help of police and roughly 150 improvised warriors to drive Gerst and his loyal battalion of about 15 men into the lagering cellars. Less determined followers of Gerst peeled away. As the standoff continued, Gerst and his troops escaped one of the lower cellars and found a defensible space in an upper floor of the brewery. A rumor spread that the rebels had run a series of explosives and had set the Jackson Brewery to blow apart. This wreaked minor havoc, but it wasn't true. Cops got hold of Gerst during the afternoon and placed him under arrest for disorderly conduct, but the fighting didn't stop. While the outnumbered Pfau-Starbuck contingent held strong, Gerst gave bail, left jail and returned to the theater of war. He was arrested a second time with several other men for attempting to throw one of the Weber men into a furnace. By nightfall, one hundred barrels of beer had been maliciously destroyed, but little other damage was done. The battle was over, and the fight for control of the Jackson Brewery returned to the courtroom.

Weber and Brigel eventually gained permanent control, and William Gerst needed to find a new job. Whether or not Christian Moerlein had attempted to lure Gerst away from Jackson several years earlier, as Weber had alleged, Moerlein clearly held him in high regard. Gerst was hired as a foreman at the Christian Moerlein Brewing Company and had risen to the

Oil on canvas depicting Friedrich Billiods, with his original 1835 Lafayette Brewery in the background. Daughter Katherine Hauck inherited the portrait, and it descended through her husband's family until it was donated to the Cincinnati Art Museum in 2013 by Cornelius Hauck. *Friedrich Billiods, circa 1847–circa 1849, gift of Cornelius Hauck, courtesy of Cincinnati Art Museum and Bridgeman Images.*

This image of the Jackson Brewery in the late 1800s illustrates the oldest part of the brewery on McMicken, as well as how the cellars were used—fermentation on the top level, aging below. *From the collection of the Public Library of Cincinnati and Hamilton County.*

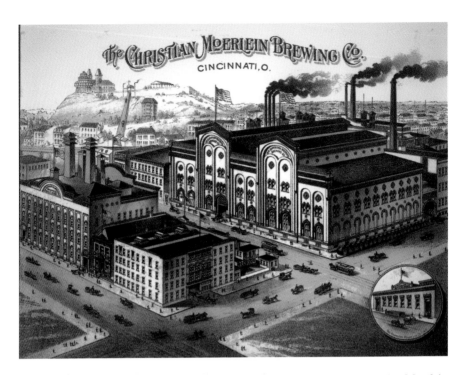

Above: The Christian Moerlein Brewing Company complex as it appeared in the late 1800s. *From the collection of the Public Library of Cincinnati and Hamilton County.*

Left: Ad for Moerlein's National Export Beer from around the turn of the last century. *From the collection of the Public Library of Cincinnati and Hamilton County.*

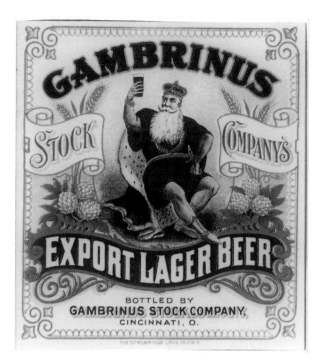

Gambrinus Stock Brewing Company was located on the east side of Sycamore Street, near Twelfth Street. *From the collection of the Public Library of Cincinnati and Hamilton County.*

Windisch-Muhlhauser's Lion Brewery advertises its seasonal bock beer. *From the collection of the Public Library of Cincinnati and Hamilton County.*

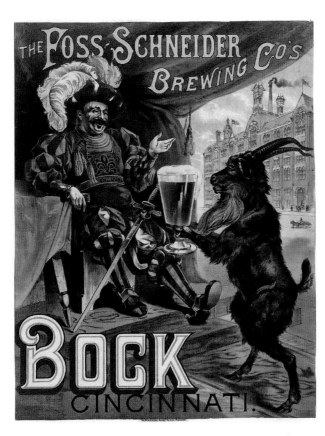

Left: Foss-Schneider advertises its seasonal bock beer. *From the collection of the Public Library of Cincinnati and Hamilton County.*

Below: The Jackson Brewing Company's lagering cellars as they appear today. *Photo by the author, www. queencityhistory.com.*

Bret Kollmann Baker of Urban Artifact Brewing Company labels a sample collected by George Burpee from the inside of a nineteenth-century fermenting tank. *7/79 Video.*

Nineteenth-century brewing vessels found in the F.&J.A. Linck Brewery's lagering cellars. The cellars were constructed circa 1855. *Photo by the author, www.queencityhistory.com.*

Above: The rooftop deck and bar at Rhinegeist Brewing. *Photo by Minnesota Jones.*

Right: Artist Brian Methe immortalized craft beer pioneer Dan Listermann for a 2017 keg tapping event at Arnold's Bar & Grill. *Brian Methe, www.bmethe.com.*

The Moerlein Lagerhouse became a critical cornerstone for the redevelopment of Cincinnati's riverfront when the 1,100-seat capacity restaurant and microbrewery opened in 2012. *Photo by the author, www.queencityhistory.com.*

Mad Tree Brewing Company was the first craft brewer in Ohio to can its beer, and the brewery opened shortly after changes in Ohio law made taprooms practical. A combination of good timing, smart decisions and great beer has led to rapid growth and a new facility. *Mad Tree Brewing Company.*

Top: Construction of two adjacent reservoir basins in Eden Park began in 1866. The lower basin, and its eighty-four-foot retaining wall, were completed in 1878. The Eden Park Pumping Station began operating in 1894. City tap water was pumped up from the river, stored in these open basins with a 100-million-gallon capacity and piped to residents without any filtration until the 1900s. *From the collection of the Public Library of Cincinnati and Hamilton County.*

Bottom: The Samuel Hannaford–designed Eden Park Pumping Station as it appeared in 2018. *Photo by the author, www. queencityhistory.com.*

Part of the Bellevue Brewing Company complex as it appeared in 2016. *Photo by the author, www. queencityhistory.com.*

Before Hudepohl-Schoenling bought Burger's trademarks and used the name for a budget brand, it was a respected independent brewery that touted its use of artesian well water. *Christian Moerlein Brewing Company and Gregory Hardman.*

The abandoned Hudepohl plant on Gest Street facing a questionable future in 2018. *Photo by the author, www.queencityhistory.com.*

Both Schoenling and Hudepohl helped keep the tradition of seasonal bocks alive through the 1980s and '90s. *Christian Moerlein Brewing Company and Gregory Hardman.*

Above: 50 West Brewing Company opened in the former Heritage Restaurant in November 2012. *Photo by the author, www. queencityhistory.com.*

Left: St. Paulus Kirche (circa 1850) on Race Street in 2009. *Photo by the author, www.queencityhistory.com.*

Above: Part of the Rhinegeist Brewing Company today, the historic Elm Street Club building was threated with demolition after it was gutted by fire in January 2010. Here, Cincinnati firefighters continued to quell flare-ups in the following days. *Photo by the author, www.queencityhistory.com.*

Left: St. Paulus Kirche in 2018, restored and given new life as the Taft Ale House. *Photo by the author, www. queencityhistory.com.*

Above: Mural on Streetside Brewing Company in Columbia-Tusculum. *Photo by Minnesota Jones.*

Right: Paul Miller, a former clown for Ringling Bros., is now "Chief Goof-Officer" for Bircus Brewing Company in Ludlow, Kentucky. He serves tasty lagers and ales—and balances kegs on his chin. *Photo by Minnesota Jones.*

Left: Elias Gomez performs several roles at Bircus Brewing Company, including pouring beer, executing astounding acrobatics and eating fire. *Photo by Minnesota Jones.*

Below: David Walters poses in the nano-brewhouse of Off Track Brewing Company in Over-the-Rhine. *Minnesota Jones.*

Right: Pedestals and Roots is a mural on the Brewing Heritage Trail by artist Philip Adams (Philadelphia). Painted in 2016, it is an abstract of the brewing process. *Photo by the author, www.queencityhistory.com.*

Below: Revival was the first public art installation on the Brewing Heritage Trail. Painted in 2014 on the side of the former Crown Brewery by artist Keith Neltner (Neltner Small Batch, Camp Springs, Kentucky), the mural celebrates the past and future of brewing in Cincinnati. *Photo by the author, www. queencityhistory.com.*

Left: Artist Jim Effler created a label for the release of Christian Moerlein Lagerhouse in 2008 that pays homage to the brewery's history and updates an iconic ad image that was previously used in the late 1800s and revived in the 1980s. *Christian Moerlein Brewing Company, Gregory Hardman and Jim Effler.*

Below: Hazy IPAs at 50 West Brewing. *Photo by Minnesota Jones.*

This photo of Jackson Brewery workers during George Weber's tenure is not accompanied by names, but the man sitting behind the keg and looking to the side may be William Gerst. (In the author's opinion, he bears a strong resemblance to later photos of Gerst.) *From the collection of the Public Library of Cincinnati and Hamilton County.*

position of superintendent by 1883, the year that William and Archibald Walker left Cincinnati and purchased the Nashville Brewing Company.

For several years, the fates of the Walker brothers and the Moerlein-Gerst team ran parallel but unconnected tracks. As the Moerlein Brewery continued to expand into export markets, the company advertised heavily in Nashville. There were unique challenges in the South. Despite some growth in southern breweries, Nashville continued to be supplied largely by breweries in Cincinnati, St. Louis and Louisville. William Walker explained that this was due to differences in the markets. Specifically, the southern beer trade was much more seasonal, with sales dropping off precipitously in the winter. Nevertheless, Walker was pleased with life in Nashville. He took active part in promoting local music festivals, and in late July 1889, he told a reporter that he was not particularly interested in exploring offers to purchase the business. "Nashville is a good enough place for me to live," he explained, "and I shall be very slow to go away." Then tragedy struck.

Early in the summer of 1889, Archie Walker died from "a combination of illnesses." He was just fifty years old. Archie's death motivated his brother to leave the business. Although he had rejected previous offers from prospective buyers, William agreed to sell the Nashville Brewery to the newly formed partnership of Christian Moerlein and William Gerst in January 1890. Moerlein and Gerst announced plans to begin immediate, large-scale expansion of the facility. Although Moerlein supplied most of the startup capital, Gerst was able to buy his partner out in just three years. He changed the name to the William Gerst Brewing Company. The brand and the business grew, and it remained under Gerst family control until 1950. The brewery became one of the largest in the South, producing 200,000 barrels per year, and it was the only brewery that remained open in Nashville throughout most of the 1900s. Although the physically magnificent brewery was closed in 1954 and demolished in 1963, the Gerst name still looms large over the Nashville beer scene, leaving a legacy that traces back to a day when George Weber made William Gerst angry enough to try to throw a man into a furnace.

Following Archie Walker's death, William Walker sold the Nashville Brewery to partners Christian Moerlein and William Gerst in 1890. They completely rebuilt the plant, dramatically increased its capacity and announced bold plans for expansion. Eventually known as the William Gerst Brewing Company, it became the largest in Nashville and one of the largest breweries in the South, producing 200,000 barrels per year at its peak. *Tennessee State Library and Archives.*

Weber won the war over control of the Jackson Brewery, but his own penchant for self-destruction would catch up to him. Consistent with his standard business practices, he (figuratively) stabbed Brigel in the back and then invited a fresh mountain of debt to cripple the brewery again. Finally, in 1887, karma struck George Weber a decisive blow. The George Weber Brewing Company owned a large malt house at the corner of Twelfth and Clay Streets, in Over-the-Rhine. On July 4, neighborhood fireworks sparked a flame. The combination of dry, flammable grain, volatile grain dust and two large ventilation shafts that ran through the building caused the fire to spread with astounding speed. A neighbor was killed trying to rescue his life savings from his nearby apartment, and a second man died when he jumped roughly seventy feet to the sidewalk attempting to escape the flames. The massive six-story building was a total loss. Only a fraction of it was insured, and the investigations that followed revealed that Weber was upside down again. The brewery went back into receivership. Weber lost his remaining ownership in the business, and the name reverted to Jackson Brewery. Weber was forced to take a job at the St. James Hotel, rising to the rank of manager before dying on the job of heart failure at the age of sixty-four. Weber's obituary read, in part, "The deceased was one of the best-known brewers in America, having been brought to his prominence by his celebrated fight over the Jackson Brewery."

THE SECOND GENERATION
WRECKS THE FAMILY BUSINESS

I f the beer baron who rose from poverty and built an empire with his bare hands, hard work, honest dealing and savvy business acumen is a positive stereotype that validates the best attributes of the American Dream, several of the children of Cincinnati's nineteenth-century beer barons justify a different stereotype. Many entrepreneurs hope that their children will follow them into the family business, utilizing the bequeathed opportunities to cement the honor of the family name. Sometimes this works out nicely. The sons of Christian Moerlein, John Hauck and George Wiedemann, for example, all grew the family businesses and avoided any particularly embarrassing scandals. Other times, the second generation is the one that gets drunk to the gills on an unearned sense of entitlement and slams a wrecking ball into decades of hard-earned progress. Adding an unlimited supply of beer to the equation made breweries particularly susceptible to the curse of the second generation.

In 1850, 70 percent of Cincinnati's business leaders had worked their way up through the ranks, including a clear majority of brewery owners who scratched and clawed through menial jobs on their way to becoming beer barons. By 1880, only 35.8 percent of business leaders had reached the top the hard way. This percentage was still higher than found in many comparable American cities, but it illustrated a broader truth about the U.S. economy in the Gilded Age: an increasing percentage of the rich were inheriting their wealth. As this occurred, a surprising number of Cincinnati firms retained their status as "family businesses," with one to three individuals in charge. Brewing companies were no exception. Even as breweries began to incorporate in the late 1800s, a clear majority of them kept the bulk of brewery stock and management positions within the family. This meant that as the founding generation of beer barons aged, the personalities, ambitions, shortcomings and occasional criminal tendencies of their children could determine the fate of the family name.

The Hudepohl and Kotte partnership is a great example. After the death of both Koehler brothers, their Buckeye Brewery closed. After the site spent a few years as additional lagering space for other breweries, business partners Louis Hudepohl II and George H. Kotte reopened it in 1885. Hudepohl and Kotte quickly increased capacity from 25,000 barrels a year to 40,000, demolishing parts of the original brewery and building a much larger facility in its place. Nine years after they started the business, the Buckeye Brewery had a capacity of 100,000 barrels per year, making it one of the largest breweries in Ohio. Unfortunately, George Kotte didn't live to see the ten-year anniversary.

On November 1, 1893, George Kotte's face turned crimson, and he developed a nosebleed while having lunch. His symptoms rapidly turned gruesome. Kotte reached for his head, "gasped and blood spurted from his mouth." Moments later, he died on the floor of a Norwood saloon. His death was as unexpected as it was gory. Following his wishes, George's wife, Kate, and her father, John Taphorn, took over Kotte's responsibilities at the brewery. The arrangement worked out well. Together, Hudepohl, Kate Kotte and Taphorn continued running a profitable and harmonious business. Then the children got involved.

George and Kate Kotte had nine children. Son Louis proved to be the most troublesome. Louis was at his father's side when he died. As a teenager, he assumed the role of "man of the house," although it was a role that he bore at his own insistence and then performed poorly. A respectable period after George Kotte's death, Kate Kotte developed a close friendship with an architect named Theodore Sanning (or "Sannig"). There were even rumors that marriage might lie in their future, but Louis disapproved. He warned Sanning to stay away from his mother. Sanning ignored him, so Louis, a brother-in-law named Henry Kaiser and a third man decided to kill Sanning one night while drinking heavily in a Vine Street saloon. Overhearing this plan as it was discussed boastfully in the bar, one of Sanning's friends went to warn him. Sanning left home for the evening, which probably saved his life. Louis and his drunken pals trashed the architect's home and office and terrified his neighbors. Ultimately, no one was seriously hurt, so the episode was forgotten. It was, however, just one instance of Louis's bad, impulsive judgment.

Louis wasn't satisfied meddling in his mother's private life. He also decided that he was better equipped to run the family business. There was a magnificent flaw in George Kotte's Last Will and Testament. He bequeathed everything to Kate and gave her full authority to manage his affairs. He also specified that everything he owned should be divided equally among his children. Kotte probably wanted his estate to pass to his children after Kate's death, but that's not what the will said. As written, the will simultaneously left all of Kotte's worldly belongings exclusively to Kate and exclusively to his nine children. As soon as he reached the age of legal majority, Louis Kotte used this flaw in the will to contest it in court. Louis believed that his status as a pampered teen rendered him far more competent to participate in running the Hudepohl & Kotte Brewery than his mother and his grandfather.

An ugly and protracted drama ensued, both in and outside the courtroom. The stress certainly didn't help Kate Kotte when she began developing health problems, and the dispute ended when she died of appendicitis on November 8, 1899. She was only forty-seven years old. Fortunately for Louis Hudepohl II, he had enough money to buy the other half of the brewery from the Kotte heirs, and they were willing to sell. Hudepohl extricated himself from the Kotte drama, and in 1900, he became the president and sole owner of the renamed Hudepohl Brewing Company.

Tragically, turmoil persisted in the Kotte realm. In addition to a fortune left by George, Kate Kotte left an estate in her own right worth roughly $30,000—the modern equivalent of around $1 million. The combined inheritance from both parents should have made life easy for the Kotte heirs, but that's not what happened. Louis Kotte, who was so confident in his financial management skills, was made executor of Kate Kotte's estate. This included investing and safeguarding money that was held in trust until five of his minor siblings reached adulthood. By the summer of 1901, there were some clear deficiencies in Louis's duties as an executor. He wasn't filing the required financial reports with the probate court, and as it turned out, this was more than a disdain for paperwork. Louis retired from the working life in his early twenties and spent his time "investing" his siblings' money at racetrack betting counters. An arrest warrant and a manhunt later, Louis Kotte was dragged back from Chicago by Cincinnati police. Entrusted with a baronial family fortune, Louis squandered all of it, leaving just fifteen cents in the trust account. Louis's three adult siblings were forced to sacrifice their own inheritance to cover enough of what Louis had stolen from his

Louis Hudepohl II had several vocations before becoming a brewer. He sold medical supplies and then entered his father's wholesale liquor business. For a while, Louis I and Louis II, along with George Kotte, also sold real estate out of the liquor store. Louis II and George Kotte revived the Buckeye Brewery in 1885. Hudepohl was gregarious and affable, an ardent Catholic and Democrat, the leader of a singing group and a proponent of preserving the German language within German American communities. *Author's collection.*

minor siblings to keep him out of the penitentiary. George Kotte spent a lifetime working hard and making wise business decisions, but a family reputation that took decades to build was sullied by the second generation with astounding rapidity.

Only half of the Hudepohl-Kotte partnership spawned bad seed. Hudepohl had no male heirs, but his sons-in-law maintained the family business without any Kotte-style histrionics. At age fifty-nine, Louis Hudepohl II died from a wrecked liver. Afterward, the extended Hudepohl family remained at the helm of the brewery until the 1980s, while the Kotte name rapidly faded from history. The Kottes, however, were far from the only baronial beer family disgraced by the second generation.

Joseph Schaller fit the mold of the beer baron archetype as perfectly as his sons fit the archetype of the second generation. Born in Lore, Baden (later Germany), in 1812, Schaller worked on the family farm until age twenty-four and then immigrated to the United States, passing briefly through New York before joining large numbers of his countrymen in Cincinnati. He worked as a street paver, backbreaking work that paid a paltry seventy-five cents per day, and then got a job making vinegar. Schaller started his own business manufacturing vinegar and expanded it into a lucrative enterprise before partnering with Johann Schiff to buy and transform the Eagle Brewery. Johann Schiff also possessed a quintessential beer baron biography—born poor and building successful businesses from scratch along with a notable political career. By the age of forty-six, Schiff had amassed enough wealth to retire, and he sold his half of the brewery to Schaller.

Five years later, Schaller took on a new partner, John Gerke. Also a poor German immigrant, Gerke's life story trumped both Schaller and Schiff in its Dickensian qualities. He spent his youth as a shepherd, farmer and common laborer, immigrating to the United States at age twenty-one. After bouncing around Indiana, St. Louis and Cincinnati, finding a variety of ways to barely avoid starvation, he got a job making bricks, working extremely long hours. He eventually opened his own brickyard, became successful and saved enough money to buy a distillery. Nine months into his ownership, the distillery and one hundred barrels of aging whiskey were destroyed by fire. Gerke rebuilt, and the distillery was almost immediately wrecked by a tornado. Again, he rebuilt. In several years, Gerke had paid off his creditors and ran a lucrative distillery, making enough money to buy a 50 percent interest in Schaller's Eagle Brewery.

Schaller and Gerke "worked together like brothers" until Gerke's death in 1876. Like many of his brethren, Gerke's death appears to have been

Hudepohl, Louis

M W M 59-9-7   4-27-02   502

3046 Cleinview Avenue   *pg .46*

City   Brewer   *1902*

Cirrhosis of liver & Kidneys - heart disease

Dr. E.M. Schwab

Theo Homer   St. Joseph Old

Like many brewers and brewery workers in the 1800s, Hudepohl died young of alcohol-related illnesses. Born on July 20, 1842, he passed away on April 27, 1902, at the age of fifty-nine. Lung ailments were the most common cause of premature death in the nineteenth-century brewing industry, attributed largely to the constant inhalation of grain dust, but alcoholism was also a risk of the trade. *Archives and Rare Books Library, University of Cincinnati.*

caused or exacerbated by alcohol, officially succumbing to a combination of heart and liver diseases. Born into poverty, he spent most of his life struggling or broke but died worth an estimated $500,000 (roughly $12 million today). John Gerke's son, George, took over his father's role on the board of directors. Initially, the relationship between Schaller, acting as principal manager, and George appears to have been smooth and amicable. Like Schaller's sons, William and Michael, George Gerke spent his formative years working in the brewery and learning the business. Something, however, began to erode the relationship between these two families. It may have had something to do with the murder charges.

At about 12:45 a.m. on March 16, 1879, two Cincinnati police officers standing across from the Washington Platform Saloon, just south of the Schaller-Gerke Brewery, heard a gunshot ring out in the crisp night air and went running down Elm Street to investigate. They found William Schaller, Schaller-Gerke's traveling salesman J.L. Hahn, Washington Platform owner Fidel Bader and two other men sauntering up the street. The moderately intoxicated men were en route from the brothel that they had just departed to Washington Platform, where they planned to continue drinking. William Schaller confessed to shooting a gun into the air, and he was briefly placed under arrest before the cops recognized him. Realizing that they had committed a serious social faux pas by arresting a wealthy brewer—Cincinnati cops routinely drank for free at brewery taprooms while on duty—the officers released Schaller. He invited them up to the Platform to demonstrate his gratitude, and all was forgotten until after sunrise.

Early Sunday morning, a twenty-four-year-old traveling insurance salesman named Harry Baldwin died from a gunshot wound in the head. Initially, the case appeared clear-cut. Evidence suggested that Baldwin had been shot near where William Schaller confessed to shooting a gun, roughly at the same time. One gunshot plus one gunshot wound was simple math. William Schaller was arrested in the brewery-owned apartment where he lived and charged with murder. The case against Schaller quickly unraveled, but the crime was never solved. Charges against Schaller persisted, including allegations that the Schaller family paid vast sums of money to plant evidence. Even if Schaller wasn't guilty of murder, the case made Schaller's associations with brothels and bars front-page news for months. As the city's first high-profile unsolved homicide, the death of Harry Baldwin was a mystery that haunted the city for decades.

There may have been other rifts between the Schaller and Gerke families, but this one was probably sufficient. The cloud never quite cleared over the Schaller name, and the Gerkes decided to part ways. The split grew bitter. On September 1, 1881, George Gerke and his siblings offered to buy Joseph Schaller's half ownership in the brewery. Schaller accepted, but then he balked and refused to conclude the deal. Gerke sued and Schaller relented, even agreeing to a major concession. Schaller agreed that he would not "enter into the business of brewing beer in the city of Cincinnati, Ohio nor permit any person to use his name in said business" for a period of fifteen years. In 1881, the business was incorporated, and the name of the august institution was changed to the Gerke Brewing Company. As important as the Schaller name had been to the development of the region's brewing industry and its reputation for quality, *Reinheitsgebot*-brewed lagers, the Gerkes tried to erase the Schaller family name like a stain.

Just five days after Joseph Schaller made a legal vow to stay out of the brewing business, a judge ordered the Main Street Brewery sold for the benefit of creditors. It wasn't the first time. Opened in the early 1850s, the brewery changed hands multiple times, with a bad habit of stopping off in insolvency court between owners. Michael, William and Peter Schaller purchased the business on November 28, 1881.

HARRY BALDWIN.

On the morning of March 16, 1879, Harry Baldwin died from a mysterious gunshot wound to the head, and brewer William Schaller was charged with his murder. "Murder on the Menu" is a monthly event at Washington Platform Saloon & Restaurant that unravels the mystery of Baldwin's death. (More about Baldwin can be found at www.queencityhistory.com.) *From the collection of the Public Library of Cincinnati and Hamilton County.*

A promotional piece from the Schaller Brothers' Main Street Brewery celebrates the new year. *From the collection of the Public Library of Cincinnati and Hamilton County.*

Although Joseph Schaller claimed to take no part in the business, various transfers and mortgages leave reason to suspect that the elder Schaller was providing more than moral support to his sons. The renamed Schaller Brothers' Main Street Brewery did, however, grow into a formidable concern in its own right. The Schaller boys—Michael, William and Peter, at least—were competent businessmen despite a variety of personal failings. They kept a vicious bulldog as a pet that attacked a brewery worker on more than one occasion, felt compelled to publicly deny selling kegs to minors and maintained a gun fetish that William's near brush with prison didn't quell. They also clearly drank too much. While he was still the modern equivalent of a multimillionaire, Peter was accidentally shot in the thigh while spending a Sunday shooting rats at the aptly named Slimer Hotel. Michael's transgressions were more serious. Because his wife believed it was a sin, she refused to file for divorce, but she was forced to move out of their home on multiple occasions due to both psychological and physical abuse that included plausible death threats.

Conflict smoldered at the Schaller Brothers' Brewery. One source of it was eliminated when Peter decided to retire in 1889. He sold his interest to his brothers, receiving most of the money in annual mortgage payments. In addition to his share of the inheritance from his father, he never had to work again, which would have been his best career move. Instead, he kept getting lured into opportunities that all ended in failure. In 1905, Peter died at the age of fifty, leaving a widow and four children. Unfortunately, he left them broke. Of the roughly $200,000 that Peter Schaller inherited (roughly $5 million today), ill-conceived business ventures and other bad decisions only left $3,000 remaining before the debts of the estate were settled.

William Schaller died in 1895 of spinal meningitis. At just forty-five years old, he was the youngest of the Schaller brothers. He was a widower with children, and nothing seems to have marred his reputation after his indictment for murder was dismissed in 1881. He died a wealthy man, never conceding any guilt in Harry Baldwin's death. Some acrimony between William and his brothers continued to wreak havoc at the brewery after his demise. Terms of William's will revealed a deep distrust of his brother and led to a court fight over the brewery. Ultimately, Michael got clear title to the brewery, and he had the mortgage debt to his brother Peter nullified in the process, adding to Peter's financial woes. He removed "Brothers" from the brewery's name, formally changing it to the Schaller Brewing Company. On March 10, 1899, Michael Schaller died in his Corryville home. The *Cincinnati Enquirer* called him "a man of family." Indeed. His two children and the wife he repeatedly abused were at his bedside when he died, although his surviving siblings seemed to be absent. The Schaller Brewing Company, however, would live on. As a corporation, it was no longer beholden to the personal abilities or failures of its namesake family.

For all their various personal foibles, the Schaller brothers knew how to run a brewery. It's more difficult to reach the same conclusion about the Kauffman heirs. On his way back from a funeral in Erie, Pennsylvania, John Kauffman appeared to catch a cold in Cleveland. It was an irritating but minor malady, so he continued his journey home and resumed work at the brewery when he reached Cincinnati. In hindsight, he was suffering symptoms of a far worse ailment. The cold got worse, and he began coughing blood. On January 15, 1886, the wealthy and tenacious brewer died at the age of fifty-five. Kauffman's famed lineup of Bohemian and Bavarian-inspired lagers, brewed with imported hops and malt and aged on ice for seven months, were selling well, and the brewery was in the process of significant expansion.

Kauffman left all his estate to his wife, Maria, which was particularly apropos since he owed much of his accumulated wealth to the inheritance that she received from her father. Maria may have been capable of adroit brewery management, but her sons never gave her the chance. The sons were not objectively incompetent. Kauffman had overseen their training, brewing education and mentorships, and they were accomplished brewers. But as more time passed in their father's absence, the more the Kauffman boys—all well into adulthood—found ways to act like unsupervised children.

As treasurer of the Kauffman Brewing Company, Michael Kauffman was embezzling money—a lot of it. He denied the charges, blaming the former treasurer, but he was ultimately trapped. Right before a forensic audit began, the assistant bookkeeper suddenly vanished from town "under peculiar circumstances." It became clear that Michael had stolen at least $24,000 while acting as treasurer. He never admitted responsibility. Instead, he said that while he was in charge of the company's finances, "nearly every member of the firm [had] a key to the safe and could take money when ever he desired." There may have been plenty of blame to go around, but Michael Kauffman died of "acute congestion of the lungs" in the summer of 1893, and money quit disappearing.

John Kauffman Jr. brought a more personal form of scandal to the brewery. He married Blanche Bree, a woman with a disruptive comportment far exceeding her diminutive size. Blanche was a concert hall singer. She had a beautiful voice and a grandiose theatrical presence that she didn't bother leaving at the theater's exit. She was often described as beautiful and had a number of admirers, although the *Cincinnati Enquirer* once cruelly described her as the "little woman with the homely face and short curls." In the modern vernacular, Blanche was high-maintenance. She lived with John Jr. in an apartment above the main brewhouse and offices on Vine Street, and her behavior became a disruptive embarrassment to the brewery. Her status as a beer hall performer, with multiple versions of her last name and different, conflicting biographies, also didn't help.

Probably acting on Maria Kauffman's instructions, brewery manager (and John's brother-in-law) Emil Schmitt gave John an ultimatum: divorce Blanche or lose your job. Faced with losing Blanche or losing his comfortable position in the family brewery, John Jr. chose the job. It wasn't the romantic choice. As things turned out, it wasn't the safe one either. Emil Schmitt, the force that was separating her from her beloved husband, became the target of Blanche's rage. She hid in a doorway with a gun and waited for her nemesis to leave the brewery for lunch. When he stepped out onto Vine with his young son, she leveled the revolver at his head and pulled the trigger. The gun misfired, and Schmitt wrestled it from her hands, grabbed her and marched his attempted assassin to the police station.

Blanche returned to singing in Vine Street theaters and beer halls. She stayed in the limelight but out of trouble for almost a month before her next attempted murder. On September 2, 1894, John Kauffman Jr. boarded the train to the affluent suburb of Glendale, where he kept a summer home. Unbeknownst to him, Blanche also boarded the train. Blanche had grown obsessively jealous of a woman who worked in a bakery across the street from the brewery. She spied on her husband, had a young boy shadow him and was even caught hiding under his bed by a startled maid. Although she still declared her love for John Jr. to be deep and endless, she expressed in her thick French accent that she had decided to kill Kauffman so that "zee girl in zee beckerei cannot 'ave 'eem."

Walking through the aisle of the train car clearly seeking someone with frenzied determination, Blanche drew the attention of several passengers, although John Jr. remained oblivious to her presence. Spotting him, she stepped up behind him, pulled a cocked gun from her dress, steadied herself by placing one hand on the back of a seat, placed the muzzle next to John's head, closed her eyes and pulled the trigger. Although the gun was almost touching Kauffman's head, the shot went wild. The ball traveled down the side of his face from ear to jaw. As John Jr. tried to process the copious blood and searing pain, Blanche re-cocked the revolver for a second shot.

THE BULLET FROM MRS. KAUFFMAN'S REVOLVER STRIKES HER HUSBAND.

John Kauffman Jr. broke several conventions when he married a French actress and beer hall singer named Blanche Bree. When brewery manager Emil Schmitt forced John Jr. to divorce Blanche, it sparked a shooting spree. She attempted to assassinate both Schmitt and John Jr. *From the collection of the Public Library of Cincinnati and Hamilton County.*

A brakeman grabbed her hand and wrestled the gun away. The wound was dangerous, but John lived and made a full recovery.

John Kauffman Jr. and Blanche Bree were eventually divorced. She only spent a few months in jail for two attempted murders. Her fine was covered by a theater promoter, who considered it an investment. She packed the house as "the beautiful ex-wife of the well-known brewer." Although legally restored to her maiden name—one of them—she performed as Blanche Kauffman, drawing crowds as a result of both her talent and infamy.

John Jr. eventually became the sole surviving heir to the Kauffman empire. He acted as president of his father's company until Prohibition forced it out of business in 1920. His second wife, Mary, found his lifeless body lying on the floor of their home in July 1926. Ironically, he had succeeded at what his first wife, Blanche, had attempted and failed. John R. Kauffman was dead of a self-inflicted gunshot wound to the head. Friends and relatives were distraught, shocked and confused. At age sixty-eight, the retired brewer seemed healthy and in good spirits. There appeared to be no justification for suicide, although a possible motive emerged in Probate Court. Mary Kauffman, widow and executrix, was forced to declare the estate insolvent. In the years following the brewery's closure, the last heir to the once prodigious Kauffman brewing fortune had gone broke. The Kauffman empire was gone. All of it.

By the turn of the century, some family-owned breweries had morphed into true corporations. Other breweries incorporated but retained tight family control of ownership, which occasionally worked out well. However, as brewing became big business, the dream of leaving empires to offspring had mixed results. The Kotte and Kauffman families were not anomalies. Christian Boss's sons took sibling rivalries to the extreme of getting into a gunfight in the middle of the Gambrinus Stock Brewery. Friedrich Billiods's grandchildren squandered an inherited fortune in such a spectacular style that the story is too complicated to tell here. Even though it sometimes took multiple generations, many of the city's breweries were eventually wrecked by family disputes or the incompetence of heirs.

WHY SOMEBODY HAD TO
MAKE A LAW AGAINST IT

By the dawn of the 1900s, it wasn't just the spoiled heirs of brewing empires who were behaving badly—so were the breweries themselves. Temperance advocates laid a lot of blame for social chaos at the feet of local beer barons. Blaming alcohol for rising crime rates, domestic abuse, vagrants, prostitution and political corruption was overly simplistic, although the "drys" aired legitimate beefs. By the late 1800s, Cincinnati had too many saloons. That wasn't just the opinion of the temperance people; it was a fact that was eventually recognized publicly by breweries and many saloon owners themselves. The first step toward fixing a problem, of course, is admitting that it exists, and that took a while. Before breweries decided to become part of correcting the excesses of the bar business, they practiced a lot of denial and diversion.

The first statewide prohibition law was passed in Maine in 1851. Ohio prohibitionists longed for a similar eradication of demon rum here in the heartland, but it was clear that Ohioans weren't there yet—at least not in sufficient numbers to amend the state's constitution. Instead of promoting prohibition legislation that was destined to fail, Ohio drys took what they believed was a three-quarter step toward their ultimate goal. They wanted to begin by eradicating saloons. By shutting down the dens of sin, alcohol would be effectively out of reach for most poor and working-class Ohioans, and both prostitution and gambling would be evicted from storefronts across the state along with liquor. Implementing this dream required both a constitutional amendment as well as broad statewide legislation. That's what the drys proposed, and it's what they got, but things didn't turn out as planned.

In 1851, Ohioans voted by a narrow margin to eliminate the tavern and saloon licensing system by amending the Ohio Constitution. As amended, the constitution now provided that "[n]o license to traffic in intoxicating liquors shall hereafter be granted in this State, but the General Assembly, by law, provides against evils resulting therefrom." Previously, cities, towns and rural townships were all empowered to issue liquor licenses to prospective business owners who wanted to open a country tavern or urban saloon (also known as "coffee houses" or "Porter houses"). This amendment stripped local governments of the right to approve, regulate and tax bars. Along with this amendment to the constitution, the temperance lobby convinced the Ohio legislature to pass a statute that prohibited the sale of alcoholic beverages for on-site consumption, a power that it now possessed thanks to the new amendment. Together, these changes in the law criminalized the saloon business.

Once saloons were criminalized, the bar business ceased operating. Every saloon in the state was closed, with the exception of those that remained open to pour glasses of fresh farm milk, often served with a wholesome side of prayer. Just joking. In reality, this legislation had almost the exact opposite result as drys intended. Some rural taverns in very conservative parts of the state were either driven out of business or forced to become "blind tigers," the illegal bar precursor to speakeasies. In towns and cities, the impact of this new, revolutionary social change ranged from minimal to imperceptible. The most immediate impact was the elimination of a notable source of local government revenue. Ironically, in fact, that is how the amendment passed. The amendment eliminating liquor licenses would not have passed with the support of drys alone. Exit polling didn't exist, but interviews with voters from the time suggest that many people—particularly saloon owners—voted to ban local governments from issuing liquor licenses because they believed that the only change that it would render in their businesses would be the elimination of license fees and taxes. It is impossible to calculate how many of these pro-liquor cynics voted for the anti-liquor amendment, but there is reason to believe that there were enough of them to make a difference in the narrow outcome. Ultimately, these voters were the only ones who got the kind of change that they were looking for.

In the absence of liquor license requirements and restrictions, the number of saloons blossomed. In addition, if there were no fees, licenses or taxes associated with selling booze, there was no reason not to incorporate small-scale bars in a wide variety of businesses—no practical reason, at least. Selling alcoholic beverages by the glass was, of course, illegal after 1851, but by the time that the law went into effect, there were more saloons in Cincinnati than there were police officers and voters didn't support the enforcement of such an asinine law. The net effect of this great temperance success was "the liquor traffic" that the drys wanted to curb entered a golden era of anarchy and gross excess. Saloons popped up everywhere, and a wide variety of businesses sold drinks by the glass.

Groceries, billiard halls and bowling alleys could all find startup capital that they needed from a brewery, but the businesses that were most likely to have a direct tie to breweries were saloons and beer halls. The "tied-house" system was an old idea that originated in Europe, but it caught hold with particular vigor in the United States during the second half of the 1800s. Although there was a variety of specific arrangements, the basic concept was simple. Breweries provided saloon owners with the capital and other things that they needed to open and run their businesses, and in exchange, the saloon would agree to exclusively carry that brewery's beer.

There was nothing inherently wrong with the arrangement. An entrepreneur got a shot at the American Dream; the brewery added a new, dependable account; and neighbors enjoyed one more neighborhood saloon. The problem was that the free market did a poor job of regulating its own health. By 1890, Cincinnati was home to roughly 2,000 saloons and about another 1,400 businesses like groceries that sold drinks by the glass. Sheer numbers created problems and made competition among saloon owners stiff. In response, saloonists relied more heavily on supplemental forms of income, like illegal slot machines, and supplemental draws and amenities, such as prostitution and craps games. Just like today, crime was driven by a number of complex social factors, but some of the math was pretty simple. By making their credit and capital available to prospective saloonists, breweries were largely responsible for filling cities with too many saloons.

In many instances, particularly in the 1870s and 1880s, breweries addressed this problem by denying it. The Schaller & Gerke Brewery boasted to the public and its customers that it was "entitled to credit for not injuring the business…by setting men up in the saloon business here and there on the condition that the latter will purchase their beer." It was a gutsy claim to make because it was only necessary to walk a few dozen feet from the Schaller & Gerke Brewery to prove that this was a lie. Just four years before making this claim, the firm helped a bartender named Fidel Bader lease the Washington Platform saloon, across the street from its brewery.

MECKLENBURG'S GARDEN — CINCINNATI, OHIO — *Established 1865*

Mecklenburg's Garden in Coryville was a Moerlein tied-house. Mecklenburg leased the establishment from the Moerlein Brewery and, in exchange, was required to exclusively purchase Moerlein beer. *Mecklenburg's Garden.*

Although it was patently false that Schaller & Gerke didn't participate in the tied-house system, its activity in this realm may have been less than some of its competitors. Like Fidel Bader, Louis Mecklenburg was a bartender who wanted to own his own saloon. In his case, it was the Christian Moerlein Brewing Company that came to his aid. Moerlein leased the saloon— known subsequently and since as Mecklenburg Gardens—and sublet it to Mecklenburg. In consideration for this opportunity, Mecklenburg paid rent and agreed to "purchase all the beer used and sold on said premises both in bottle and kegs from the Christian Moerlein Brewing Company."

It is difficult, maybe impossible, to determine the extent of the tied-house system in Cincinnati or to conclude how it differed from other American cities. It didn't become a common practice in the United States until roughly the 1880s, although brewer Friedrich Billiods owned property on Vine Street that he rented to Francis Voglebach's saloon by 1859. When this saloonist went out of business, he was replaced with a new bar operator. The Lafayette Brewery wasn't big enough to make a meaningful contribution to the scourge of nineteenth-century crime, but Billiods certainly did his part to keep his small piece of the world sopping wet. He owned three adjacent properties on Vine Street, and all three of them simultaneously hosted saloons for a while. This wasn't a coincidence. At least one of these leases prohibited the storefront from being used for any purpose *other* than as a saloon. Billiods's leases did not specifically require his tenants to purchase his beer, but that doesn't mean that unrecorded—possibly even unwritten—agreements didn't include such terms. If so, it suggests that some Cincinnati breweries were importing the tied-house system well before it became commonplace in other American markets. By 1881, in fact, it was already estimated that one-fifth of the city's saloons were "virtually owned by the brewers."

Some breweries did a much better job of preserving their role in the saloon trade than others. The John Hauck Brewing Company, like Moerlein, had no qualms with specifying in its leases that saloon operating tenants were required "to sell and exclusively use on said premises the beer

Simon Arnold stands in front of Arnold's Saloon on Eighth Street, circa 1878. A John Hauck Brewery sign beside him suggests that the saloon primarily or exclusively sold Hauck beer. *Arnold's Bar & Grill.*

manufactured and sold by the John Hauck Brewing Company," but often these arrangements were part of side agreements. They could have been included in leases on backbars, bar furniture and fixtures, for example, or they could simply be gentlemen's agreements. Every piece of furniture, shelving, glassware and keg cooler in a saloon could be purchased with the help of a brewery's credit, bought or leased directly from the brewery or loaned to a bar by a brewery perpetually and for "free" as long as nobody else's beer crossed the threshold.

The Ohio legislature wasted a lot time in the 1880s passing legislation that would effectively act as a liquor license without the necessity, or courage, of amending the state constitution to specifically return to a licensing system. Bills were passed that taxed saloons and required the closure of any saloon that failed to pay. Since saloons were already illegal, this was a backdoor approach to granting legal status to any bar that paid its tax bill. The Supreme Court found, logically enough, that the legislature had effectively created a form of liquor license. Since the Ohio Constitution as amended in 1851 still made liquor licenses unconstitutional, the tax law would be ruled unconstitutional. This would be followed by the passage of a similar law, followed by a similar Ohio Supreme Court decision.

Finally, in December 1886, a political shift in the court caused the "Dow Law" to stick. Every saloon in the state had to pay a hefty tax or face being shuttered, and failure to pay the tax on time resulted in crippling fines. With just four days between the court's decision and the deadline, saloonists across town ran to the courthouse. Lines stretched for hours on the last day to pay, with the treasurer's staff foregoing lunch and dinner and working into the wee hours processing payments. As the dust settled, the treasurer calculated that there were roughly 2,140 saloon proprietors in Hamilton County that paid the tax. Roughly 80 percent of these paid the bill on their own, while about 30 percent had their taxes paid by either a brewery or a wholesale liquor dealer. Despite severe penalties, an additional 800 to 900 establishments didn't pay the tax because they refused to, simply couldn't or were unsure whether or not they were permitted to pay the Dow tax. Brothels were the most common example of the last category. This doesn't provide an accurate count of local tied-houses, but it suggests that the staggering number of saloons in Hamilton County rendered the overall percentage of tied-houses relatively small in comparison to some other cities.

The Dow Law was a blessing and a curse for the beer business. It helped prune some of the smaller dives that were more trouble than they were worth as beer accounts, which also improved the business of larger saloons and brewery-owned tied-houses. Initially, the Dow Law also legalized Sunday beer sales for the first time in Ohio's history. In its one major concession to brewers and bar owners, the law allowed municipalities to vote themselves either wet or dry on Sundays. Cincinnati, of course, wasted no time passing an ordinance that legalized the sale of beer and native wines on the Sabbath. The alderman who introduced the proposed ordinance deemed it a mere "formality." The council treated it as such, suspending the ordinary rules to pass it quickly and without fanfare, but it was a necessary requirement for legalizing beer sales on Sundays. What the alderman meant, apparently, was that it wouldn't really change anything since the law against Sunday sales was already being ignored.

Two years later, the Sunday question took a precipitous turn for the worse. Sunday sales had always been illegal in Ohio, and the law had typically been treated as a dead letter. There were exceptions. In 1882, there was an increase in the fine and a brief enforcement fervor. Hundreds of saloonkeepers were arrested for opening on Sunday, bonded out and returned to their bars to finish the workday slinging drinks. It was a waste of time for the prosecutors, judges and cops and an irritation for the saloonists, so things went back to normal and the Sunday law received only a little more attention than the law that criminalized saloons seven days a week. The local option provision in the 1886 Dow Law legitimized existing reality and temporarily restored some respect for the legal system in general.

Both changed abruptly in 1888, when the legislature voted to abolish the local Sunday option. All Sunday sales were criminalized again, and the penalty for breaking the law was raised to a $100 fine (roughly $2,500 today) and up to thirty days in jail. Saloonkeepers were indignant. At a May 1888 meeting of the General Protective Association of Saloon-Keepers, the members voted to simply ignore the law in collective protest, and the Brewers' Protective Association vowed to stand behind them. Local breweries resolved not to sell beer to private parties on Sunday because it hurt the business of saloonkeepers that remained open in defiance of the law, and they contributed funds to the resistance, which consisted of litigation and bailing bartenders out of jail.

Eventually, however, breweries grew increasingly concerned with public relations damage that saloons could reap. Cincinnatians liked to drink on Sundays, but they disliked open, unchecked disregard for the law, and they felt compelled to object—publicly, at least—to the baser forms of vice, like prostitution and gambling. The saloonkeepers' acts of rebellion ultimately proved futile. By 1895, Cincinnati's mayor was claiming that

This Moerlein tied-house on Elm Street depicts several common aspects of nineteenth-century saloons. A fork and bowl suggest a free lunch. All the customers are men with the exception of two women found near the "Sitting Room" section of the business. *Brewery District CURC and the Brewing Heritage Trail.*

public intoxication was down precipitously, the saloon trade had improved its reputation and "[a]ll liquor places are closed on Sunday, and whatever traffic is carried on is done surreptitiously and in the quietest manner possible." He was undoubtedly overstating the case, but the additional risks associated with Sunday sales does seem to have subdued Sunday Funday a bit. All liquor places were not closed on Sunday, but they were quieter—and an increasing number of establishments decided that opening on Sundays wasn't worth the liability.

Cincinnati breweries were at the forefront of organizing as an industry to fight collective challenges. Throughout the nineteenth century, brewers participated in several successive organizations. These occasionally weakened or disintegrated, but local breweries remained well organized and symbiotic, at least for competitors in a cutthroat business and a saturated market. In 1897, the region's twenty-six breweries reorganized as the Cincinnati, Covington and Newport Brewers' Exchange. By joining this organization, the local breweries all agreed to be bound by a set of self-imposed regulations. Members could only sell beer for a standard price established by the Exchange. They also agreed to limit types of advertising and curbed their generosity toward saloons. Breweries were no longer permitted to give free ice to saloons, provide them with bar furniture, equipment, glassware or "gifts of any kind." Breweries could not "put a man up" in the saloon business, pay his rent or other expenses, including the $250 annual Dow Law tax. To hold themselves true to their word, the breweries collectively deposited roughly $100,000 in trust and signed an agreement to be bound by Exchange rules, which included getting fined for breaking these rules. Local breweries agreed to these terms to avoid self-destruction through increasing competition. Over the previous ten years, the price of a keg of beer had fallen from $2.75 to less than $1.30—roughly 47 percent. Brewers claimed that profit margins were razor thin and that it was impossible for any of the city's breweries to survive a price war without cheapening their product and damaging Cincinnati's reputation for "pure and unadulterated" beer.

They were also trying to rein in some of the more destructive elements in the saloon business. A beer in the late 1800s cost five cents at a bar regardless of whether it was a dive or a posh hotel. At least that was tradition. It wasn't a law or a formal requirement, but it was what consumers consistently expected to pay. In a city awash with saloons, someone was bound to look for a competitive edge by offering a better deal. This first came in the form of schooners, extremely large glasses. Serving schooners meant that a dive could give drinkers more beer for the money while still selling "a glass of beer" for five cents. Breweries bound together, with the rousing support of most saloon owners, and quashed this practice by refusing to sell beer to schooner bars. Similarly, "buy one get one free" specials were also curtailed, along with a price reduction to three-cent beers.

Even in 1897, it was hard to earn a living on three-cent beers, so there was a cascade of effects from these price reductions. Saloons needed to make more demands for free things and financial assistance from breweries, ask for cheaper beer or both. In addition, financially strapped saloons were more susceptible to looking toward other avenues of income, like slot machines or direct involvement in prostitution. It had become "a well-known fact" that breweries were subsidizing hundreds of saloons that would otherwise go out of business without a seemingly endless supply of freebies. These saloons were parasites to the rest of the bar business, as well as the breweries. Brewers claimed, in fact, that five unspecified breweries had been driven into insolvency during the preceding two years as a result of propping up failing saloons. (One of these was likely Foss-Schneider.)

Although respectable saloonkeepers appreciated attempts to curb three-cent beers, they resented many other measures adopted by the Brewers' Exchange, and they voiced these objections vociferously in a meeting of the

Saloon Keepers' Association called at the Washington Platform. Saloonists were so incensed that some vowed to start buying their beer from the "foreign" breweries that were gaining a foothold in the Greater Cincinnati market—brands like Pabst and Anheuser. Brewers responded that the saloon subsidies in Cincinnati were "without parallel in any other city in the country." Pointing out some of the excesses of the local saloon trade, the brewers noted that growlers were often being sold for take-out at less than it cost the bar to fill them, and that lunch specials that promised customers a filling lunch and two beers for ten cents were economic suicide. These were valid points, but rifts between the brewers and saloonists would continue to emerge and fester until the bitter demise of both.

Rifts would also continue between breweries themselves. Although they agreed to be bound by the rules of the Brewers' Exchange for their mutual survival, and all deposited substantial sums of money that could be drawn on to pay heavy fines, cheating and lying were a lot easier one hundred years before the Internet. When asked about the number of saloon leases that they held, several breweries gave suspect replies. The Christian Moerlein Brewing Company, the largest in the city with real estate holdings and leases all over (and out of) town during the 1800s, claimed not to know the number of saloon leases it held, but a brewery spokesman thought it was "about six." Both Foss-Schneider Brewing Company and Hudepohl's Buckeye Brewing Company claimed to hold "four or five" saloon leases. Gerke Brewing Company admitted that it held "about ten" and that several of these properties were operating at a loss. Windisch-Muhlhauser estimated that it would wind up losing between $3,000 to $5,000 on eight different saloon properties. Gambrinus Stock Brewing Company, Banner Brewing Company and Bellevue Brewing Company claimed to only hold two or three each and expressed satisfaction with their tenants. The Jackson Brewing Company claimed not to hold any brewery leases in Ohio, although rumor held that it lost money on out-of-town arrangements. Sohn, Herancourt and the Jung Brewing Company all denied having any tied-houses at all. It's possible that all these statements were true at the moment they were made in 1897, but regardless of what they pledged to the Brewers' Exchange, local breweries had no intention of abandoning the tied-house saloon trade.

This was especially true of the Jung Brewing Company. In the spring of 1898, the company went on a surreptitious leasing spree, acquiring numerous properties throughout the city but placing a priority on grabbing corner storefronts in the West End, along with prime space downtown and Over-the-Rhine. Within six months, it entered into more than a dozen

A Herancourt
Brewery tied-
house. Herancourt
revolutionized local
beer in 1851 but was
driven out of business
by Prohibition. *From
the collection of the Public
Library of Cincinnati
and Hamilton County.*

saloon leases. Jung's modus operandi was to specify as little as possible about the business in the leases. Whenever possible, the company clearly preferred to lease property without describing its use, and it insisted on a provision that allowed it to sublet the premises at its discretion. Some properties or owners required more. Several leases refer to saloons, and one particularly prudent landlord insisted that Jung agreed to operate the property "for a quiet orderly Saloon," adding that any sublease required written consent.

Breweries frequently owned investment properties that were not directly related to brewing, as well as apartment or mixed-use buildings that contained lagering cellars underneath for overflow aging and storage space. Sometimes they leased storefronts in these buildings to saloon operators, and sometimes they specifically prohibited saloons, restricting the use to the current or proposed business. The Jung Brewing Company illustrated why this was prudent. It subleased a prominent corner on Sixth Street in a building that was owned by rival brewer, Christian Boss, of the Gambrinus Stock Brewing Company. Although it signed an agreement not to "set men up" in the saloon business in 1897, between then and 1901, Jung entered into more than two dozen saloon leases. It did, however, keep the terms of agreement with the operators private, shielding the exact nature of the arrangement between the saloonkeeper and the brewery.

The Jung Brewing Company was particularly flagrant in its acquisition of saloons, but it wasn't alone. In 1899, the Ohio State Brewers' Association met in Cincinnati, and brewers from across the state voted unanimously to adopt a resolution that prohibited any brewery in the state from leasing property for saloon purposes. There was, however, an important caveat: Ohio's brewers enthusiastically supported this restriction on their own business practices but suspended enforcement of the rule "until other state organizations of brewers adopt such resolutions." Actually, other states already had. What Ohio brewers were really looking for was a binding national consensus. It was a valid concern, as while Ohio brewers were trying to roll back the tied-house problem at both state and local levels, out-of-state breweries like Pabst Brewing Company from Wisconsin were signing leases and establishing their own tied-houses in Cincinnati. For all its entanglements and pitfalls, the tied-house system was embedded in the industry, and legislation would be required to extract it.

Saloon owners accused breweries of monopolistic behavior. They had a point. Collectively, local breweries blacklisted people for selling schooners or three-cent beers, and they cut off bar owners if any brewery alleged that the saloonist owed it money. They also established a price for a keg of beer that none of them deviated from—except when they did. In 1901, the Herancourt Brewing Company was insolvent and under the management of a court-appointed receiver. One of the receiver's first decisions was to declare that being under court protection meant that the brewery was no longer obligated to comply with the rules of the Brewers' Exchange. Therefore, Herancourt dropped the price of a keg from the established $3.50 ($7.00 per barrel) to $3.00. It had taken several years to inch the prices back up, and the other breweries went ballistic. Herancourt's receiver, however, stuck to his guns, claiming that the price reduction was necessary to compete because, despite their sanctimony, other breweries were secretly cutting their own prices in violation of Exchange rules. The Jung Brewing Company was specifically accused by name, and the brewery may have been supplying its stable of tied-house saloons at reduced rates.

Ohio's bar owners also struggled in their attempts to save their collective profession through self-imposed rules. In a statewide convention in 1902, Ohio saloonkeepers adopted a resolution to abolish free lunches. According to legend, the free lunch promotion was born in Chicago shortly after the Great Fire of 1871, when a bar owner named Joe Mackin started giving away a free oyster with every drink. If Mackin was really the first, it didn't matter for long. The practice spread through Chicago almost as fast as the fire had, then throughout other American cities just as quickly. An oyster almost immediately morphed into sides of roast beef and hams on the bar, and in the spirit of competition, saloonkeepers throughout urban America were soon conducting promotions that lost money. Once customers began to

The Chicago Bar, on the corner of Walnut and Court Street, advertises a hot and cold free lunch, night and day. (The Court Street Market is on the right side of the photo.) *Kenton County Public Library.*

expect a free lunch, saloonkeepers were stuck. Nobody wanted to be the first barkeep on the block to stop the practice, so resolutions were inadequate to end the economically disastrous tradition.

Brothels both posed and faced a separate set of problems. It was a felony to run a brothel, and state law imposed a penitentiary sentence on anyone selling liquor in affiliation with a house of ill fame. This law, like most of the state's vice laws, was largely ignored. Taxing saloons had the de facto effect of legalizing them, but there was no similar understanding with brothels. Proprietors operated with little regard for the Dow Law tax until a 1902 modification to the law required brothels to pay a $350 annual tax for selling liquor to patrons. Unlike with saloons, this tax was imposed without any reciprocal immunities in exchange, even though the tax acted so much like a liquor license that it was typically referred to as "a license" by both the public and the press. Saloons with sitting rooms already paid the tax, so state officials could only come up with a list of seventy pure brothels that served liquor in Hamilton County without paying Dow taxes.

Although they lacked a formal organization, brothel owners banded together and hired legal counsel to challenge the constitutionality of a law that forced businesses to pay a tax while simultaneously declaring the businesses illegal. This had nothing to do with breweries directly, but it drew public attention to the fact that Cincinnati's brothels were regular accounts for the breweries and given regular service like a saloon, hotel or any other business. It is likely that some of the city's brothels also received direct support from breweries in one capacity or another.

In 1904, the Cincinnati, Covington and Newport Brewers' Exchange was disbanded and replaced by the Brewers' Board of Trade. It was the same organization and carried over the same rules and procedures with a few modifications. The primary difference was the name. After seven years, it occurred to the members that brevity was a virtue. Carrying over all the existing members and adding some newer breweries, it had twenty-one members. The organization took credit for placing "the liquor business on a higher plane" and pledged to continue this progress under the new name, continuing to work toward ensuring the respectability of the saloon trade. It was a hard yet often ambivalent fight, but brewers got a little "help" from the state thinning out the saloon herd.

In 1906, the Ohio legislature increased the Dow Law tax from $350 to $1,000 per year—roughly the equivalent of raising the annual cost of a bar's liquor license renewal fee to $25,000 today, while the price of a beer remained at $0.05, or the modern equivalent of roughly $1.50. The measure was so draconian that very few people believed that it would pass, and saloon owners, cigar makers, liquor dealers and brewers were all taken aback when the vote was announced. The dramatic increase in the tax was not tailored to clean up the saloon business because there was no causal relationship between size and respectability. Some of the largest, most prominent bars in town were full of illegal slot machines, and prosperous theaters and beer halls were favorite haunts of prostitutes, whereas many of the smallest saloons were quiet, respectable family businesses or modest attachments to grocery stores. The saloons that were most profitable, in fact, often tended to be the sleaziest, rowdiest dives.

The precipitous increase in fees (a measure that was known as the "Aikin Law") had a dramatic effect. Statewide, an initial 3,306 saloons were forced to close. Some parts of the state were affected more than others. Roughly 63 percent of all saloons in Summit County were shuttered, reducing the number of watering holes from 310 to 113. As a matter of pure percentages, Fayette County was hit the hardest by losing 2 of its 3 saloons. It was a bloodbath in Cuyahoga County, home to Cleveland, where 875 saloons were driven out of business. Hamilton County lost the second-largest number, seeing the initial closure of 364 establishments. Cuyahoga was still left with 1,870 bars, and Hamilton emerged with 1,606—roughly half the number that had existed when taxation began in 1886—although the number would continue to fluctuate with late payments and new businesses driving the total up to 1,793 and then falling to 1,763 in 1907.

Alarmed by the inroads that were being made by temperance and Prohibition forces nationwide, the Ohio Brewers' Vigilance Bureau was formed to investigate immoral behavior, expose the worst dens of iniquity and publicly demand their closure. The bureau also possessed an acute interest in hypocrisy. The first arrests to be made at the bureau's insistence occurred in Columbus, where two establishments were raided by police at the bureau's urging for being "frequented by fallen women." One of these prostitution-focused dive bars was located on State Street, just a block and a half from the capitol. The vigilance force was just getting rolling. It had identified and was continuing to investigate an additional thirty-three saloons for a variety of reasons, including catering to known felons, harboring prostitutes and violating midnight closing laws. The bureau noted that the worst dives in town were "within a stone's throw of police headquarters."

In Cincinnati, the bureau began by demanding the closure of the Majestic Concert Hall on Vine Street. It was chosen for reasons that were both objective and purely political. "Sitting rooms" were the focus of moral crusaders in Cincinnati. The euphemism was used in different ways. Most commonly it referred to an open room where men mingled with prostitutes before going somewhere else, but some sitting rooms were the rendezvous point themselves.

Many of the city's most prominent breweries owned or leased tied-houses with sitting rooms. However, the Cincinnati wing of the Vigilance Bureau conveniently overlooked all of these establishments when it decided to demand only the closure of the Majestic Concert Hall, accusing its owner of committing a sin that transcended harboring prostitutes and maintaining sitting rooms. At the Majestic, teenage girls as young as twelve could often be found falling into a life of ill repute. Something else caused the Majestic to stand out among the crowd: it was owned by a Cincinnati city councilman named Dan Bauer. As Percy Andrea, who was both president of the Jung Brewing Company and chairman of the Ohio Brewers' vigilance committee, explained, the Majestic was "the one place in the city conducted practically under warrant from the Mayor himself."

Andrea told the press that "as long as the Chief Executive countenances such a place," the Vigilance Bureau would be "severely handicapped in dealing with [other places] of a similar character."

Moral crusaders who were not affiliated with the beer or liquor businesses pointed out the flaw in this logic. Rather than grandstanding over the closure of one politically well-connected concert hall, brewers could instead shut down countless other establishments by simply refusing to sell them beer, stopping subsidies or evicting their most disreputable tied-house tenants. The dramatic increase in the liquor tax caused more businesses to become reliant on breweries to pay or front their $1,000 Dow Law tax, so that by 1907 an estimated 50 percent of all Dow Law payments made in Hamilton County were "paid either by brewery checks or by the breweries themselves." Hamilton County's assistant county treasurer alleged, in fact, that breweries were paying the Dow tax for a majority of the city's brothels, most of which would be forced out of business without this assistance. For the moment, however, the city's breweries would need to take these matters under advisement. Brewers remained vociferous about their commitment to separating the saloon trade from prostitution and gambling, although it was unclear what they were going to do about it. Speaking as chairman of the Brewers' Vigilance Bureau, Percy Andrea would later claim that local breweries had tried to cut off bad actors, but even when every brewery in town cooperated, an out-of-town firm was happy to fill the void.

Ohio's brewers, distillers and wineries began to join forces to advocate for a return to the liquor license system in Ohio. In the past, the collective adult beverage lobby had opposed essentially any restrictions or hindrances on alcohol sales. Around 1908, the group changed strategy. Laws were challenged more selectively, and industries that had historically balked at regulation started advocating for it. The adult beverage industries believed that license systems that limited the number of saloons by population, enacted character qualifications for license applicants and provided for the loss of licenses for violations of vice laws were the only hope for preventing more drastic legislation, meaning statewide prohibition. With the support of breweries, Ohio enacted and began sporadically enforcing laws that acted like a license without being called one. Convicted criminals were no longer allowed to operate saloons, nor were saloon owners allowed to participate in or even condone prostitution or gambling on their premises.

Breweries, however, continued to accumulate tied-houses. If anything, the practice became more important to the industry. In 1909 litigation between board members of the Bellevue Brewing Company, the court noted that "the

Good
for
Little
Tots

Barbarossa Beer
is good for the
children be-
cause of the
care with
which it is
brewed by the Moerlein process, after the good old honest
German fashion—and of the best materials. It is as pure as
can be, healthful and invigorating.

ORDER DEPARTMENT:
TELEPHONE CANAL 2400.

This 1905 ad explains why Moerlein's flagship Barbarossa was "good for the children." *From the collection of the Public Library of Cincinnati and Hamilton County.*

business of all brewing companies throughout the country depended largely upon [breweries] being able to secure locations for saloons, where they can control the sale of their beer." That same year, *McClure's Magazine* chastised the nation's breweries for filling American cities with too many saloons, estimating that the brewing industry had invested $70 million in American saloons. It was a national problem, but one that was more acute in some parts of the country versus others. The United States Brewers' Association frankly concurred that both Ohio and Indiana were "over-salooned," placing the blame on inadequate license laws, although the breweries continued to contribute to the problem by propagating and sustaining far too many bars. By 1911, several local breweries were each paying the Dow tax for between

50 to 140 saloons, which added up to roughly 50 percent of all the saloons in Hamilton County. Saloon owners paid the breweries back on monthly installments, but they were still indebted to the brewers for fronting lump sums that they couldn't muster on their own.

Tied-houses had grown even more prolific elsewhere. In Indianapolis, it was estimated that 75 percent of all saloons were controlled directly or indirectly by breweries. Although the industry tried to laugh off attacks by religious leaders and moral crusaders, it was harder to dismiss criticisms and warnings that came from their own ranks. At a national brewing convention, the president of the Houston Brewing Company warned attendees that investigations were proving that "a majority of the vicious dives in all cities were either owned or controlled by the brewers, who had the power to regulate them or close them entirely," and that they were going to feel a growing public wrath if they did not avail themselves of one of these two options. Cincinnati breweries largely ignored this advice, until the State of Ohio decided to force them out of the bar business.

Ohio held a state constitutional convention in 1912. Several dramatic, progressive changes were recommended and adopted by Ohio voters. Reinstitution of a liquor license system was among the changes. Speaking on behalf of the liberal, pro-license forces, Percy Andrea blamed temperance fanatics for creating disreputable saloons when they succeeded in abolishing the liquor licenses system in 1851 and declared "the final overthrow of that most pernicious coalition of interests known to modern times—the unholy alliance between the criminal dive-keeper and his creator, friend and sponsor, the Anti-Saloon League." Although brewers were pleased with the constitutional revival of a license system, some specific provisions of the license legislation were more than they bargained for. The total number of saloons was capped at one for every five hundred residents, and proprietors had to meet character and fitness qualifications for holding a license. Licenses could also be revoked if a bar was caught permitting gambling or prostitution on the premises.

Brewers supported all these provisions. What took them aback was the abolition of the tied-house. Although breweries were still permitted to own real estate that they leased to a saloon, they could no longer hold any pecuniary interest in the saloon itself and could not require the saloon to carry their beer—exclusively or at all. A brewer's lease to a saloon could not be different in any respect than it would be to any other business. Legally, at least, a strict partition was drawn between the saloon business and the brewing business. Any saloon that had an exclusivity agreement with a

The Bellevue Brewing Company, originally called Klotter & Sons, opened in 1866 on the north side of a bend in the Miami & Erie Canal. It was a midsize local brewery. Suffering from bitter internal conflicts within the board of directors, the company was struggling in the 1910s and closed at the outset of Prohibition. (The building has been known best in recent years as "The Mockbee.") *From the collection of the Public Library of Cincinnati and Hamilton County.*

brewery would be denied a license. This wreaked more havoc in some cities than others. In Toledo, the Huebner Toledo Brewing Company controlled three hundred saloons in $1 million worth of brewery-owned real estate, and an estimated 90 percent of the city's saloons were tied-houses. Fewer than eight saloons in the entire town owned their own bar fixtures. Breweries controlled hundreds of Cincinnati saloons, but the saloon business was generally more independent here.

The total number of saloons in the state of Ohio reached its peak in the early 1900s at roughly 13,000. Under the new license law, the maximum cap would be between 5,100 and 5,200. In Hamilton County, 539 saloon owners were denied a license. Without prior warning or compensation, their livelihoods had been declared illegal. Although the loss of businesses was a bitter pill to swallow, former saloonists in every village, town and city throughout the state accepted their fate and gave up the ghost—with one notable, irritating exception: Cincinnati. Here, roughly 100 saloonkeepers remained in operation without a license and in open defiance of the law. At the governor's vehement insistence, however, even Cincinnati was forced to heel by the end of 1913.

Cincinnati breweries didn't exactly get out of the tied-house business as the law required. Some just took it underground. Although the law only permitted one person or company to own one license, and it precluded breweries from requiring saloons to carry their beer, breweries worked a black market in saloon license transfers. While most people who obtained a license wanted to stay in the saloon business, others just wanted the opportunity to sell the license at a handsome profit and find a new vocation. Due to their scarcity, a liquor license on the resale market ran between roughly $2,500 and $4,000. Operating, furnished and stocked saloons with a valid license sold for up to $10,000 (roughly $250,000 today). That was a lot of upfront capital for most people, but not for breweries, so they could front the money to a willing seller and accept payments from a buyer, provided that the buyer agreed to exclusively carry their beer. This was blatantly illegal, but it happened.

Generally speaking, however, breweries accepted the new license terms, partly because it was the law but also because they recognized the need to reform their image. In 1916, breweries across the country started voluntarily reducing the alcohol content in their beer from a typical 7 percent ABV (alcohol by volume) to around 4 percent. This was accompanied by a renewed push to market beer as a healthy, "non-intoxicating" alternative to hard liquor. Although all the changes were disruptive and costly—at least so brewers believed—these drastic changes in the production and sale of beer would surely pacify enough of the public to stop Prohibition. Of course, that's not what happened.

DARK BEERS MAKE A COMEBACK AND THE SHERIFF GETS INTO THE BEER BUSINESS

Statewide prohibition was first enacted in Maine in 1851. The law prohibited both the sale and manufacture of alcoholic beverages. During the next four years, twelve additional states and one U.S. territory followed suit and banned booze. Briefly, it seemed that Americans would rid themselves of the scourge of demon rum by the end of the 1850s, but immigration patterns helped suffocate this puritanical dream in its crib. The Irish Potato Famine started in 1845, lasted until 1852 and continued to have broad impacts on the country for decades. Roughly 1 million Irish fled Ireland in these years, with U.S. cities being their most popular destination. German immigration also continued, with some uptick and changes in patterns following the revolution and counterrevolution in 1848. The result was that just as the temperance movement was successfully taking over the American political system, thirsty Irish and Germans were filling American cities, becoming citizens, voting and reversing the tide.

By 1855, the prohibition wave had already waned. Statewide prohibition amendments and legislation were reversed or simply became dead letter law by around 1860. The non-united states were busy trying to destroy themselves between 1861 and 1865, and then Reconstruction took most of the South's attention for a while. By 1900, only three states were still trying to enforce prohibition laws. Temperance, however, did not go away. The Woman's Christian Temperance Union was founded in 1874, and the brilliantly Machiavellian Anti-Saloon League was organized in 1893. The Anti-Saloon League realized that the ultimate key to success rested in strategic takeovers of state-level government, and its strategies worked. It lobbied for local option laws like the one adopted in Ohio in 1902 and strengthened in 1908. These laws allowed parts of the state to vote themselves dry.

Starting in Georgia in 1907, the League revived and modernized the statewide prohibition campaign. Following success in Georgia, thirty additional states went entirely dry prior to national Prohibition. Even in Ohio, where large majorities of wets in the cities successfully blocked statewide measures on several occasions, the Anti-Saloon League made plodding, consistent progress. After Ohio's local option law was modified in 1908 to make going dry easier, sixty-two of the state's eighty-eight counties banned alcohol. In 1914, statewide prohibition was again placed on the ballot in Ohio. It was defeated, but just narrowly, and numbers should have been alarming to any wets who were paying attention. With more than 1 million votes cast, prohibition was only defeated by 84,152 votes, and 75,696 of those votes that kept the state wet came from Hamilton County. Cincinnati was carrying roughly 90 percent of the burden of keeping the state of Ohio from falling dry, and eventually the Queen City's drunks were just outnumbered. Ohio voted itself dry, with statewide prohibition going into effect on May 26, 1919. This was followed by the implementation of national Prohibition on January 16, 1920.

Bedlam was predicted. The chamber of commerce estimated that eight thousand Greater Cincinnati workers would lose their jobs and that 1,044 saloons would go out of business. Locally, distilleries would also fail, and of course, the region's thirty local breweries would all be shuttered. Cincinnati's mayor gloomily announced that Prohibition would force the city to "face the most serious financial situation in its history." City officials predicted the direct loss of $570,000 in city revenue, $60 million in annual business and $15 million in property investment. Ultimately, the prediction that all the region's breweries would close came mostly true. There would be only one true survivor, but the carnage was not immediate. Local breweries took several approaches to Prohibition, which determined how long they clung to life.

The Christian Moerlein Brewing Company took the most realistic approach to Prohibition by exercising its right to die. In the summer of 1917, Moerlein had the foresight to enter the near-beer market a few years before other breweries hastily entered the market by necessity. It made Moer-Lo "from the finest hops and the best cereals under the most ideal conditions." Advertising for the near-beer was not that different from the brewery's real beer campaigns. Moerlein continued to advertise its flagship

Barbarossa label as a "Temperate Drink," "a most wholesome beverage" that was not only delicious but also acted "as a tonic and strength-builder." Moerlein promised that Barbarossa "refreshes the weary, strengthens the weak…promotes digestion and stimulates the stomach's action." Consumers could be forgiven for failing to understand the difference between Moer-Lo and other, full-strength beers that they had, for years, advertised as healthy, invigorating and perfect for children. Moer-Lo was, however, something even more wholesome. The most conscientious of parents could have a case delivered to their door and let the "whole family try it." Moerlein wasn't smart for making Moer-Lo because it sold well. It appears that it didn't, but the company almost certainly gained extremely important knowledge from its early near-beer experiment. Moerlein invited the public to judge Moer-Lo, and people rendered their verdict by sticking to real beer. By the time other breweries were trying to convince themselves that near-beer was simply the future of brewing, Moerlein already knew that it was the taste of financial death.

This turn-of-the-century mother is unwilling to share her "mommy juice," but *not* because her daughter is too young to imbibe. Moerlein's brews were good for young and old and endorsed by all the best physicians. *From the collection of the Public Library of Cincinnati and Hamilton County.*

By the fall of 1919, the Christian Moerlein Brewing Company had thrown in the towel. Prohibition was the law and near-beer didn't sell, so the brewery started selling what it could: bottling machinery, boilers, engines, ice machines, pumps, compressors, glass enameled bright tanks, empty bottles, beer cases and delivery trucks. In the spring of 1920, it started stripping fixtures and advertising the sale of various sizes of steam, water and ammonia piping, valves and fixtures and "brewer's hose." Then the company listed all its real estate, focusing on the versatility of the different parts of the brewing campus. The brewhouse, bottling plant and icehouse could all easily be converted to new, useful warehouse or manufacturing purposes. Then, on October 31, 1921, John Moerlein, the seventy-five-year-old son of Christian Moerlein, heir of a doomed empire, passed away at his home. The Christian Moerlein Brewing Company was dead, although unlike other brewing families, the various Moerlein heirs made money on the liquidation of the company.

Louis Hauck also preserved the family's wealth by bowing out early. The brewery closed in 1919, although the company was less fatalistic than Moerlein. It leased space to compatible industries, letting most of its equipment go dormant but keeping it intact. The E. Kahn Sons meatpacking company leased the brewery's stockhouse and replaced aging beer with 3 million pounds of cured meat. The Red Top Malt Extract Company took additional space, eventually buying the brewery itself. At the end of Prohibition, the brewery was fully intact. The Hauck family never returned to brewing, but money made on beer established a charitable foundation that still survives.

The dismal pallor that enshrouded the Gambrinus Stock Brewing Company on Sycamore was almost fatal. Gambrinus was in its third generation of Boss family ownership when Prohibition hit. Christian Boss bought the brewery from pioneer brewer Pierre Jonte, converted it to lager production, expanding greatly, and built a successful firm. Son William Boss took over the reins until his forty-five-year career came to an unexpected end. Although he was not considered seriously ill, the sixty-three-year-old William Boss died following a "nervous breakdown." That's how his thirty-two-year-old son, William A. Boss, became president of the company.

With the criminalization of the family business looming, Boss's wife said that he "worried over prohibition until he was nearly crazy." On St. Patrick's Day 1919, he became unhinged. Boss had lunch with several brewery employees and floated cheerfully through the celebratory mood in the taproom before slipping into his office and retrieving a gun. He scratched out a short note that read simply, "I am in the hands of my friends, and I request Undertaker Sullivan to bury me from my mother's home." Then he stepped into a lavatory and shot himself in the left side of his chest. Holding the gun in his left hand, he must have pulled the trigger with too precipitous of an angle to hit his heart. Ultimately, the wound was ugly but not particularly dangerous. Boss recovered, although the once-proud Gambrinus Stock Brewing Company did not. It brewed a near-beer named Gam that promised to possess the "old Gambrinus merit," but it didn't. After just a few months of trying to rely on Gam to keep the lights on, Gambrinus folded. The brewery buildings were sold, and part of the brewery became a parking garage.

Other breweries went down with more of a fight. The first brewery busts took place in November 1920. Agents brought in from out of town visited one hundred saloons and eight breweries, taking samples of purported near-beer and analyzing the actual alcohol content. When the tests were completed, the Hudepohl Brewing Company, Herancourt Brewing Company and Jackson Brewing Company were all seized by the federal revenue collector. All operations were shut down, employees were kicked out of the facilities and armed guards stood vigil at the doors twenty-four hours a day. The breweries may have been assuming that Prohibition officials would let modest violations of the law slide. If so, they were wrong. Although the tests showed that beers sampled at saloons and the three offending breweries only contained between 1.11 percent to 2.96 percent alcohol by volume, this was enough to violate the Volstead Act, which prohibited the manufacture of beer (or any beverage) containing more than 0.5 percent.

The beer was mild, but the potential penalties were harsh. All three breweries faced possible revocation of the federal permits that allowed them to brew near-beer, along with fines that could have ruined the companies. Internal Revenue officials presumed that all three breweries had been manufacturing illegal-strength beer since the beginning of Prohibition and that they had failed to pay a collective $1.5 million in taxes as a result. Herancourt appears to have faced the largest possible penalty of $577,000. Ultimately, all three breweries settled. In exchange for $15,000 fines, they got to continue making near-beer and avoided hundreds of thousands of dollars in assessments for back taxes. In theory, brewery officials also avoided jail time, although not even the most ambitious federal prosecutors had made any serious attempt to lock up brewery executives for making real beer—not yet. That would come later.

Both Hudepohl and Jackson would live to brew another day. In fact, both would live to face more Volstead Act violations. Herancourt, however, did not recover. The brewery had been struggling financially even before Prohibition hit, and being reduced to brewing actual near-beer was the final straw. Herancourt was still trying to emerge from insolvency proceedings, and stockholders tried to hold the court-appointed receiver personally liable for both the $15,000 fine and roughly $15,000 in legal fees. The company couldn't withstand both Prohibition and infighting, and the plant was sold to the International Union of United Brewery, Flour, Cereal and Soft Drink Workers of America, which converted it into the American Ice & Storage Company in an effort to save the plant and replace brewery jobs. Nationwide, by this time roughly 50 percent of the union's members were unemployed.

It somehow became an accepted fact in Greater Cincinnati's history of Prohibition that the breweries that managed to stay open "reaped large profits for several years with production of near-beer." There is, however, absolutely no evidence to support this widely repeated belief. If a brewery or two managed to eke out a profit from near-beer, it was the exception to the rule. When the Jackson Brewery was charged with brewing 2.96 percent beer, a member of its board of directors testified that the brewery had incurred "great expense" installing equipment to dealcoholize beer in compliance with federal law and that since Jackson was relegated to manufacturing near-beer, monthly financial statements showed that the company was making "no profit whatever."

The Schaller Brewing Company provides the clearest insight into why some breweries survived and others, like Gambrinus Stock and John Kauffman, consistently lost money until they closed. Schaller survived the death of all three Schaller brothers and lived on as a viable concern into the early days of Prohibition. Then near-beer sent the business into a death spiral. By January 1921, the brewery was broke and seeking protection from creditors in Insolvency Court. Schaller executives asked the court to appoint Michael Hilsinger as receiver. Hunter S. Thompson once said, "When the going gets weird, the weird turn pro," and there is no more fitting explanation for why Michael Hilsinger was placed in charge of a brewery. He was undeniably smart, but most of his experience appears to have been in saloon management, a vocational path that he pursued competently although not always legally. This made him the perfect man for the job. Anything that Hilsinger lacked in knowledge of the brewing profession he compensated for with his moral pliability. Schaller didn't have bad debt. It just wasn't making money for one key reason: very few people wanted to buy near-beer. Once the court placed Hilsinger in charge of business affairs, he met with the brewmaster and hatched a plan. They decided to make a new near-beer with better prospects. The improved product would differ in two fundamental ways. First, they changed the malt to produce a darker, richer brew. Second, they gave it roughly a 4 percent alcohol content.

Near-beer didn't sell, but real beer did. The Schaller Brewing Company's profits took a distinctly positive turn, and Hilsinger received accolades and the most meaningful form of praise: a raise. His $50 a week salary was raised to $125, and the court ordered Hilsinger to pay himself back wages reflecting the change. All was going great at the brewery until it was raided by federal Prohibition agents on September 9, 1922. Near-beer was made by first producing beer of an illegal strength and then using a process to reduce the alcohol content to at or below 0.5 percent. That meant that it was not inherently illegal for a brewery to *possess* illegal-strength beer, so agents needed to follow a beer delivery truck from Schaller to saloons and confiscate it at the point of delivery in order to prove that the brewery was *selling* illegal-strength beer. Agents also raided the brewery itself, confiscating "good beer" from the taproom and off shelves where it was destined for delivery to clients.

The Schaller system was simple. The brewery's dark beer contained 4 percent alcohol, and its light-colored beer was legal near-beer. Saloons received deliveries of both, paying $9.20 a barrel for the near-beer and $18.00 a barrel for the "good beer." A saloon owner testified at trial that the only way he could determine whether a beer delivery contained "near" or "good" beer was by a "wink of the eye, a nod of his head and the price given to him by the driver." Saloons sold the good stuff to people they trusted, and Hilsinger placed the additional $8.80 made on each barrel of dark beer in one of two safe deposit boxes that he maintained in a downtown bank—$9.20 of each barrel of "good beer" was accounted for, while the money in the safe deposit boxes acted as a form a petty cash drawer. Hilsinger explained that this was about practicality. He could use this money for making repairs and performing essential business without getting court approval as the receiver, but the extra $8.80 added up to more than petty cash. When Hilsinger was appointed receiver of the brewery, the company was down to $28.40 in its bank account. By the time Schaller was raided, Hilsinger had squirreled away $35,000 in one of the safe deposit boxes alone, and the brewery's on-the-books business was also doing well. Since Hillsinger's tenure began, the $28.40 in the ordinary business account had been joined by an additional

$100,000 in receipts. It was an amazing turnaround. It wasn't too good to be true, but it was too good to be legal.

Hilsinger claimed that the only difference in the dark beer was the quality and that Schaller customers were simply discerning enough to pay twice as much for a truly good, non-alcoholic beverage. You had to be both drunk and stupid to swallow this, and nobody did. A popular rumor provided the best explanation for why Hilsinger kept the extra money in a safe deposit box. According to the din on the street, several local politicians were receiving $5 in protection money for every barrel of real beer that was sold by multiple Cincinnati breweries. If so, it was a bad investment. Prior to the Schaller case, the government had been satisfied to hit breweries selling illegal beer with hefty fines, as had been the case with Herancourt, Hudepohl and Jackson, but Prohibition Commissioner Roy A. Hanes decided to make Schaller a test case for a change in policy. Hilsinger, former brewery president Michael Keck and account collector Joseph Herrman were all charged with criminal conspiracy to violate the Volstead Act. While the company faced fines totaling approximately $50,000, each of the three defendants faced two-year federal prison terms and $10,000 fines. The jury took a little over three hours to find all three defendants guilty. Hilsinger was sentenced to one and a half years in federal prison and $6,000 in fines. Keck received one year and one day in the federal pen, along with a $500 fine, and Herrman was sentenced to serve six months in the Montgomery County Jail in Dayton and pay $1,500 in fines and costs. These sentences marked the first time in America since Prohibition became law that brewery officials were sent to prison for selling beer.

Hilsinger remained free on bond pending an appeal of his sentence. During that time, the Insolvency Court took up the matter of whether he should be removed from his position as receiver of the brewery. He was, but not because of the criminal conviction. The court found that the company no longer required a receiver. Hilsinger had paid all its debts, was producing a profit and had accumulated a net total of $73,821.30 in the bank—not bad considering the expense of graft and bribes. Despite some curious lack of detail in the accounting, everyone was pleased. Hilsinger was awarded $20,000 in compensation in addition to his weekly salary. This helped with his fine and lost income, but the Hamilton County Insolvency Court judge couldn't do anything to keep him out of federal prison. Hilsinger's, Keck's and Herrman's sentences were all upheld. Herrman went to jail, and on December 4, 1924, Hilsinger and Keck started serving their terms in the federal penitentiary in Atlanta. Commissioner Roy A. Haynes expressed his satisfaction with the verdict, crowing that "the enforcement of the eighteenth amendment here in Cincinnati is constantly improving."

Cincinnati's brewers were less enthusiastic about this victory for law and order. Risking fines was one thing. Risking the degradation and disgrace of a prison term was another. It is unclear how many of the city's breweries were making illegal-strength beer at the time of Hilsinger's conviction, but almost all of them would be a good guess. Federal prosecutors readily admitted that other breweries were breaking the law, but the Schaller raid cooled things down and the Schaller criminal convictions temporarily turned the spigot off all over town. Hudepohl sought alternative means of income. The brewery started to sell malt extract, which was legal, but a zealous Prohibition agent filed charges against the brewery because he bought a five-gallon can of the extract that was accompanied with "a recipe for making good beer from the contents." Hudepohl's license to manufacture near-beer was temporarily revoked but quickly reinstated. The company eventually quit brewing non-alcoholic beer on its own for financial reasons. Hudepohl stayed in business through Prohibition distributing soft drinks and near-beer made by other breweries, but the company allowed its brewing equipment to go dormant.

As Prohibition dragged on, the stakes got higher. Violations of the law grew more blatant and more deeply corrupt as breweries needed to find and rely on some form of protection. The Mohawk Brewing Company was one of the breweries making real beer when Schaller was raided. Brewery officials got nervous and tried to go straight for a while. Fear couldn't turn red ink black, so Mohawk dove back into the real beer business with better insurance. Rather than selling directly to the public on a wink-and-a-nod system, Mohawk bought into a network of runners and crooked law enforcement. Unfortunately for brewery executives George H. Osterfeld and Joseph Osterfeld, their protection had holes in it. The brewery was raided on August 3, 1925. Federal agents shot at a delivery truck driver as he fled the scene with a load of contraband, and agents stormed Mohawk, seizing sixty full barrels and thirty-four half-barrels of real beer. Once again, its alcohol content was low, testing at just 2.5 percent, but it was well beyond the legal limit. It was easy to understand the temptation to break the law. While people didn't want near-beer at around twelve dollars per barrel, café owners paid prices ranging up to between forty-five dollars and sixty per barrel for good beer—a commodity that was selling for less than ten dollars per barrel before Prohibition. What was shocking about the Mohawk bust was the public officials who also faced criminal charges.

Harry "Butch" Worthman was arrested and charged with conspiracy. Worthman sold influence and connections. A Cincinnati city councilman posted his bond. Richard B. Witt was a much more sensational defendant in the alleged conspiracy to keep Cincinnati awash in good beer. At the time of his arrest, Witt was the very popular sheriff of Hamilton County. According to federal prosecutors, Mohawk as well as other Cincinnati breweries were making real beer. Worthman used his truck and a web of trusted connections to distribute it to various forms of speakeasies, and Sheriff Witt provided protection from local prosecution and tips about raids. Ultimately, all the defendants in the case, ranging from Worthman to truck drivers and brewery executives, pleaded guilty as charged, and several agreed to testify against the sheriff.

The case against Witt was compelling, partly because he failed to deny several suspicious or scandalous allegations. It was true, Witt confessed, that he was conducting private business with the Mohawk Brewery. In addition to being sheriff, Witt was a contractor. His firm was doing roof work at Mohawk, and this apparently caused him to stop by there frequently. Witt's visits, however, were not restricted to the roof. He had a good, long friendship with brewery officers George and Joe Osterfeld. Not only was he aware that they were making full-strength beer at Mohawk, but he typically drank a few "good beers" himself when he stopped by on business or general social calls. Despite their friendship, the Osterfelds testified against Witt. They said that he had vouched for "Butch" Worthman. He always asked about how the relationship with "Butch" was going when he stopped by to drink illegal beer, and he played an active role in the "good beer" conspiracy. Sheriff Witt even hauled beer in his company's truck on occasion, and immediately after the raid, he told the Osterfelds, "It looks as if we were double-crossed."

That was the story according to the Osterfelds and other witnesses. Sheriff Witt told a slightly different story. He admitted drinking at the brewery and occasionally joining other "business men" there for private lamb chop and steak dinners. He even continued to stop by and drink with the Osterfelds after the raid, but according to the sheriff, the raid never came up in their conversations. He flatly denied the rest of the allegations. Sheriff Witt said that he didn't know anything about a beer ring or illegal sales, didn't provide protection to anybody and didn't know "Butch" Worthman. Some of the denials bordered on comic, but Witt kept his composure and conviction. Only Worthman, the confessed bootlegger, confirmed Witt's version of events. It took the jury just an hour and forty minutes to reach its verdict. They declared Sheriff Witt not guilty, and the room erupted in "one of the greatest demonstrations ever witnessed in the United States District Court in Cincinnati." The crowd assembled in the courtroom clapped their hands and cheered until both the judge and the clerk needed to bang their gavels repeatedly to quiet the din. When court was dismissed, a crowd of well-wishers rushed the sheriff. Businessmen and lawyers lined up to congratulate him, and one young man broke from the crowd to embrace the sheriff in a hug. Witt was so overcome with the affection of his constituents that he had to fight back tears. It was a touching scene in the annals of Cincinnati corruption.

Witt went free while six members of the conspiracy who pleaded guilty were all sentenced to jail time or fines. Cooperation in the trial was looked on favorably, however, and brewery president George Osterfeld was only sentenced to six months in the Miami County Jail (which was also used as the local federal lockup). Joe would join him there for four months of the term, and other brewery employees escaped with fines. The judge believed that "Butch" Worthman was a liar, so he slapped him with a year and a half in the Atlanta Penitentiary. (Atlanta, Georgia, was the federal prison used by the U.S. Southwest District of Ohio at the time.) George and Joseph Osterfeld took solace in their religious belief that confession brought absolution, but the family felt disgraced by the convictions and shielded George and Joe's seventy-six-year-old mother from the news of the raid, trial or jail sentences. The Mohawk Brewing Company was padlocked by the federal government and willfully dismantled by the stockholders.

During the weekend before the Monday raid on the Mohawk Brewery, rumor said that Prohibition agents let four hundred barrels of "good beer" made by a different brewery escape their grasp. Newspapers didn't print the name of the alleged offender, but one thing seems certain: it was not the Crown Brewing Company. Crown brewed a near-beer named Tang during Prohibition. Its advertisements for Tang, however, were extremely suggestive. There were essentially two types of beer during Prohibition: near-beer, which contained less than 0.5 percent alcohol, and "good beer," which was a universal euphemism for beer with an illegal amount of alcohol (real beer). Like Schaller's illegal-strength beer, Tang was a "Special Dark Brew." It "tast[ed] like more." Tang "[brought] back memories of olden days"—when beer could get you drunk. The most common theme in Tang's advertising was the use of the euphemistically loaded adjective "good." It was a "good drink" that was available "Wherever Good Drinks Are Sold," and the "full zest" of Tang acted as a "real tonic for tired nerves."

The advertising for Tang was so pervasive and so flagrant in its implications that it seems unlikely that all of it contained an illegal amount of alcohol, but it may have been a way of informing consumers that some batches of Tang were better than others, depending on where you bought it. If Crown stayed in the real beer business, though, it got spooked—or tipped off—prior to the raid on the Mohawk Brewery. On February 10, 1925, company stockholders were advised that the board of directors had "ordered the discontinuance of the manufacturing department because the business cannot be continued without incurring large losses." Stockholders were advised that the brewery had remained open in the hope that Congress would come to its senses and legalize beer again, but Crown was out of money. The jig was up.

It's possible that no keg or bottle of Tang ever contained an illegal amount of alcohol. The company might have been relying on subtly deceptive advertising practices. Ernst Uhlmann provides the best support for this theory. Uhlmann had a unique right to be bitter about Prohibition. In 1898, Uhlmann became the "father of near beer" when he patented a process for dealcoholizing beer. As the brewmaster at Crown until his death in 1922, Uhlmann likely created Tang. It's possible that his personal knowledge of the dealcoholizing process allowed him to make a superior product.

Amid increasing local enforcement of federal Prohibition laws and dismal sales of near-beer, the party ended at the Crown Brewing Company in 1925. *Author's collection.*

Unfortunately for Uhlmann, however, even fewer people cared about quality near-beer in the 1890s than in the 1920s. Dealcoholizing beer was such an unpopular idea that Uhlmann let the patent expire well before the first few years of Prohibition could have made him filthy rich.

Prohibition was no more popular in Northern Kentucky than it was in Ohio. In fact, Commissioner Roy A. Haynes spoke approvingly of Cincinnati's relative respect for the law in comparison to other cities, whereas Newport and Covington were lambasted by federal agents as "black spots" of liquor enforcement. Despite the fact that Kentucky's state prohibition law empowered every cop in the commonwealth to enforce Prohibition, by late 1921 not a single arrest had been made for Volstead violations in Campbell or Kenton Counties (where Newport and Covington are located). Of course, Kentuckians may have simply shrugged off generations of tradition and given up drinking in mass, but that's not what federal agents found every time they raided one of the multiple speakeasies, "blind pigs" or raucous roadhouses in Northern Kentucky. Raids suggested that whiskey, moonshine and full-strength beer ran freely in the northern reaches of the commonwealth. There were a lot of reasons for this. The Wiedemann Brewery was one of them.

Saturday night, January 29, 1927, federal agents surrounded a truck, halting the delivery of beer kegs to Heidelberg Gardens, south of Newport. Agents watched the truck leave the George Wiedemann Company and followed it. Following seizure of the truck, Prohibition forces stormed Wiedemann and confiscated sixteen barrels of beer that contained 4 percent alcohol. Thirteen defendants were charged with an ongoing conspiracy. According to federal prosecutors, the Wiedemann Brewery had distributed 1,534,638 gallons of illegal alcohol (roughly 99,000 kegs). Federal officials padlocked the brewery and, in addition to seeking criminal penalties, sought the forfeiture of the entire brewery and affiliated real estate, valued at approximately $1.5 million. It was much higher stakes than previous brewery cases in Greater Cincinnati. Despite the seriousness of the case, there were problems getting both Charles Wiedemann, brewery president, and Carl Wiedemann, vice-president, to show up for trial. The reasons were different. Charles, one of founder George Wiedemann's sons, was seventy-one years old and declared too ill to attend the trial by his physicians. Charles's son Carl was just irresponsible. At the opening of proceedings, the trial was delayed, to the great dismay of the judge, while a defense attorney and a U.S. marshal motored around Newport looking for Carl. They found him in a saloon at the corner of Brighton and Eleventh Streets. He was drunk. While the case was pending, Carl was also arrested for drunk driving in Newport—a much harder feat to accomplish in 1927 than today.

Ultimately, most of the blame was laid at the feet of Carl Wiedemann. Family lore and the accepted oral history of events holds that famed "King of the Bootleggers" George Remus, a personal friend of Carl's, oversaw the distribution aspects of Wiedemann's illicit beer sales. This is unlikely. Remus was in prison, jail or legal proceedings for bootlegging between January 1924 and April 1927. However, Carl doesn't seem to have been organized or responsible enough to have managed the region's most widespread illegal beer network alone, so members of organized crime were probably involved. Carl lived a colorful life. Born and raised rich, he made his own fortune on a racehorse and then appears to have lost all of it on the same horse. He was found guilty along with the rest of his coconspirators in the Wiedemann trial. The defendants were fined a collective $40,000. The ailing Charles Wiedemann was spared jail time, but Carl was sentenced to two years in the Atlanta Penitentiary. He was contrite, promising to be "the man I was years ago and not what I am today" by the time of his release. The George Wiedemann Company escaped government forfeiture of the brewery, and it reopened under family leadership following Prohibition.

Finally, as an overinflated stock market prepared to crash, contributing to a national Depression that would help end Prohibition, the Jackson Brewing Company had one more local brewery scandal left in the vat. Real beer was discovered at the brewery again in December 1928, leading to a January 1929 federal indictment against Jackson's brewmaster, two Cincinnati lawyers (one of whom was a former legislator) and the State of Ohio's acting treasurer, Bert B. Buckley. All were charged with conspiring to bribe a Prohibition agent. Although Jackson was the only brewery hit with indictments, U.S. prosecutors alleged that multiple Cincinnati breweries were working with Treasurer Buckley and other state officials to install a friendly Prohibition enforcement agent in Cincinnati. In exchange for providing advance notice of raids, the agent would receive a $300 per week salary from the breweries. Other kickbacks and graft were implied but not prosecuted, and unproven allegations included a senator and Ohio's governor. Treasurer Buckley was not as lucky as Sheriff Witt. He denied the charges against him, but he was convicted and sentenced to two and a half years. Jackson's brewmaster spent four months in jail, and one of the lawyers also went to prison. Finally, having survived much longer than most and living through two criminal trials, the Jackson Brewery shut its doors.

Prohibition is remembered mostly as a disastrous policy that produced organized crime and rampant corruption, undermined the rule of law and the integrity of the justice system, turned honest people into criminals and exacerbated irresponsible drinking patterns. All true, but Prohibition also worked. It didn't work as intended, and the accepted version of history is that its harm outweighed its benefits, but it worked. It wrecked the brewing and distilling industries. Americans drank more than 70 percent less during the first years of Prohibition than before, and although alcohol consumption rose as sobriety lost its novelty and bootleggers replaced professional brewers and distillers, average U.S. consumption of booze did not reach pre-Prohibition levels again until a peak in 1973, after which it declined back to below pre-Prohibition levels by the late 1980s. Prohibition caused Americans to drink less for *generations*. In the first nine years of the "Noble Experiment," the federal government spent $141 million in enforcement and collected $460 million in fines, penalties and taxes, leaving a fiscal net revenue of $319,323,308. By contrast, America currently spends roughly $50 billion per year on the War on Drugs, and as of the printing of this book, this expenditure has produced the highest incarceration rates in the world, failed to curb an increase in drug use and done nothing to stop an overdose epidemic. The War on Drugs would kill to have Prohibition's statistics.

LIQUID BREAD LINES

The great irony of repealing Prohibition was that it made it more difficult to get a drink in a lot of places. Of the 1,345 American breweries that were operating across the nation in 1915, just 31 of them were able to resume production within three months after federal legislation legalized 3.2 percent beer. Of the 21 breweries that were open in Cincinnati in 1916, only the Bruckmann Brewing Company was still making near beer by the end of Prohibition. It wasn't simply that Bruckmann's equipment was turned on and humming. The company had also upgraded and updated its machinery and processes, installing twenty-four new fermenting tanks months before it could use them to produce real beer. While Prohibition strangled the U.S. beer industry, technology and technique improved dramatically in the global brewing industry during Prohibition. While U.S. brewers were letting their facilities sit dormant—or busy dismantling miles of pipe to sell for scrap—the rest of the world was busy learning how to make pre-Prohibition brewing practices look like the Dark Ages. Even facilities like Hudepohl, which had managed to keep the roof dry and the lights on, found their once-mighty beer plants obsolete.

Bruckmann came out of the gate swinging. The company had a license to brew and sell small amounts of real beer for medicinal purpose during Prohibition. It was given permission to begin "experimenting" with real beer production while it was still illegal, and it received a permit to begin manufacturing 3.2 percent beer on April 1, 1933, six days before federal legislation legalized beer sales. In the closing hours of April 6, a cheerful crowd started gathering around Bruckmann's to listen to a ceremony welcoming in a new era and, more importantly, to start buying beer at 12:01 a.m.—the literal minute that it became legal. Bruckmann Brewery was one of just four breweries in the state of Ohio that was licensed and ready to start selling beer on the day of its return—and the only one in Greater Cincinnati. Demand exceeded supply, and Ohio legislators used the exorbitant cost of beer, as high as seventy-five cents a glass in some restaurants, to grandstand against beer profiteering.

Some breweries opened with old equipment. The new Red Top Brewery even made it central to its image. The Red Top Malt Extract Company had been using most of the shuttered Hauck Brewery already, so it took over the rest of the facility and transformed into the Red Top Brewing Company. Hauck had been famous for a "made in the wood" lager, and Red Top entered the beer business by reviving this classic taste. It used Hauck's nineteenth-century lagering cellars full of white oak vats. Red Top's brewery superintendent reported that the "casks and vats are as good as they ever were" and that the all-copper brewing system was ready to use after running some upgraded refrigeration lines. After standing dormant for thirteen years, the plant still needed roughly $300,000 in repairs, renovations and updates, but it would enter the market quickly with an initial 100,000-barrel capacity. Over time, Red Top needed to adjust to survive. Hauck's lager was made in an era when beer was still aged for months. Technology rendered this unnecessary in the post-Prohibition world. German breweries, which had provided the inspiration for Cincinnati's lagering cellars, now only took three weeks to produce a batch of beer from brew day to bottling. Modern refrigeration had made lagering cellars obsolete. Red Top's promise not to release any beer until it had been sufficiently aged in oak was quaint but out of touch.

Foss-Schneider was just one of several breweries that overestimated the ease of its resurrection. Many breweries struggled. Some, like the Schaller Brewing Company, which predicted that it would be open within sixty days after beer was legalized, floundered and, ultimately, never reopened. In 1898, a contingent of capitalists trying to simultaneously buy almost all of the city's breweries was surprised by two aspects of the local business. First, after hearing so many accolades about the Queen City's beer, they were "rather disappointed" to discover a lot of old equipment and techniques and only judged five or six local plants to be "thoroughly and modernly equipped." Second, they commented that "outside of New York there was no city in which the breweries occupied sites that were in such an improved and developed part of the city, and whose grounds were therefore so valuable." Due to the city's age and its long brewing history, Cincinnati's breweries were uniquely situated in the urban core. This was also true of Wiedemann, which inhabited a huge swath of real estate in the middle of Newport. As a result, Cincinnati brewery buildings were more susceptible to alternative reuse during the 1920s. Crown became a plumbing business, Kauffman was sold to an electrical business, most of Moerlein's brewhouse was a furniture warehouse, Gerke became Bauer Dairy, Germania was converted into an ice cream plant and most of Gambrinus Stock was turned into a parking garage.

Nevertheless, Greater Cincinnati got back into the beer game with vigor. By the summer of 1934, there were eleven operational breweries. Four of them were pre-Prohibition firms that were still run by the same families and extended families of their founders: Bruckmann, Hudepohl, Foss-Schneider and Wiedemann. Five others utilized pre-Prohibition facilities under new ownership: Red Top took over the former Hauck Brewery, Clyffside brewed in the Mohawk plant, Old Munich was housed in a small fraction of the former Moerlein complex, Burger used Windisch-Muhlhauser's Lion Brewery and the Jackson Brewery reopened with new owners. Both Clyffside and Jackson employed their nineteenth-century hillside lagering cellars in their branding. Clyffside's flagship beer was Felsenbrau, which roughly translated as "a beer brewed in lagering cellars," and Old Jackson Lager was aged in the old massive stone cellars. There were also new facilities, including Schoenling Brothers and Heidelberg in Covington.

Before Prohibition, Greater Cincinnati breweries were collectively producing more than 2 million barrels of beer per year. Due to technology and shortened brewing times, the region surpassed this mark by 1940 with fewer breweries. Production numbers continued to increase even as some breweries failed. By 1947, Cincinnati's nine breweries were producing 2,276,772 barrels of beer per year, despite the fact that they were still recovering from grain shortages and other hardships resulting from World War II. In 1918, just before Prohibition, local beer production had fallen to 1,617,583 barrels. Based on volume, Cincinnati was more of a beer town than ever before. It accounted for more than 44 percent of all beer produced in the state of Ohio. The *Cincinnati Enquirer* declared that Cincinnati had "recovered its position of eminence in beer-making."

In real time, Cincinnati appeared to be headed back to the glory days of brewing by the mid-1930s, but in hindsight, it was already on a trajectory toward extinction. Bruckmann Brewing Company took advantage of the scarcity of beer in the early days of the post-Prohibition era, but it wasn't positioned to do so on the same scale as breweries like Anheuser-Busch, Miller and Pabst. Breweries that were ready to serve thirsty markets, and that had the capital for rapid expansion, kicked off an inevitable course toward market consolidation before the Eighteenth Amendment was even repealed. Cincinnati's one lone brewery multiplied quickly, but the reopened or new breweries were all relatively small in the 1930s. Before Prohibition, the combined output of the Christian Moerlein and Hauck breweries was greater than all eleven local breweries that were operating in 1934, and by reopening a greater number of its pre-Prohibition plants, Cleveland temporarily surpassed Cincinnati as the state's biggest brewing center (until the 1940s). By 1936, the number of breweries had increased to twelve and production was climbing steadily, but there were warning signs of doom ahead. The market was changing.

At its nineteenth-century peak of intoxication, Greater Cincinnati consumed roughly two-thirds of all the beer that was produced by local breweries, but in 1936, only 50 percent of the beer produced in Greater Cincinnati was consumed here, even though the total production was lower. People were drinking less, so markets were expanding geographically. Consumers had also developed a preference for packaged beer over draft. Sales of cans and bottles jumped perceptibly, while keg sales fell. In their pride and self-confidence, Cincinnati breweries failed to understand why all of this added up to their demise, but it did. Colonel C.F. Von dem Bussche, president of the Greater Cincinnati Brewers Inc., reported with pride that while half of all local beer was being shipped to California, Maine, Florida and all points in between, very little beer made outside of Cincinnati was sold locally.

Draft beer was more prone to spoilage than packaged beer. It required refrigerated shipment. That was expensive, and it helped give local beer an advantage in the draft market, but the same thing could not be said for packaged products. As glasses of draft were increasingly replaced by bottles and cans, it mattered less whether a beer came from Cincinnati, Milwaukee or St. Louis. Cincinnati beer enjoyed a good reputation, in part due to the city's pre-Prohibition history, but as beer got lighter and more homogenous, that started to matter a lot less. Cincinnati was destined to become increasingly reliant on the brand loyalty of local consumers, and that was like building a house on silt. By 1935, while Cincinnatians were looking forward to their renewed preeminence in the world of American beer, the nation's five biggest breweries had already captured 14 percent of the national market. By 1958, this share had increased to 31 percent. This meant that most American beer was still being made by hundreds of local breweries scattered across the United States, but the writing was on the wall.

During the late 1800s, big breweries like Christian Moerlein had grown, in part, by embracing new technologies that increased efficiency. This became even more important in the mid-1900s. By the 1960s, the majority of the nation's breweries were too small to compete effectively in the new marketplace. Big beer had expanded capacity, embraced technological advances and doggedly grown market shares to an extent that rendered roughly 50 percent of the nation's breweries obsolete in the new American marketplace. Local and regional breweries were faced with four basic options: expand, merge with other breweries, find a unique niche and fill it or die.

The brewing industry had become locked into a full-scale war of attrition by the 1970s. Brands were dying or getting gobbled up by bigger companies, while some breweries scrambled to fill a boutique market. Technology drove much of the concentration in the industry, but it wasn't the full story. Advertising was also a critical part of the formula. Billboards might have made you thirsty for a Bruck's, Red Top or Old Jackson Lager in the 1930s, but television made it impossible to keep brands like Budweiser out of the comfortably insulated Cincinnati market by the end of the 1940s. Regional breweries didn't have the resources to compete in national ad wars, particularly as the ad campaigns grew increasingly savvy. By the 1980s, even the children of loyal Hudepohl and Wiedemann drinkers blasphemously preferred national brands, and by 2009, just three breweries controlled 80 percent of the U.S. market.

These national trends all played out locally without any major deviations. The breweries that held on the longest owed most of their longevity to continual growth and merger, and the ones that just wanted to make good beer on a regional scale were the first casualties. The Jackson Brewery's cursed history didn't end with new ownership. It was purchased by the Squibb-Pattison Corporation in March 1933. The following summer, its cellars were stocked with Old Jackson, a beer advertised as being "full malt, full flavored, full quality" and "full of life and health," but there were already problems. Squibb-Pattison had violated securities law in the way that it issued stock, and it was heading into financial trouble. Jackson went into Insolvency Court, again, and was offered for public auction in December 1934. Creditors blocked a sale and tried to right the ship, but they were ultimately unsuccessful. The federal government slapped a lien on the

The Foss-Schnieder Brewery was producing 130,000 barrels of beer per year by the mid-1890s, making it the seventh-largest brewery in Greater Cincinnati. It reopened after Prohibition but never regained its footing and closed permanently in 1938. *Cincinnati Historical Society Library, Cincinnati Museum Center.*

brewery for failing to pay taxes in 1938, 1939 and 1940, and a long, colorful saga came to a permanent end in 1942.

The Foss-Schneider Brewery enjoyed an even shorter post-Prohibition honeymoon. It suffered massive damage during the Great Flood of 1937 and was forced to shut down for several weeks. This exacerbated the brewery's "embarrassed financial conditions," and it went into bankruptcy. Attempts were made to reorganize the debt and the business, but they failed, and a promising sale fell through. The real estate and every aspect of a fully functional brewery were offered up at public auction in 1938, but the brewery was dead. Everything was liquidated, and every physical trace of a magnificent brewery that dated back to 1849 was eventually demolished.

Old Munich lived a short, unproductive life in part of the former Moerlein Brewery. In May 1933, plans were announced to invest more than $200,000 in renovating part of the former Moerlein brewhouse and purchasing new brewing equipment. The owners quickly found themselves in over their heads, and the business was sold and renamed the Tyler Brewing Company in October 1933. In less than eight months, Tyler tripled the plant's capacity. Tyler Brewing flirted with prosperity but was out of business by 1937.

The Christian Moerlein Brewing Company disavowed any plans to reopen, but part of the company's management quickly had a change of heart. The Christian Moerlein Brewing Company Inc. (technically a different company than the one without the "Inc." in the name) issued 420,000 shares of common stock in the fall of 1933, with the plan of raising close to $6 million for the construction of an entirely new 500,000-barrel brewery. Plans called for locating a new site, but the ambitious vision was quickly dashed. The nation was in the grip of the Great Depression, and selling stock for a speculative venture was harder than anticipated. Three months after stock was offered for sale to the public, all the money that had been raised was returned to would-be investors. As a matter of legal housekeeping, the original Christian Moerlein Brewing Company, formed by Christian Moerlein in 1881, was officially dissolved in 1934. The new Moerlein corporation held an option on land for a while, but the new Moerlein never got off the ground.

Plugging along as a good, medium-sized brewery may have helped keep Bruckmann alive during Prohibition, but the company's conservative management probably helped kill it in the post-Prohibition world. In hindsight, Bruckmann should have taken the opportunities of 1933 to grown into a major player, but it didn't. By the late 1940s, Bruckmann was still contemplating expansion, but it was too late. Then came a bitter family estate battle that lapsed into a fracture in the company's board of directors. President William Bruckmann claimed that the company was solvent and doing fine, but the disgruntled faction of the board alleged that it was mismanaged, hemorrhaging money and operating at a net loss.

The dispute was resolved with the sale of the brewery in the fall of 1949. Herschel Condon, the new owner of the brewery, had three big plans for Bruckmann: switch the heritage brand name in favor of his own; make a lighter, "zesty" beer; and dump an astounding amount of money into advertising. The second two prongs of this formula would turn big breweries into behemoths in the 1980s, but Condon didn't pull it off, partly because Condon was no Don Draper. Condon was inspired to buy the brewery in order to produce his flagship Modern Style Beer, which, according to ads, was "expressly created for those who drink beer for taste enjoyment." Despite the snappy catchphrase "taste enjoyment," Condon's "zestful," "mellow," "modern," "brisk," champagne-like beer without an "after taste" didn't catch on. In 1950, all the brewing equipment, machinery and trade name of the former Bruckmann Brewery were placed up for auction, and a beloved beer brand died an embarrassing death.

In 1947, Red Top Brewing Company, Burger Brewing Company and Hudepohl Brewing Company were the three biggest exporters in the region. All had a capacity of more than 1 million barrels a year (although none was actually producing this much), and all three were expanding. There were six breweries remaining in Cincinnati and three in Northern Kentucky, and they kept dropping dead like teens in a slasher flick. Heidelberg would only remain independent until 1949 before it was subsumed by Bavarian Brewing Company, which was then acquired by International Breweries Inc. in 1959. Bavarian would continue to brew under the auspices of this corporate conglomerate until 1966, when the last beer was brewed in Covington until the modern craft beer era.

Mohawk Brewing Company in Over-the-Rhine never recovered from the Prohibition arrests of its management and announced that it had no intention of reopening in the '30s. The brewery did reopen under new management as the Clyffside Brewing Company. Clyffside produced creative ads and stayed in business more than a decade, but it was purchased by Red Top in 1946. Red Top made the recently remodeled facility part of its aggressive expansion. Brewery officials said that the acquisition of Clyffside would make Red Top the largest brewery in Cincinnati and one of the twenty largest in the United States. The company was staying alive by expanding its capacity, advertising heavily and growing into new markets, but wars take the strong along with the weak and Red Top had become an unlikely casualty by 1956.

Part of the national consolidation of the brewing industry can be attributed to World War II. Grain rationing and other restrictions on non-essential industries helped deprive American beers of a lot of their previous flavor, which had already taken a hit during Prohibition. As the content of cans and bottles grew increasingly similar, labels and advertising grew more important. Burger Brewing Company took a locally novel approach to this problem. Although it couldn't afford to compete with national advertising campaigns, it carved out a niche by sponsoring radio broadcasts of baseball games, both locally and in other markets, including the sponsorship of both major- and minor-league broadcasts. Radio sponsorship of the Cincinnati Reds between 1942 and 1965 helped increase company sales threefold. Affiliation with local sports teams helped keep Burger in the game and helps explain why it was one of the largest exporters in the region in the late 1940s.

However, as the market tightened in the '50s and '60s, the company started to struggle. Harkening back to the nineteenth century, Burger dug a well under its brewery and started brewing exclusively with artesian spring water. The decision was primarily financial, a plan for eliminating city water fees, but the company also placed its natural water supply at the forefront of its advertising. Unfortunately, this switch to artesian water in 1968 sealed the company's doom. The beer may or may not have been better, but it was definitely different. This alienated a lot of loyal consumers, and sales declined. In its Annual Report to Shareholders for the fiscal year 1971, the Burger Brewing Company reported a net annual earning of just $393,404, which the board of directors reported being "understandably gratified with," given the general economic pattern of the United States and the "most severe competition to date in the brewing industry." Ultimately, Burger was forced to sell its brands, trademarks and packaging to the Hudepohl Brewing Company in 1973, terminated employees without notice and allowed the 1-million-barrel capacity plant to go dormant. Opened in 1866 as the Windisch-Muhlhauser Brewery, more than one hundred years of brewing history was laid to rest. Hudepohl eventually used the name to brew an economy beer, the brewery buildings fell increasingly into disrepair and, in 1993, the nineteenth-century brewhouse was demolished.

Windisch-Muhlhauser's Lion Brewery reopened under new ownership and the new name Burger Brewing Company after Prohibition. Beloved and respected for decades, Burger was forced to close and sell its brands to Hudepohl in 1973. In 1975, there were plans to turn the property into a shopping and entertainment complex that envisioned use of its massive lagering cellars, but they fell through; the building decayed and was demolished in 1993. *From the collection of the Public Library of Cincinnati and Hamilton County.*

Conrad Windisch and Gottlieb Muhlhauser established the Lion Brewery in 1866. Producing 175,000 barrels per year by the 1890s, it was one of the region's four largest breweries at the turn of the century. *From the collection of the Public Library of Cincinnati and Hamilton County.*

Schoenling Brewing Company proved to be the dark horse in the race for twentieth-century survival. At the end of Prohibition, the Schoenling Ice & Fuel Company delivered coal and ice to retail customers. Schoenling prospered, but the business model was headed toward extinction. Every home would eventually have an electric refrigerator in the kitchen, and gas-fueled furnaces and boilers were diminishing the demand for coal. In 1933, Edward Schoenling Jr. wanted to buy a keg of beer for a party, and he discovered how difficult that was in the months following the return of legal beer sales. A line at the Hudepohl Brewery stretched around the block, and a policeman was required to keep it orderly. Repelled by the crowd, Schoenling tried his luck at the Bruckmann Brewery, where he found a similar scene. Schoenling was both frustrated and inspired. Unlike the dying coal and ice businesses, the beer industry clearly had more demand than it could supply, so Schoenling approached his family with a plan to build a brewery. It was a hard sell at first, but they finally agreed, and on Good Friday 1934, the Schoenling Brewing Company sold its first beer. The new brewery got off to a rocky start. Years later, Schoenling admitted that its beer wasn't very good in the '30s and that a complete lack of brewing experience was a problem. The brewery went through several brewmasters before finally finding its groove. Eventually, however, the company began to grow by leaps and bounds, increasing output from 42,029 barrels in 1937 to 193,360 barrels in 1957.

Schoenling entered the 1960s as one of the largest and strongest breweries in the region, and it ended the decade as one of only four regional breweries left standing. The other three were Hudepohl, Burger and Wiedemann, which soon lost its independence. Wiedemann struggled during the '60s and was forced to make difficult choices. In 1967, the company was purchased by Wisconsin-based G. Heileman Brewing Company. This was part of the trend of national consolidation. Companies like Heileman purchased regional breweries. This expanded capacity and improved distribution for the parent company, while allowing it to capitalize on the loyalty of local beer consumers. Heileman upgraded equipment at Wiedemann, and by brewing additional brands at the facility, production increased. In 1971, Wiedemann became the first brewery in the history of Greater Cincinnati to brew 1 million barrels of beer in a year, but while business improved at Wiedemann,

Before entering the beer business in 1934, the Schoenling family delivered ice and coal. *From the collection of the Public Library of Cincinnati and Hamilton County.*

officials steadily lost more of their autonomy to their corporate parent. As Heileman continued to acquire more breweries across the United States, many of them much larger and more efficient, the Wiedemann Brewery started to become an obsolete piece of a much larger portfolio. Despite producing 1.3 million barrels of beer in 1982, Heileman closed Wiedemann the following year. Beer would not be brewed in Newport again until the Haufbrau House opened in 2003, followed by Wooden Cask Brewing Company, across the street from the former Wiedemann site in 2016.

Although it faced a near-death experience and survived in a coma longer than a soap opera character, Hudepohl Brewing Company was resilient. In an era that forced breweries to grow, merge or find a niche to fill, Hudepohl eventually did all three. It rebuilt part of the original brewery in Over-the-Rhine in 1933, but the company also began brewing and continually expanding a second plant on West Sixth Street, which combined the nineteenth-century Lackmann Brewery with extensive new construction and modern equipment. In 1958, the Over-the-Rhine facility was closed, and the company engaged in aggressive expansion and modernization at the new plant. Hudepohl also expanded its portfolio by purchasing the Burger brands.

When Americans shamefully embraced light beer en masse in the 1970s, Hudepohl rolled with the demand for watery beer and did well with Hudy Delight. By 1982, Delight held 40 percent of the regional market share on light beer sales, second only to Miller Lite. The company also carved out a niche in the infancy of the craft beer movement. In homage to Cincinnati's greatest pre-Prohibition brewery, Hudepohl introduced a craft beer called Christian Moerlein Select in 1981. Marketed with the tagline "Quite Simply a Better Beer," Moerlein was a dark, rich amber lager made with imported hops and aged for six weeks. This premium beer was part of Hudepohl general manager Bob Pohl's strategy for using the brewery's modest size to its advantage. Hudepohl promotional materials explained that a smaller brewery could make higher-quality brews. After years of American beer getting lighter and more homogenous, Pohl gambled on the belief that an underserved market wanted more flavorful, distinct beers, and he was right. Moerlein was a hit. Recalling Cincinnati's pre-Prohibition German tradition of shunning beers made with rice, corn or other adjuncts, Pohl submitted the beer to German officials, resulting in Christian Moerlein Select becoming the first American beer to officially pass *Reinheitsgebot* standards.

Hudepohl followed the success of Moerlein Select with premium seasonal and limited-release beers, including Hofbrau, Ludwig Hudepohl Bock

The First
American
Beer
to pass
Germany's
Highest
Standards

Hudepohl Brewing Company
Cincinnati, Ohio U.S.A.

Hudepohl introduced one of America's first craft beers in 1981, named Christian Moerlein Select. It became the first beer in American history to officially comply with *Reinheitsgebot*, the Bavarian beer purity law dating back to 1516. *Christian Moerlein Brewing Company and Gregory Hardman.*

and Ludwig Hudepohl Special Oktoberfest. The beers played on the city's brewing heritage and were released with pomp and circumstance. The first shipment of Moerlein was delivered to Arnold's Bar & Grill, the city's oldest bar, in a horse-drawn carriage. Hudepohl successfully found and claimed a niche market, but it wasn't enough. After several years of growth in the early '80s, sales started to flag again by the mid-'80s. Following significant internal disagreement over the future of the company, Hudepohl and Schoenling publicly announced a merger on November 3, 1986. In reality, it was more of an acquisition by Schoenling. All production was shifted to the Schoenling plant on Central Parkway, and Schoenling president Ken Lichtendahl became president of the combined Hudepohl-Schoenling Brewing Company.

The merger was beneficial. Hudepohl's business, particularly its premium beers, was focused within a 150-mile radius of Cincinnati. By contrast, much of Schoenling's growth was attributable to Little Kings Cream Ale. The beer was the product of serendipity. Patrons at Ted Gregory's bar wanted a beer to drink as a chaser with whiskey shots. In 1958, this request from a good account led Schoenling to develop a cream ale, a style of beer that derives a sweet, creamy character from the ample use of corn in the mash. The flavor complemented bourbon, and the beer was packaged in a seven-ounce bottle so that it wasn't necessary to purchase a full beer to use as a chaser. This specially designed beer-half of a boilermaker took off. Consumers liked the taste, and they loved the little green bottles. Little Kings developed a large cult following and a sixteen-state distribution.

Combined, Hudepohl and Schoenling played to different strengths. Christian Moerlein was introduced to broader markets by piggybacking onto Little King's distribution network. Sales increased, and by the late 1980s, Moerlein was being distributed more broadly across the United States and exported to West Germany, Canada and Japan. As the last man standing, Hudepohl-Schoenling also became "Cincinnati's Brewery," wrapping itself in local pride. At the same time, the company also began contract brewing, the business of brewing other firms' beers on a contractual basis.

Nationally, between 1984 and 1990, the market share of America's three largest breweries—Anheuser-Busch, Miller and Coors—increased from a combined 64 percent to 81 percent. Advertising took most of the credit. By the mid-1980s, the nation's largest breweries were spending close to three dollars in advertising for every keg of beer that they produced, and regional breweries simply couldn't compete. National brands spent more on a single Super Bowl ad than the entire annual advertising budget for companies like Hudepohl and Schoenling. As big breweries poured astronomical sums of money into funny, memorable ad campaigns, Hudepohl-Shoenling's share of regional draft beer sales dropped from roughly 50 percent in 1989 to less than 10 percent of all draft, bottles and cans sold regionally in 1992. Conversely, Anheuser-Busch controlled roughly 43 percent of the local market by 1992.

Hudepohl-Schoenling also lacked a clear vision in the 1990s. Hudepohl's introduction of Christian Moerlein was visionary, whereas Hudepohl-Schoenling chased trends, including dry beers and ice beers and expanding into the wine cooler market. Finally, in 1996, the Hudepohl-Schoenling brewery was sold to Jim Koch's Boston Beer Company. Under the terms of the agreement, Hudepohl-Schoenling retained ownership of its brands, and Boston Beer, in addition to brewing its own Samuel Adams Boston Lager at the plant, would continue to brew the Cincinnati brands on a contractual basis. Hudepohl-Schoenling also retained the right to continue operating a microbrewery adjacent to the main facility. This was an opportunity to start over, start small and rebuild as a craft brewery just as Cincinnatians were beginning to support the emerging craft beer market, but that's not what happened.

In 1999, Cleveland-based Crooked River Brewing Company purchased what was left of Hudepohl-Schoenling—"Cincinnati's Brewery"—and in 2001, Boston Beer stopped brewing the brands on behalf of its out-of-town owners. Although products like the decidedly non-*Reinheitsgebot* brew Christian Moerlein Honey Almond could still occasionally be found on tap handles and retail shelves, and Little King's Cream Ale could still be purchased in more than a dozen states, Cincinnati's iconic brands were no longer owned or brewed locally. Both the nineteenth- and twentieth-century Hudepohl buildings were dormant; Burger, Gambrinus Stock, Walker, Schaller, Herancourt and Wiedemann had all been razed; and Jackson, Mohawk, Crown, Bellevue, Germania and what was left of the once-mammoth Christian Moerlein complex all sat in varying degrees of disrepair. Several were vacant. Greater Cincinnati's long, proud brewing history seemed to be functionally dead.

The Boston Beer Company retained Hudepohl-Schoenling employees and invested heavily in the brewery. As of the writing of this book in 2018, improvement and expansion is ongoing, and Boston Beer is notably increasing its local presence and identity. The company is solely responsible for keeping midsize brewing alive in Cincinnati during the 2000s. However, Boston Beer is frequently left out of the narrative of local brewing because it inhabits an odd ground. For understandable reasons, Boston Beer has historically been reticent to tout how much of its Boston Lager is manufactured in Cincinnati, so despite being the largest brewery in town, located in an iconic facility and adjacent to the Over-the-Rhine Brewery District, the Boston Beer Company has previously felt foreign, although this has been changing rapidly. The brewery has become the largest sponsor of Cincinnati's Brewing Heritage Trail, helping bring local beer history to life, and it opened an experimental nanobrewery and taproom across the street from its West End production facility in late 2018. Boston Beer Company founder Jim Koch, a Cincinnati native whose father and grandfather both worked in local breweries, noted at the taproom opening, "My family has been part of Cincinnati's brewing heritage for almost 100 years." Speaking of the former Schoenling plant, Koch said that "keeping open the last brewery in Cincinnati was really important to me and to my dad."

REINVENTING FLAVOR

In 2005, Mike Cromer pulled together the staff of Barrel House Brewing Company after the annual, raucous Bockfest and delivered painful news: Barrel House was closing, effective immediately—sort of. The brewpub opened for one more day. Working the shift was entirely voluntary, and the members of the Barrel House family who chose to participate in this living wake got to split the last day's profits. Then the first modern era of craft beer in Greater Cincinnati came to an end.

Although several things made it stand out, Barrel House wasn't the city's only craft brewery in this first resurrection of quality beer. Oldenberg Brewery opened in Fort Mitchell, Kentucky, in 1987. Jerry Deters, a contractor, built Oldenberg to resemble a nineteenth-century brewery. The complex contained a small brewing system, entertainment center, restaurant and brewpub. German-born Hans Bilger was hired as brewmaster, bringing extensive academic and practical brewing experience. Oldenberg specialized in German-style lagers, including a pilsner and a "Schenk," a variety that traditionally referred to type of "young beer," light-bodied and low in ABV. These styles allowed Oldenberg to make quality beers that were still recognizable and approachable to the light beer–swilling Greater Cincinnatians of the late 1980s. Oldenberg also became home to the American Museum of Brewing History and Arts, an extensive, world-class collection of breweriana.

In 1991, Oldenberg roughly doubled its capacity to twenty-five thousand barrels per year and kept growing. It opened a branch location called Holy

Grail Brewery and Grill in Coryville, near the University of Cincinnati. In 1996, the company raised $2 million in capital for renovations, expansion and extension of its brands. Although Oldenberg appeared poised to lead a local revolution in beer—just as Cincinnati's last regional brewery was facing extinction—Oldenberg Brewing Company was sold. New owners continued to operate the Fort Mitchell facility until 2001. Oldenberg changed the landscape, became an institution and then disappeared. It did, however, leave a legacy. Oldenberg conducted beer camps and beer classes, events that helped spread the local knowledge and appreciation of good beer, as well as improving a lot of homebrew and sparking a few brewing careers. (The author of this book also received his first craft beer tutorial during training to become an Oldenberg bartender.)

Main Street Brewery opened on Main Street in Over-the-Rhine in 1994. It was a quality, typical brewpub of this era. It had a warm atmosphere, was restaurant-focused, had good food and brewed good beer on a small system.

The following year, Barrel House Brewing Company opened around the corner, on Twelfth Street between Main and Vine. Physically, Barrelhouse was close to the epicenter of Cincinnati nightlife on Main Street, but the difference in a block required a quantum leap in the perception of potential customers. At the time, the street was usually deserted and poorly lit. Over-the-Rhine contained several hundred vacant, rotting buildings and was consistently ranked as the highest crime neighborhood in Cincinnati. Mike Cromer, an accountant for GE, and his partner Dave Rich had never run a brewery before. They hired Rick DeBar, a respected brewer; got a long-term lease on an industrial building; and opened the doors.

Mike Cromer was one of a few dozen people who believed wholeheartedly in the need to save Over-the-Rhine from wrecking balls and restore the beauty and vitality of the city's most storied neighborhood. Several generations of his family had lived in OTR and the adjacent West End—where his great-grandfather ran a bootlegging operation during Prohibition—and Cromer rooted most of the theme of Barrel House in the history that surrounded it. The beer menu contained a basic explanation of the brewing process for a local population that was still largely unfamiliar with craft beer, and the food menu invoked a litany of names from Cincinnati's discarded past. Infamous beer halls, burlesque theaters, bootleggers, writers and painters all got their own beer, pizza or sandwich.

More importantly, the beer was exceptional. Barrel House pushed well beyond the boundaries of local beer palates. The yeast for its unfiltered Hefeweizen came from Germany. The same year that Americans were being bombarded with a national ad campaign that warned them against the peril of "bitter beer face," Barrel House featured an IPA. On the other end of the spectrum, it brewed a dark, rich porter and a seasonal Helles Bock. At first, none of this mattered much. For the first few years, Cromer spent most of his days surveying the taproom and asking, "Where is everybody?" Cromer and the team were in the middle of an untraveled street, in a neighborhood that scared the hell out of most of the city, serving beers that the public didn't understand yet. Guerrilla marketing was the answer. They printed windshield flyers that looked exactly like parking tickets and summoned the recipients to appear before the bartender. They offered deep discounts on food, brought in the best live bands in town and never charged a cover. Giving away the farm with the hope of getting it back one pint at a time was a risky strategy, but it worked. Barrel House became the place to be—at least for those who were smart enough to get it.

They also supported beer festivals, including taking over responsibility for Over-the-Rhine's Bock Beer festival. By the dawn of the twenty-first century, Barrel House was brewing to capacity. Roughly 50 percent of its business was derived from taproom sales and roughly 50 percent came from bar accounts that it serviced from the back of a Chevy Blazer. Everything was roses until the brewery was hit with several misfortunes. On April 7, 2001, a Cincinnati policeman chased a young, unarmed African American man named Timothy Thomas into a dark alley in Over-the-Rhine. Thomas, who was wanted on multiple misdemeanor offenses, refused to comply with an order to put his hands in the air, and the officer shot him. Thomas became the most recent of a series of African American men to be shot and killed by the CPD, and his death became a rallying cry. Riots and looting erupted in Over-the-Rhine. In one of the more surreal moments, Cincinnati police officers lined up along Central Parkway in riot gear and held a line of demarcation that kept the residents of Over-the-Rhine out of the central business district. The officer was acquitted of a negligent homicide charge in September. A boycott and the fear of more rioting followed, which mingled with the general sense of fear that pervaded the entire country after the September 11 terrorist attacks.

The civil unrest of 2001 crippled small businesses downtown, particularly in Over-the-Rhine. Restaurants and bars were hit especially hard. For years after any rational basis for fear had dissipated, astounding numbers of Cincinnatians steered clear of downtown. The much-lauded Main Street renaissance sputtered. Business after business struggled and closed. The Main Street Brewery closed in 1999, well before the riots, and reopened in

2000 sans the brewing equipment. It closed as the Jump Café & Bar along with a series of other Main Street institutions, names still fondly remembered by people who were around at the time: Neon's, Jefferson Hall, Kaldi's and Courtyard Café all eventually succumbed. The neighborhood entered a new era of challenges.

Leadership at the Cincinnati Art Academy in Mount Adams made a bold, brave and highly controversial decision to become part of the solution. The revered institution purchased the Rosethal Printing Building on Twelfth Street—home of the Barrel House Brewing Company. While advocates of Over-the-Rhine applauded the decision to move the school to the struggling neighborhood, it drew a visceral response from people who believed that the Art Academy was placing its students in danger. Locating above a brewery added an additional element to the controversy, so the Art Academy tried to force Barrel House out of the building. Litigation ensued. The court eventually upheld Barrel House's right to remain in business under its long-term lease, but the situation was untenable. Cromer and Rich agreed to sell the business and the rights to their lease. A company from Indiana purchased the brand and began bottling Barrel House brews in the West End. Without a taproom, Barrel House couldn't survive. It struggled and eventually closed in 2010. (As of the writing of this book, the portion of the Art Academy building that was inhabited by Barrel House Brewing Company remains vacant—more than thirteen years later.)

Several local microbreweries and brewpubs popped up, struggled for one reason or another and closed between the late 1980s and the early 2000s. In 1996, national brewpub chain Rock Bottom Brewery opened on Fountain Square, and in 2003, Hofbrauhaus Munich opened its first American Hofbrauhaus in Newport. Although neither is homegrown, both companies invested in the revitalization of downtown Cincinnati and Newport's waterfront, and both kept pouring tasty beers through dark times.

SOME BEER BUBBLES AREN'T JUST IN YOUR HEAD 2.0

Mike and Kathleen Dewey took the humble first steps toward ushering in a new era in local brewing when they started Mt. Carmel Brewing Company in 2005. It started small. Investing $10,000 of their own money, they erected Mt. Carmel's original commercial brewing system in the storm cellar of their 1924 farmhouse in Anderson Township. It was a family business. Mike, who owned his own commercial construction firm and had taught himself to brew, made the beer. He also used his construction and engineering background to install and repair some of his own equipment. Kathleen, with a background in real estate sales, took over office management. The brewery grew, and the Deweys quit their day jobs. At first, they brewed, marketed and self-distributed out of their house. Thanks largely to their entrepreneurial spirit, Mt. Carmel kept growing. The Deweys built a two-thousand-square-foot addition to their home to accommodate a new brewhouse. They bought a bottling line, began package sales and signed a wholesale agreement with a distributor. By 2012, Mt. Carmel was producing 4,500 barrels per year, and the beer was available in all of Ohio's eighty-eight counties, as well as ten counties in Kentucky. The kids' playroom was converted into a gift shop and a taproom was added as growth continued both through distribution and on-site sales. In 2018, a large event center was built beside the old farmhouse, and Mt. Carmel was reaping the rewards of getting to the craft beer revolution early in the game.

The local, modern craft beer business can be viewed in three general eras. Oldenberg, Main Street Brewery and Barrel House were part of a pioneer generation from the late 1980s through the mid-1990s. Although each of these businesses was different in the execution of the concept—Oldenberg was a formidable complex that included a beer museum—they were all "brewpubs," meaning that restaurants were an important aspect of their business. This was more of a necessity than a choice. While the decidedly downsized Hudepohl-Schoenling Brewing Company was struggling to sell enough Christian Moerlein through traditional distribution methods to stay alive, the new craft breweries could both distribute their product as well as enjoy much higher profit margins from on-site sales, but there was a catch. At the time, in both Ohio and Kentucky, the only practical way to sell beer at a brewery for on-site consumption was to make the brewery "ancillary" to a restaurant. Even though the brewery was the focus of the business, a combination of state and local laws drove the brewpub model. The national chain Rock Bottom Brewery dates to this period as well. In the 1990s, most people simply assumed that a craft brewery was attached to a full-service restaurant.

Mike and Kathleen Dewey kicked off a new, brief second era in regional brewing because they began brewing a craft beer purely for wholesale distribution. It was a risky plan, and less tenacious people might have failed. Nevertheless, the Deweys weren't alone for long. Listermann, Rivertown and Blank Slate would also open in this pre-2012 era. The third wave came after Ohio made it cost-effective to open taprooms in 2012. Mad Tree and Rhinegeist were pioneers in this third wave that built into a tsunami. Christian Moerlein played a conspicuous but unique role by straddling these eras and successfully combining several business models, including the mother of all brewpubs.

Dan Listermann has played an unparalleled role in the growth of Greater Cincinnati's current craft brewing industry. Listermann started his brewing career with a crime and a disaster. As a college student at Miami University, Dan bought a homebrew kit at a local pharmacy. It was 1973, five years before Jimmy Carter signed federal legislation that legalized homebrewing. Prior to that, making your own beer was like making your own whiskey—illegal. Dan made a few terrible batches of bootleg brew, most of which was used to fill fire extinguishers in his frat house. He went back to letting professionals make the beer that he drank. Then, in 1988, Dan's former college roommate called him up and said that he planned to try homebrewing again. Listermann thought that it was terrible idea. Scarred by his past, he

Mt. Carmel Brewing Company kicked off a new era in local beer history when Mike Dewey took a homebrewing hobby pro. Mike and his wife, Kathleen, opened the brewery in 2005. Its first brewhouse was located in a storm cellar adjacent to the family's 1924 farmhouse. *Photo by the author, www.queencityhistory.com.*

didn't understand why anyone would try brewing their own beer, but he reluctantly agreed to participate. This time, the hobby stuck.

In 1991, Dan was sitting at a bar and allowed his mind to wander from the stage show. As an engineer by profession, he had a random epiphany. He believed that he could make a better device for filling beer bottles, so he did. Listermann gave the prototype to the Bloatarian Brewing League, a local homebrew club. The club tested it and loved it, and Listermann Home Brewing Supplies was born. Two years later, with the full support of his wife, Sue, Dan Listermann resigned his position as an engineer and focused entirely on designing, manufacturing and selling his own homebrewing equipment, quickly becoming the primary and most respected source for homebrew supplies and homebrewing wisdom in the region. Listermann and his staff inspired, weened and encouraged a new generation of homebrewers, several of whom eventually made the leap into the professional realm. Dan and Sue Listermann purchased the current home of the Listermann Brewing Company in 1995, although it wasn't until 2008 that the homebrew business started to morph into a brewery.

Listermann Brewing Company didn't start with a business plan. It started with serendipity. Someone offered to sell Dan a small, used two-barrel commercial brewing system. He bought it, acquired the necessary brewing license and started to produce small batches of boutique beers, selling kegs to bars and hand-bottling some of the brews, selling them for carry-out at the homebrew store. Fate intervened again two years later. In 2010, local brewer Kevin Moerland approached Listermann with a proposal to rent some of the brewhouse to work on test batches for a group of investors that was thinking about opening a new brewery. At the time, Listermann Brewing was barely making enough beer, or money, to justify the $4,000 annual brewery license fee. Kevin's proposal brought new inspiration, and with Moerland's help, drive and knowledge, Listermann was transformed. Dan the engineer repurposed and redesigned some old dairy equipment, which helped roughly quintuple the brewery's capacity. More importantly, Moerland oversaw a dramatic change in the beer. Quality and consistency improved, a taproom was added—designed after an 1875 Listermann family saloon—and the building was reconfigured to make more room for serving space. Dan quit manufacturing homebrew equipment, and the Listermann Brewing Company became a quirky, award-winning neighborhood brewery.

In 2018, Listermann's annual capacity was still a modest 1,800 barrels per year, but the spunky little brewery's reputation has exceeded its size and Dan Listermann has obtained cult status in the region's beer world. Plans call for expanding the capacity of the current brewhouse, although it is limited by the size of the building and the lot that it sits on. Head brewer Jared Lewinski envisions growing the business by opening new neighborhood Listermann breweries throughout the state, expanding the brand and its beers while preserving the funky, local Listermann vibe.

Other breweries that opened in the first decade of the twenty-first century followed different models and have enjoyed or suffered different fates. Rivertown Brewing Company followed the same basic business model as Mt. Carmel. Partners Randy Schiltz and Jason Roeper opened Rivertown in 2009. Plans did not include a taproom because Ohio law made them cost-prohibitive. Rivertown opened in an industrial office park in Lockland with the mission of selling kegged and packaged beer. Proximity to the interstate was more important than ambiance. Schiltz and Roeper expected to produce a very modest five hundred barrels per year in '09 and were pleasantly surprised when they had to scramble to satisfy a demand for three times that amount. Hitting the market several years before the floodgates burst, Rivertown landed lucrative contracts with large grocery store chains and started taking over tap handles all over Greater Cincinnati. Timing helped, but it wasn't enough. Schiltz and Roeper worked hard, and they made good traditional beers as well as variations on traditional styles, including a Helles lager, an oatmeal stout and a vanilla porter.

By subsequent standards, Rivertown was inexpensive to get off the ground, but it started with a great deal more risk than Mt. Carmel or Listermann. After being rejected by dozens of banks, the startup finally received a $250,000 loan. Another $75,000 came in from personal and private investors. Roeper found a good deal on some used equipment, and Rivertown was in business. The bank that finally gave Rivertown the green light didn't have to worry about getting repaid. For the next several years, the brewery grew 100 percent annually. By 2012, when taproom legislation changed in Ohio, Rivertown had expanded from 2,500 square feet to 12,000 square feet. Schiltz and Roeper added a taproom that summer, but their location, tucked away in an office industrial park, wasn't ideal for retail sales. In 2015, Rivertown decided to move. The company found a piece of land in Monroe, Ohio, and began constructing a new facility. By this time, Rivertown was producing ten thousand barrels per year and projected doubling its growth again within two years.

When Rivertown opened its new $6 million brewery with a full-service restaurant in 2017, it was a monument to success. The new twenty-six-thousand-square-foot facility sat on eight acres of land. The Monroe brewery could produce up to 40,000 barrels of beer annually, with space to expand into a 140,000-barrel facility. Jason and Lindsey Roeper summarized the vision for Rivertown as "dream big dream beer." Rivertown co-founder Randy Schiltz was not present at the grand opening. The partners had a split in 2014, precipitated by several factors. They disagreed on what the future looked like, and they also held a persistent underlying difference in the beers that they wanted to brew. Both men were award-winning homebrewers before becoming heralded professional brewers, but Schiltz enjoyed making the traditional styles that characterized Rivertown's early days. Roeper, by contrast, had always enjoyed sours. When differences of opinion became irreconcilable, Roeper bought out Schiltz's ownership. Then, in 2015, he rebranded the company, changing both the packaging and the product. Rivertown started focusing more on sours and brewing less traditional beers. Schiltz, meanwhile, went his own way to build a brewery that was consistent with his own vision.

Several patterns emerged as craft beer rapidly gained popularity, both nationally and locally. Some people began entering the business with detailed business plans and ample funding, while others simply took their love affair with beer to the logical next step. Scott LaFollette founded Blank Slate Brewing Company for love, as well as with a lot of sweat. After homebrewing for more than a decade, LaFollette began searching for a space that he could turn into a small production brewery with local distribution. He identified a rental space in a small warehouse, located on a short road between Eastern Avenue and Lunken Airport. Since craft brewing was still a relative novelty in Cincinnati in 2010, Scott met with residents of the Columbia Tusculum Community Council to explain the brewery, its low emissions and minimal impact. The neighborhood was supportive, but LaFollette still had hurdles ahead. It was a time when the city building department and the county Municipal Sewer District were still trying to wrap their heads around the concept of microbreweries. LaFollette completed the various licensing and approval processes through 2011 and became a professional brewer in 2012.

LaFollette named the brewery Blank Slate. Several factors inspired the name. First, he quit his job as a polymer chemist to begin an entirely new journey. Second, the space was an empty industrial box, and thirdly, LaFollette explained that he was starting "with no preconceptions of what a brewery should be." He was a man shrugging off the corporate grind to become an artisan, willing to go where creative beer led. Although they often change over time, most breweries begin with flagship beers, brews that they keep on tap year-round and use as an introduction to the brand. LaFollette rejected the concept of flagships. He wanted to focus on seasonals and always offer consumers something new, creative and delicious.

Blank Slate's brewhouse was assembled with equipment that LaFollette purchased over a three-year period while he found a location and began the licensing process, and he connected and plumbed a lot of the system himself. With help from family and friends, LaFollette also built out most of the brewery on his own, saving money and leveraging his life savings at every opportunity.

Timing, however, struck LaFollette some vicious blows. In 2012, the craft beer world changed dramatically in Ohio when the state legislature finally made it practical for breweries to operate taprooms. Prior to this change in the law, breweries either focused on distribution to bars and package retailers, like Mt. Carmel and Rivertown, or they fit the mold of the 1980s and '90s brewpubs, operating full-service restaurants. Allowing true production breweries to sell beers by the glass in taprooms opened a new and lucrative route to making breweries profitable. This changed everything. Unfortunately for Blank Slate, the brewery was roughly 90 percent finished before the change in the taproom law, and the small, sparse warehouse was poorly equipped for adding a bar. LaFollette's business cards read "Proprietor, Janitor, Yeast Farmer" as a joke, but they also conveyed a literal truth. Through the first few years of Blank Slate's existence, the brewery only had two employees, counting LaFollette. Already straining resources to open and start brewing, it simply wasn't feasible to modify the plans that late in the buildout. Finally, with self-deprecating humor, LaFollette announced in the fall of 2014 that after two and a half years of having "the dubious distinction of being the only (local) brewery without a taproom," Blank Slate was finally opening its Pour House, a modest serving area carved out of the front of the brewery. With seating for forty-five people, the Pour House was cozy, but at a time when Rhinegeist was planning to add a deck that could seat two hundred on top of its airplane hangar–sized taproom, "cozy" was of limited value.

In 2015, Blank Slate expanded and started canning. The business grew, but by the time all the pieces were in place, the craft beer world had changed dramatically. The floodgates had opened. New breweries were popping up at an astounding pace, many backed by millions of dollars in investment, aided by teams of marketing firms. In a city full of breweries, Blank Slate beers still stood out. Ultimately, however, exceptional beer was not enough. In the summer of 2017, the local beer world was shocked and saddened to hear that Blank Slate Brewery had closed its doors and ceased operations. Blank Slate became the first casualty of the post-2012 era.

Greg Hardman entered the craft beer business circuitously. He didn't begin as a homebrewer or a chemist. Hardman entered the beer world as a sales rep, working for a distributor that served Athens, Ohio. As a recent graduate of Ohio University, the position allowed him to remain close to friends and copious amounts of cheap beer. Hardman sold quantity, not quality. His target demographic was OU students who filled cavernous bars on penny beer nights. Ironically, however, this was an unknowing first step toward building a craft beer business. Hardman sold discount labels like Burger Beer in such high volumes that he attained legendary status at the Hudepohl Brewing Company, and he periodically visited the Cincinnati brewery. During one of these visits, Hardman watched some of the last bottles of Hudepohl brands roll off the bottling line at the West Sixth Street plant before the company was subsumed by Schoenling. Although he was from Cleveland, witnessing part of the slow death of Cincinnati's independent breweries left a deep impression, one that would eventually have profound impacts on his career and the future of Cincinnati beer.

In the intervening years, Hardman's proficiency as a salesman, innate sense of marketing, a business degree and an ample supply of confidence allowed him to climb the ranks of the beer industry, eventually becoming president and CEO of Warsteiner Importers Agency, the North American sales, marketing and operations arm of the Warsteiner Brauerei Brewery in Germany. It was a lucrative and venerated position, but Hardman wanted something else. He wanted his own empire. In the machinations that followed the sale of Moerlein and Hudepohl to the Crooked River Brewing Company in Cleveland, Hardman saw the opportunity to purchase the fledgling brands, and he did so in 2004. Although Hardman's original vision only included the craft Moerlein label, dire straits for the once-regal brands caused the Hudepohl-Schoenling portfolio to become part of the deal. Hardman purchased most of the city's best-known beer brands, and in 2008, he reunited Little Kings with its former family.

This began a reclamation of the city's brewing past. Initially running the company from an office in Middletown, Hardman restored local ownership of the Hudepohl-Schoenling brands. He then began a multi-year quest to brew Moerlein, Hudepohl and Schoenling in Cincinnati again, a process that came in several steps. The Christian Moerlein Brewing Company continued to brew its beers on a contractual basis in other states while plans were developed and executed to open a production brewery in Cincinnati. Specifically, Hardman wanted to return Moerlein and Hudepohl to their original home: Over-the-Rhine. The neighborhood was still extremely troubled at the time, boasting the highest crime rate of any neighborhood in the city. It was both risky and visionary to tie the future of the company to this location, and some of Hardman's more conservative advisors thought that he was crazy when he named the first new flagship beer brewed under the revamped Moerlein brand "Over-the-Rhine Ale" in 2007.

Hardman's commitment to the struggling neighborhood was more than the name on a label. He continued to search for the appropriate location for the company's new production facility. With the help of Michael D. Morgan—a lawyer, real estate agent and, at the time, executive director of the Over-the-Rhine Foundation—Hardman offered to buy a

The taproom at Christian Moerlein Brewing Company's production facility is located in the former Kauffman malt house, and it is representative of a unique pattern of dome, pillar and arched construction that was typical of nineteenth-century malt houses. *Photo by the author, www.queencityhistory.com.*

manufacturing building in the heart of Over-the-Rhine's Brewery District in 2009. Although it required a leap of faith, it was the perfect location in many ways. As the former Husman Potato Chip Factory, the building was zoned and certified for food and beverage production and had ample water and energy and space for commercial brewing on a large scale, including tens of thousands of square feet for future expansion. The building also encompassed the nineteenth-century Kauffman Brewery malt house, with two layers of lagering cellars below ground. This added nineteenth-century ambiance. Reaching the terms of purchase, getting signatures on a contract and closing the transaction was difficult. The owners weren't speaking to each other, and a debt collection firm in Texas owned a lien on the property that was greater than the purchase offer. Morgan (who is also the author of this book) spent more than a year and a half of pro bono work completing the transaction.

After all parties agreed on a purchase price, the bank that was supposed to be providing the loan quit returning Morgan's calls. Morgan then found a new lender, a private investor, and held the deal together until 1621–23

Moore Street became the new Cincinnati home of the Christian Moerlein Brewing Company, which also encompassed the Hudepohl-Schoenling Brewing Company. Hardman announced his intent to move all brewing operations to the facility but explained that the process would take time. The first beer produced in the 125,000-square-foot building was brewed in a small, homebrew-sized system in a tiny corner of the future brewhouse. Brewed for Arnold's Bar & Grill, where the first keg of Christian Moerlein Select had been delivered by horse and wagon in 1981, the March 22, 2013 tapping of Arnold's 1861 Porter marked a humble next step in the gradual homecoming for the Moerlein and Hudepohl brands.

Hardman was doing something extremely ambitious: he was opening two breweries at once. The high-profile Moerlein Lagerhouse on the riverfront drew a lot more attention than the production brewery. Located within the forty-five-acre Cincinnati Riverfront Park, the Lagerhouse began with a partnership between Christian Moerlein and the Cincinnati Parks Department. The company signed a forty-year lease for the site of the $4 million brewpub. Cincinnati Riverfront Park was designed to be self-funding, and Moerlein's annual rent was essential to making the park's financial plan work. In return, the Parks Department provided Moerlein with one of the city's best pieces of real estate, next to Great American Ballpark, south of the Banks, a few blocks east of Paul Brown Stadium and facing the beautiful Smale Riverfront Park, the river and the Roebling Suspension Bridge.

After several construction delays, the Moerlein Lagerhouse opened in early 2012. Featuring panoramic views from all four sides of the two-story structure and an indoor-outdoor combination of 1,100 seats, the Lagerhouse was not a typical brewpub, and the man in charge of the five-thousand-barrel production brewery was not a standard-issue brewer. Richard Dube, the brewmaster who would oversee production at the facility, was nationally known and respected. A French Canadian by birth and a microbiologist by training, Dube previously worked for Molson and Labatt's and headed brewing operations for Boston Beer Company during the years that it turned Samuel Adams into a household name. Dube quit brewing and became a high school teacher for a while, but he was inspired to get back into the game when he saw Hardman's nationwide search for a brewmaster.

Once the Lagerhouse opened, Hardman turned his attentions back to the production facility in Over-the-Rhine, finishing improvements and buildout, installing a brewhouse and beginning the multi-stage process of brewing the city's classic brands in Cincinnati again. In addition to reinventing the

Moerlein craft brand, Hardman also revived beloved non-craft labels like Hudy 14-K and Burger, as well as releasing a new Hudepohl Amber Lager. Along the way, he leveraged nostalgia on several occasions, including the 2015 release of HuDey. Christening himself a "modern-day beer baron," and rarely missing an opportunity to add a beaver fur top hat to a tux, Hardman has been a relentless self-promoter, and he has never suffered from a lack of confidence. In 2010, he vowed to extend Little Kings distribution to virtually all the lower forty-eight states and then to use the brand as a distribution base for the Hudepohl, Burger and Moerlein labels, essentially reinstating the solid but botched plan that accompanied the Hudepohl-Schoenling merger in the late 1980s.

Moerlein remains a major player in the craft beer business, and the company is diversified with economy labels. Under Hardman's tenure, the Christian Moerlein name has found a footing in almost every beer industry business model employed over the past forty years. The production brewery in Over-the-Rhine is attempting to revive the glory days of Hudepohl-Schoenling as a regional brewer, while also operating a taproom in the post-2012 model, and the Moerlein Lagerhouse has taken the brewpub of the 1980s and '90s into a new stratosphere. In addition, Hardman's approach to the craft beer business, basing the image of the company on the resurrection of a proud past, has been unique, and the company's commitment to Over-the-Rhine and the preservation of the city's brewing heritage has been laudable. For all these reasons (and a few more), Moerlein doesn't fit neatly into one of the modern eras of craft beer. The company straddles the pre- and post-2012 eras, and with Hardman leading the band, Moerlein tends to walk to the beat of its own drummer.

Mad Tree Brewing Company, by contrast, clearly belongs to the most recent wave of craft breweries. Mad Tree defined and set the bar for the post-2012 taproom era of local beer—although that wasn't the original plan. Mad Tree brewers and owners Kenny McNutt and Brady Duncan met at Beer of the Week Club, a casual gathering of friends and acquaintances who came together with new or eclectic brews that they would sample and discuss, sort of like a book club with less reading and a lot more drinking. In truth, it sounded kind of lame to Brady, and he had to be talked into going. Fortunately for Cincinnati beer drinkers, peer pressure worked. Brady and Kenny met at Beer of the Week, became friends, kept expanding their palates and started to homebrew, separately at first. Mad Tree's story doesn't start with prodigies. McNutt and Duncan took the long, unappetizing trip through batch after batch of awful beer that most homebrewers walk in the beginning. Duncan recalled buying supplies for a batch of Oktoberfest at Listermann Brewing Supply. The staff at Listermann explained that since the style was a lager, it would need to be fermented at refrigerated temperatures. That was, however, inconvenient, so Brady ignored the advice and produced an undrinkable soup. Homebrewing together, Duncan and McNutt invested in better equipment, learned from their mistakes and eventually started to make great beer.

As they grew more passionate about the hobby and more proficient at brewing, McNutt and Duncan started to dream about opening their own brewery. Around 2010, this talk graduated from idle conversation into a committed vision. Although they lacked professional brewing experience, McNutt and Duncan had impressive credentials. McNutt held a BS in computer engineering and an MA in electrical engineering, and Duncan was using an academic background in public relations, marketing and an MA in enterprise integration to build a career at P&G. The future partners compiled a smart, data-based business plan and started seeking funding and investors in 2011. Although professional and well informed when dealing with bankers who didn't understand the potential of the industry, McNutt and Duncan took a novel approach with private investors: honesty. They brought great beer to prospective investor meetings, shared a few, laid out the plan and the possibilities and then told their prospects, "There is a decent chance you're going to lose your money."

It was true. There were real risks, but Mad Tree caught hold and grew like a wildfire. McNutt and Duncan were overwhelmed by the support of the community. They brewed exceptional beer and people drank it—a lot of it. Mad Tree's original five-year plan called for annual production to reach 9,500 barrels per year, relying on distribution in six or seven states to reach this goal, but a year after opening in 2013, it was already producing more than 11,000 barrels annually, selling all of it locally and having trouble keeping up with demand. Taprooms were still cost-prohibitive in Ohio when McNutt and Duncan wrote their original business plan, but they revised the vision with the change in the law. Buying cheap used furniture and pouring a sealed concrete bar top themselves, they built out the original taproom for about $10,000, and the surrounding community started filling it nightly.

Three years after opening, Mad Tree saw the need for massive expansion. The company purchased a derelict manufacturing facility in Oakley for a reported $3.55 million and began an $18 million project to transform the space into roughly fifty thousand square feet of brewhouse and taproom space, with a ten-thousand-square-foot beer garden. It was a huge step up. Despite tripling the size of the taproom, thirsty crowds braved inclement weather to stand in long lines just to get into the maxed-to-capacity brewery in the weeks after Mad Tree 2.0 opened.

Several factors explain Mad Tree's success. Duncan and McNutt are smart businessmen who have surrounded themselves with good partners and advisers. Mad Tree was born from a realistic plan, and as the brewery began to succeed, the owners reinvested heavily in the future of the business. They also possess a true passion for beer, a commitment to quality and a desire to keep innovating. Many breweries—from the 1850s to last week— suffer a deficiency in one aspect of this formula or the other. Mad Tree has also benefited from some serendipity and a little luck. The original brewery location offered good space and affordable rent and sat over an aquifer that allowed the brewery to access its own well water.

Unlike the John Walker Brewery or Burger Brewing Company before it, Mad Tree did not rely on the mineral content of its well water to affect the flavor of its beers, not directly at least. Working with well water allowed Mad Tree's brewers to gain a valuable education in how to strip a water supply down to its purest form and then rebuild the mineral content to compliment individual styles and beers. Starting each beer with decisions about the content of the water is part of what allows Mad Tree to brew a wide range of styles and distinct flavors. Mad Tree also benefited from fortunate timing. Duncan and McNutt had the opportunity to modify their original plans to include a taproom and open while modern taprooms were still a novelty. It also became the first craft brewery in the state to can its beer, a move that bucked the historic stigma of cans.

By 2018, Mad Tree was producing roughly 29,000 barrels of beer per year, packing its taproom and distributing in Ohio, Kentucky and eastern Tennessee. The current facility, however, can be expanded to reach a capacity of 180,000 barrels. Local distribution has remained strong despite unprecedented levels of competition, and by the fall of 2018, Mad Tree was on its way to becoming one of the top ten selling craft beers in the state of Tennessee. McNutt and Duncan have also attributed part of the success of the business to a skilled, dedicated staff and a family atmosphere.

Competition grew quickly. One year after Mad Tree opened, partners Bob Bonder and Bryant Goulding were implementing a plan to turn 250,000 square feet of the nineteenth-century Christian Moerlein Brewery's bottling plant into the Rhinegeist Brewing Company. If Rhinegeist lacked some of the romance of the breweries that preceded it, nobody cared. Bonder was president of a coffee shop chain. He possessed a lot of business savvy and specific knowledge of distribution networks. Goulding, who relocated from California, brought a wealth of knowledge about the craft beer industry with him from the West Coast. Chemist Jim Matt was recruited to fill the role of head brewer. More importantly, Rhinegeist rolled into Cincinnati's Brewery District with truckloads of capital.

J.R. "Eddie" Orton III left Cincinnati for California decades ago, but he retained a fondness for his old hometown as he built Orton Development Inc. According to its website, Orton "has specialized in large-scale, highly challenging rehabilitation and redevelopment projects" since 1984. The abandoned and neglected Moerlein bottling plant epitomized this mission when Orton Development purchased the property in 2008. It was particularly fortunate for Cincinnati that Orton owned the property when a portion of it burst into flames on January 8, 2010. It took firefighters more than three hours to tame the blaze, and it was necessary to tamp down flareups for the next few days. If the building had been locally owned and uninsured, it would have been demolished, and a critical piece of Cincinnati's brewing history would have been lost. Orton, however, held the resources and the knowledge to save the former Elm Street Club (typically misidentified as the former Moerlein cooperage or "barrel house"). It was also fortunate that Orton's projects have historically been self-funded, eliminating the need to find visionary bankers, which are roughly as common as flying pigs. Orton envisioned a brewery in the building and, after considering several options, struck a deal with Bonder and Goulding.

Through this combination of capital and professional knowledge, Rhinegeist was born with the promise of resurrecting Over-the-Rhine's brewing heyday. When it opened its doors to the public in June 2013, Rhinegeist appeared to be a different animal. The taproom was mammoth. Within eighteen months, Rhinegeist amped up production from roughly 3,600 barrels per year to more than 10,000. In December 2014, the company became the first to donate funds to the controversial streetcar project, volunteering an annual contribution of $5,000 to support operation. It was a philanthropic act but also one that was clearly in Rhinegeist's best interest. As the northern end of the streetcar route, Rhinegeist accurately predicted that the streetcar would "transport more beer fanatics to our brewery." It did—tens of thousands of them. Rhinegeist bought the brewery property from Orton Development for $4.2 million and then invested an additional $2.2 million into expanding

Rhinegeist Brewing Company opened in the former Christian Moerlein bottling plant in 2013 and later expanded into the adjacent Elm Street Club (which is frequently called the former Moerlein barrel house). *Photo by the author, www.queencityhistory.com.*

production capacity and further renovations. In 2015, expansion permitted the brewery to roughly triple production, brewing around thirty thousand barrels. With lines out of the door of its cavernous taproom, Rhinegeist also added a seven-thousand-square-foot rooftop deck. In addition, the once-endangered Elm Street Club portion of the complex was converted into a special event center and an independent restaurant.

While Rhinegeist was busy printing money in its taproom, most of the business's growth was occurring in the wholesale market. Mt. Carmel owner Mike Dewey and Rivertown co-owner Jason Roeper both attributed their relationship with distributors for much of their success—if not for their sanity. Distributors are the traditional means of getting beer into bars and stores. They have the connections, sales staff, trucks and drivers to make expansion much easier. This middleman's role, of course, comes with a cut of the profit. If you're Mike Dewey, who sometimes worked seventeen-hour days—partly because he had to sell and service all his own accounts—a good relationship with a distributor is a life-changing moment. Rhinegeist, however, went a different route. It possessed both the wherewithal and the foresight to begin self-distribution. This is one of multiple decisions that helped transform Rhinegeist from one of the city's largest craft breweries into a seemingly unstoppable force of nature. As the craft beer market became increasingly crowded, breweries had to accept being just one of several—eventually many—local craft brews sold by their distributor. Rhinegeist, by contrast, employed a sales staff to sell and deliver one brand of beer: Rhinegeist. The brewery has also continued to expand its reach in multiple states through traditional distributorship. In 2017, Rhinegeist was the largest craft brewery in Greater Cincinnati, producing a reported seventy thousand barrels annually.

From Mike Dewey turning his basement hobby into a profitable brewery to the meteoric rise of Mad Tree and Rhinegeist, it started to appear to a lot of people that it was impossible *not* to get rich running a brewery. Somewhere around 2014, the market began to look as lucrative as it did to men like George Herancourt, Christian Moerlein, Paul Andress, Frank Linck and dozens of other aspiring beer barons in the 1850s. The floodgates opened. This is the point in the story where the scope of this book compels the author to overlook a lot of amazing people, inventive breweries and delicious beers. According to a list compiled by www.CincyWeekend.com, Greater Cincinnati was home to around fifty-four breweries by the fall of 2018, with several more in some stage of development or construction. By necessity, the post-2012 history of local beer will mention a few additional breweries and leave exploration of the rest up to thirsty readers.

While nationally renowned brewmaster Richard Dube enjoyed the cumbersome title of "Vice President of Brewing and Quality" at Christian Moerlein, he tried to recruit Evan Rouse to the Moerlein team on four separate occasions. Rouse declined each time. Although decidedly different in age, Dube was familiar with Rouse from homebrew competitions and other brewing circles. Years before, Evan Rouse accompanied his father, Greg Rouse, on a trip to drop his brother, Jake, off at college. Afterward, they stopped into a brewpub for lunch. Evan was just sixteen, so he couldn't order a beer, but he was fascinated by the scrver's explanation of the brewing process and the way that breweries created different styles. On the way home, the millennial used his iPhone to order a homebrew kit, and with parental consent, he began brewing in the family's garage. Starting to learn the art at such a young age, Rouse was brewing excellent beers while he was still a minor.

Braxton Brewing Company opened with its industrial garage motif in 2015, bringing brewing back to the city of Covington and rapidly rising in sales. *Photo by the author, www. queencityhistory.com.*

Rouse became an assistant brewmaster at Hofbrauhaus Newport. While he held this position, Dube tried to bring him onto his team, recognizing a promising protégé. That didn't happen. Instead, Dube resigned from his position at Moerlein in 2014, and Rouse asked him to become a partner in a new brewery. Aside from Dube, the new brewery was largely a family affair. Evan's father, a vice-president at dunnhumby USA, helped bring valuable connections to the project, and brother Jake eventually became the CEO. The brewery's name, Braxton, came from Braxton Drive, the address of the Rouse home in Union, Kentucky, where Evan began homebrewing.

Before Braxton opened, Jake Rouse told the *Cincinnati Enquirer*, "The people who are leading the craft-beer movement, and who are passionate about unique and hand-crafted beer, are also the same people who are really involved in this startup and technology revolution." Although this might have come as a surprise to the dozens of local brewers who entered the tactile, sensory art of brewing largely to avoid being tied to smartphones and computer screens, it accurately distinguished the brewery's philosophy from many others. Naashom Marx, the City of Covington's business development manager, predicted that Braxton would "provide the space for [tech] geniuses to connect on a different level." The taproom was designed with corporate "innovation spaces" in mind and was equipped with iPhone and Android chargers.

Keith Neltner, a brilliant local artist and designer, gave Braxton a logo and look that elaborated on its garage motif, and the taproom had a distinct feel when it opened in 2015. As for the beer, Evan Rouse explained that the brewery was "aiming for multiplicity," with the goal of brewing "just about everything under the sun." In the time since, Braxton has remained true to this vision, brewing a wide array of creative offerings, including several brewed in partnership with Cincinnati-based Graeter's Ice Cream. Braxton has also remained true to its vision for its taproom, which became a communal gathering and workspace, with the feel of a coffee shop in the early hours of the day. Braxton had an impact beyond itself, serving as a cornerstone and a catalyst for the rapid redevelopment of the Covington business district that surrounds it.

In May 2017, Braxton opened a second location in Bellevue, Kentucky, called Braxton Labs (located behind Party Source). Braxton took over the former Ei8ht Ball Brewery space, including its forty-tap bar, and has been using it as innovation and experimentation space for the brewery, as well as a way of carrying a lot of intriguing and unusual guest taps. CEO Jake Rouse seemed prophetic when he announced, "We're going to run [Braxton] a lot like a technology company. And quite frankly, there's nothing growing as fast as beer, other than technology." In the time since, he seems to have been proven correct on both counts. It is unclear what this means for the future of beer, but by all outward appearances, it has worked well for Braxton. The tech-centric brewery with its ironic industrial theme is continuing to spread its footprint while retaining and growing a loyal consumer base. Tech probably plays a role, but good beer doesn't hurt.

As a local craft beer pioneer at Rivertown, Randy Schiltz reentered brewing on his own terms in the post-2012 era, giving Newport its first locally owned craft brewery in the process. He was originally from Kansas, and craft beer played no role in Schiltz's formative years. As a young adult working in Europe, it was an English bitter that changed his perception of beer. He realized that it could be light-bodied, refreshing and still full of flavor, and he was hooked—love at first sip. Later, while living in California, Randy fed his thirst for great beer, but his income hadn't quite caught up with his palate, so Schiltz decided to start homebrewing because he loved both good beer and saving money. Brewing remained nothing more than

Randy Schiltz explains the brewing process to University of Cincinnati students who are touring the brewery as part of the course "Hops & History." Wooden Cask opened in 2016 and features English-, Irish- and Scottish-style ales. *Photo by Mickey Edwards.*

a hobby as Schiltz climbed the professional ranks at Toyota, a career that brought his family and him to Greater Cincinnati. Frustrated with the chain of command in his corporate management gig, Schiltz took a leap of faith, left a lucrative job and turned a brief acquaintance with Jason Roeper into a new plan for the future. Schiltz and Roeper built Rivertown and grew a reputation for making great beer. When that partnership came to an end in 2014, Schiltz started looking for a location to open a brewery that was true to his own vision.

Focusing his search in Northern Kentucky, Schiltz found the right location at 629 York Street in Newport. Built in 1887, the building was an infamous 1980s punk rock bar and later home to the Yellow Cab company. Old and poorly maintained, it was a building with a lot of potential and a lot of problems. With the help and saintly support of wife Karen Schiltz, Randy worked exhausting days swinging sledgehammers, ripping up old bowling lanes (and repurposing them as tabletops in the taproom), driving a forklift and installing equipment. Finally, in the fall of 2016, Schiltz had built the brewery that he wanted—largely with his own hands.

Wooden Cask Brewing Company specializes in English, Scottish, Irish and some traditional German styles, with a particular focus on variations from northern England, where brews like brown ales and porters are lighter and crisper than their southern relatives. Wooden Cask does not share the same luck of timing that Schiltz had in his previous venture. Rather than facing two or three serious regional competitors, Wooden Cask swims in a crowded sea, but the brewery has maintained disciplined quality standards and has remained true to its vision. Growth has been gradual but steady, which is basically the plan. In 2016, Schiltz told the *Cincinnati Enquirer*, "I would rather move slowly in the right direction than blaze out in the wrong direction....Brewing beer should be about fun." Although, as Schiltz knows quite well, it is also about a massive amount of hard work. Wooden Cask entered the Ohio market in the summer of 2018.

West Side Brewing Company opened in 2017. Brian Willett, his uncle Jim Remmel and cousin Kurtis Remmel, all West Siders, partnered with Joe Mumper, a Newport resident with a successful background in venue and event management. Locating in Westwood was integral to the vision and identity of the brewery, and West Side's affection for its neighborhood has been reciprocated. Rather than carving out a niche with creative variations or uncommon brews, the brewery has focused on producing consistent, exceptional examples of traditional styles. Similar to Brink Brewing

West Side Brewing Company opened in 2017, was embraced by the community and quickly gained a reputation for making quality, traditional beers. *Photo by the author, www. queencityhistory.com.*

Company in College Hill, West Side is proud to be an integral cornerstone to broader neighborhood revitalization. However, the brewery also began canning and exporting to the east side of the Western Hills Viaduct as well as Kentucky in 2018.

As the number of regional breweries has exploded, it has forced new breweries to think much more critically about what sets them apart from the pack than was necessary in earlier years. Some may have mapped out a course for longevity by intentionally staying small, at least for the near term. Brink Brewing appears to have no immediate goals of growing beyond a vibrant neighborhood bar that brews great beers. There is a lot more room in the market for this business model than there is for dozens of startups whose owners all plan to become billionaires with national distribution, and Brink's philosophy portends a future full of neighborhood breweries. Woodburn Brewing has also been part of a neighborhood renaissance in Walnut Hills, carving out a niche by brewing extremely creative brews and uncommon styles. Off Track Brewery, in north Over-the-Rhine, is following a different model but also plans to stay small. Off Track started in 2018 with a nano system, and by the

In 2018, Jon and Betsy Newberry completed a multi-year journey to revive one of the region's most revered local brands when they opened the Wiedemann Brewing Company, producing craft beer and serving traditional bar food in a former St. Bernard funeral home. *Photo by the author, www.queencityhistory.com.*

end of the year, it was self-distributing to one account, the Dunlap Café, Over-the-Rhine's last dive bar and Off Track's de facto taproom.

Jon and Betsy Newberry took a page from Greg Hardman's playbook by reviving a classic regional brand. In 2018, after several years of looking for a location and seeking financing, they opened the Wiedemann Brewery in St. Bernard. Located in a former funeral home, it combines a production brewery with warm, historic space, great bar food and a revival of Wiedemann's long history. Although Wiedemann opened with a wide variety of styles, the Newberrys were most excited about brewing the beer that made pre-Prohibition Wiedemann such a respected brand, a true Bohemian pilsner.

Whether the strategy is to focus on styles that other people either aren't making or aren't making particularly well, brewing creative variations on traditional styles, staking the future on doing classic beers better than the rest of the crowd, diversifying into other products, staying small, growing quickly or building huge taprooms, local breweries can no longer simply make good beer. They need to have a solid plan to succeed—or survive. When Paul Miller, a former Ringling Bros. clown, decided to open a circus-themed brewery in Ludlow, Kentucky, he conducted a nationwide search for a brewer. Several whom he met with were dismissive, derisively telling him that his brewery was based on a gimmick. Miller's reply was, "Of course it's a gimmick." From Miller's perspective, every brewery opening today is looking for a way to set itself apart from the herd. They're all looking for a gimmick. Miller is just more honest about it—and good at it. Additionally, and critically, the brewery is dedicated to producing great beer, including lagers, Belgians and some styles that have traditionally been uncommon in the local craft lineup. People may take the trip to Ludlow for the novelty of watching the bartender balance a keg on his chin or eat fire, but they stay for the beer—and to see what crazy thing comes next.

URBAN ARTIFACT BREWS
A 150-YEAR-OLD BEER

Some breweries are meticulously planned. Some are serendipitous. Urban Artifact's origin story is both. Bret Kollmann Baker and Scotty Hunter met at Ohio University. Bret made an announcement to a chemical engineering class that he planned to start a homebrewing club, and Scotty became one of three dependable members. They started brewing OU style—in the front yard of an old house. They drank too much and shared a dream of opening a brewery, but they both graduated with serious degrees and got adult jobs. They also both left the state of Ohio. Bret lived in Kansas City and then upstate New York. Scotty moved to Arkansas, but they stayed in touch. Both hated working for big corporations, so plans to open a brewery started to become much more earnest.

Kollmann Baker and Hunter realized that by 2013, a brewery needed to fill an underserved niche to have the best chance at success. Sour beers were not their first thought. They considered focusing on craft lagers, styles that have been traditionally underrepresented in the craft beer revolution of the 2000s. Geography was also a factor. They weren't inherently tied to any location, and they observed a dearth of craft breweries in the southeastern United States. Cincinnati was one city that they considered among many, until Cincinnati chose them.

In 2014, Stephanie Kollmann Baker finished graduate school. She and her husband, Bret, carved out the time to hike the length of the Appalachian Trail, starting in the Northeast. They didn't finish the trip because Bret bought a brewery somewhere around Connecticut. That's the serendipitous part. Scott Hand, one of Urban Artifact's three owners, also dreamed of opening a brewery, but beer was just part of his vision. He wanted to build the city's best live music venue. After considering the Jackson Brewery building in Over-the-Rhine, Hand and his partners homed in on a historic church in Northside. St. Patrick's Church was for sale, and it seemed to be a perfect match for Hand's vision. The sanctuary provided dramatic space for live music. The former Catholic school gymnasium had most recently served as a commercial bakery, meaning that it had much of the infrastructure needed to become a commercial brewery, and the school cafeteria looked like a good taproom and smaller music venue. It also included a rental property, a beer garden–sized yard and a parking lot. Hand and his two partners made an offer. It was accepted, and they were approved for a loan to purchase the property and build out a brewery with a taproom and music venue. Then Hand's capital partner dropped out of the deal two days before it was scheduled to close. He got an extension on the contract but was in a precarious predicament. After his offer to buy St. Patrick's had been accepted, the owner received a much better backup offer. She wanted the deal with Hand to fall through, and the clock was ticking.

Hand turned to social media, taking an unlikely scatter shot at finding a substitute for his former partner. Bret Kollmann Baker and Scotty Hunter didn't know Scott Hand, but they had a mutual friend who tagged them in a post. Scotty investigated, sharing some spotty communications with Bret, and he also met with Scott Hand. Hunter shared a business plan with Hand for a brewery featuring wild yeast and sour beers. The plan was well thought-out, including Bret's method for brewing sours and the reasons why Bret and Scotty had concluded that sour beers were part of a future trend in the industry. Everything fell into place, except for the fact that Kollmann Baker was somewhere in the wilderness with extremely limited cell service. When he passed through the next town on the trail, Bret found an increasingly frantic set of messages from Hunter. The Kollmann Bakers abandoned their plans to hike to Georgia and caught a flight to Cincinnati. Kollmann Baker and Hunter cashed out their 401k accounts and borrowed money from family and friends, and a week and a half later they owned an abandoned church in a partnership with virtual strangers.

There were a lot of ways that this could have gone horribly wrong, but Hand, Hunter and Kollmann Baker each fell into his own role, including a lot of work that wasn't in the original vision. Scotty took over sales. Scott

Urban Artifact Brewing Company opened with the mission of brewing wild yeast and sour beers in the former St. Patrick's Church in Northside in 2015. *Photo by the author, www. queencityhistory.com.*

Hand was the architect and general contractor, built the music component of the plan and began designing all the brewery's labels and marketing pieces. Bret worked long days as a laborer before he could put his brewing knowledge to work. Less than nine months after purchasing the property, Urban Artifact served its first beers in April 2015. Timing both challenged and helped Artifact. It opened as the wave of local brewery startups was just beginning to swell into a tsunami, a time when distributors weren't overwhelmed with new labels yet but after the post-2012 sweet spot when it looked like owning a brewery was a guaranteed route to riches. Initially, Urban Artifact also struggled with the knowledge and tastes of consumers. Some adjustments in the beers were driven by the market, but the market itself also changed. Kollmann Baker accurately predicted that sours were the future in 2014. By 2018, the most common theme among the region's breweries was a plan to start offering sours or to expand their sour lineups. Locally, Artifact was comfortably—sometimes *uncomfortably*—ahead of this trend. The brewery built a niche on a Midwest fruit tart style. Never using anything but fresh fruit in its beers, Artifact built a loyal following and a stellar reputation.

Bret caught the *Brettanomyces* ("wild yeast") that Urban Artifact used in its first beers by climbing into the church bell tower and leaving a jar of wort covered in a cheesecloth there long enough to capture wild, airborne yeast. Capturing useable "wild yeast" and the *Lactobacillus* (a bacteria that produces lactic acid) that is often used as a souring agent in beers involves patience—and a willingness to smell and taste dozens of jars filled with unknown bacteria and fungi. Kollmann Baker estimated that, on average, out of one hundred jars of wort placed in an environment where the brewer hopes to capture wild yeast, fewer than three jars ultimately capture something useable, a strain that will ferment and that contains pleasant, fruity notes. The rest either taste bad or get ruled out by aroma, smells that Bret describes as "baby diaper, electrical fire, or vomit." A chemical engineering degree and an impressive career background help make Kollmann Baker a consummate professional as a brewer, as well as a bit of a perfectionist, but there is also something about his process for collecting yeast and a volatile streak that gives him a "mad scientist" vibe. That made Kollmann Baker the perfect person to brew a beer with a pre-Prohibition yeast strain, brought back from the dead Frankenstein-style.

THE AUTHOR LAPSES INTO FIRST PERSON

I'm part of this story, and I don't want to rely on the uncomfortable, cringe-inducing practice of referring to myself in the third person to tell it. I teach a course called "Hops & History" at the University of Cincinnati. The class tours several active breweries during the semester, always ending with Urban Artifact. After class is dismissed, I often remain and abuse Bret Kollmann Baker's hospitality. Following class in 2017, our conversation led to an unlikely adventure. I told Bret about a wooden fermenting vat that had been found in a previously sealed-off lagering cellar on Race Street. The vat itself was a mystery. Long since stripped of the ammonia-based cooling systems that kept Cincinnati's lagering cellars a dry, cool, constant temperature, the cellars are now humid and damp much of the year. Several contain remnants of aging barrels or wood infrastructure, but it has all rotted into black, moist lumps, unidentifiable except for context and telltale pieces of rusting metal. Yet somehow, when Model Management Group knocked through a bricked-up doorway during redevelopment of 1818–24 Race Street, it discovered a solid, intact wooden fermenting vat sitting in a sealed and forgotten subbasement lagering cellar.

The cellar was constructed by the F.&J.A. Linck Brewery around 1855. After the brewery went out of business in 1860–61, it was leased to a collection of rival brewers through 1873 (see the chapter "Some Beer Bubbles Aren't Just in Your Head"). After that, the history of the cellars gets fuzzy. The ground-level malt house was razed and replaced with a large tenement building in the 1870s, and the cellars were eventually sealed off. Model found the additional story under its building by happenstance. It punched through the passageway to the cellars hoping to find an empty building cavity that could be used to run mechanical systems to the upper floors.

After several delicious Artifact brews, Bret sparked my curiosity by speculating that, although highly unlikely, yeast could have survived in this mysterious, mid-nineteenth-century fermenting vat. On April 25, 2017, with Model Management's consent, I descended into the former F.&J.A. Linck Brewery cellars with Bret Kollmann Baker, Artifact head brewer Josh Elliott and George Burpee, along with Dan Phenicie, Drew Money and the rest of a crew from 7/79 Video, a production company that agreed to film this wild goose chase out of a combination of friendship, curiosity, professional boredom and the promise of free beer. The men from Artifact scraped and swabbed the inside of the vat and spigots, pulled small splinters of wood from crevices and pulled samples from various surfaces in the surrounding cellar. All these potential sources of either *Lactobacillus* or *Brettanomyces* were placed into mason jars of wort and sealed.

Roughly six months later, Bret, Josh and I met in the Urban Artifact taproom to unseal and test the more than one hundred different samples. Many simply tasted like wort, meaning that they weren't fermenting. Others smelled vile—baby diaper, vomit, etc.—and some had ominously turned black, indicating a potentially hazardous bacterium. If samples showed signs of carbonation and smelled okay, we tasted them. Roughly a dozen of the best candidates were then allowed to ferment for several more months before Kollmann Baker and Elliott narrowed down the best three possibilities. These samples were shipped off to Omega Yeast, a Chicago beer yeast lab, to be DNA tested and assessed for viability.

In late March 2018, Kollmann Baker and Elliott from Urban Artifact, Dan Phenicie, Drew Money and Adam Rabinowitz from 7/79 Video and I all took a road trip to Chicago to get the results. On the way, we discussed the likelihood that one of these three samples contained a useable yeast strain. Bret and Josh both agreed that it was highly unlikely that they had captured

Author Michael D. Morgan, lead brewer Joshua Elliott and brewmaster and co-owner of Urban Artifact Bret Kollmann Baker sample jars of wort that have been aged with wild yeast as well as a variety of other unknown fungi and microorganisms to determine which samples have the potential to ferment and to produce a drinkable beer. *7/79 Video.*

good "wild yeast," and it was almost statistically impossible that they had found a living, viable beer yeast strain that had somehow survived from the days when the cellar was full of fermenting and aging beer. Nevertheless, Omega Yeast's tests concluded that one of the three sample jars contained a previously unidentified strain of *Saccharomyces cerevisiae*—brewer's yeast. The test could not date the yeast, making the true era of its origin unknown, and it wasn't clear how this yeast strain could have survived for generations in the conditions where it was found. But that's what appeared to have happened.

Urban Artifact used the yeast to brew a golden, sour version of a Maibock (a German-style beer that is traditionally released in late spring). Cincinnatians got their first taste of the beer at a limited release of the test batch on November 9, 2018. Based on its mysterious origins, as well as the name of the F.&J.A. Linck Brewery, the beer was christened "Missing Linck." While the Christian Moerlein Brewing Company and the Wiedemann Brewing Company have restored iconic brand names, Urban Artifact may have resurrected a living piece of beer history.

BACK TO THE GIANT WITH THE AXE

What does history tell us about the future of local beer? Your guess is as good as mine. If you were paying attention, you saw parallels between the past and today. The total number of breweries in Greater Cincinnati capped out at around thirty-six prior to Prohibition. That occurred in 1860, the pinnacle of the lager gold rush that started a decade earlier. In the years that followed, some breweries grew, many went bankrupt and this peak number of individual breweries was not reached again until around 2016. Post-Prohibition, there was a second rise and fall of local beer. In 2018, the number of regional breweries had risen to more than fifty and climbing. Craft beer is currently in an era that resembles the 1850s in some remarkable and disturbing ways. Beer has gotten rapidly better. Some new beer barons have arisen. Fortunes have been made, and this has contributed to an explosion of startup breweries.

You may have noticed a few eerie similarities between some nineteenth-century brewers and some of the modern variety. If history is a guide, what will happen in the coming years is that a few breweries will continue to grow. As they do, some will level off and hang on for a while, and others will die. Eventually, the multinational, multibillion-dollar brewing conglomerates will consume or crush local craft beer across America, similar to the way that large national breweries destroyed regional brands in the twentieth century. If history repeats itself, there is a bloodbath ahead, but history never really repeats itself. It's full of cycles and repetitive trends and behaviors, but they always play out a little differently each time around. Rarely, but sometimes revolutions succeed where others failed, bringing permanent change. That's what needs to happen if we expect to maintain the wealth of local breweries that we beer lovers have been blessed with at this moment in time. That is going to require Americans to act in unprecedented ways. We'll have to be more supportive and loyal to local breweries than we were to local hardware or grocery stores. However, if there are two things certain about the moment that we're living in, it is 1) beer has never been better, and 2) it's impossible to predict the future. Every day that beer reaches new heights, the world keeps getting weirder. My advice is to savor the moment and support your local brewery, and if you see Big Beer step off against the wall and raise its axe, grab as much beer as you can save and run.

SELECT BIBLIOGRAPHY

For space concerns, extensive, meticulous citations of anonymous newspaper articles and advertisements have been jettisoned from this bibliography. Exclusions include items from the following papers: *Cincinnati Commercial*, *Cincinnati Daily-Enquirer*, *Cincinnati Enquirer*, *Cincinnati Post*, *Courier-Journal* (Louisville, KY), *Daily Courier* (Louisville, KY), *Daily-American* (Nashville, TN), *Daily-Union-and-American* (Nashville, TN), *Detroit-Daily-Free-Press* (hopefully self-explanatory), *Louisville Daily Journal* (ditto), *Evansville Daily Journal* (Evansville, IN), *Nashville-Whig*, *New Orleans Daily Crescent*, *New York Daily Times* and *Richmond Enquirer* (Richmond, VA). This book has also made liberal use of Hamilton County Probate Court, Estate Records and Will Records and the Hamilton County Recorder, specifically its Deed Records, Lease Records, Mortgage Records and Misc. Records. A complete bibliography can be found at www.QueenCityHistory.com.

Armon, Rick. "Ohio Alcohol Makers Rise." *Cincinnati Enquirer*, November 20, 2011.

Bernard-Kuhn, Lisa. "Brew Pub Postponed." *Cincinnati Enquirer*, September 17, 2011.

———. "City and Moerlein Brewing Up a Deal." *Cincinnati Enquirer*, June 25, 2010.

———. "Soon, Riverfront Park Will Take Us to the River." *Cincinnati Enquirer*, February 7, 2011.

Campbell, Polly. "New Era Brewing: It's Time to Raise a Stein to Local Oktoberfest Beers." *Cincinnati Enquirer*, September 12, 2012.
————. "New Microbrewery Planned for Next Year." *Cincinnati Enquirer*, November 18, 2011.
Cincinnati Enquirer. "Christian Moerlein's Head Brewer Leaves Company." "Business in Brief," March 1, 2014.
————. "Rhinegeist Brewery to Open with Party Next Saturday." "New & Noted," June 21, 2013.
Cincinnati Post. "Prodigal Beer Welcomed by Happy Nation: Brew Legal in 19 States as 13-Year Federal Draught Is Formally Ended." April 7, 1933.
City & County Directories, 1819–1930. Public Library of Cincinnati and Hamilton County. Digital Library, retrieved from http://digital. cincinnatilibrary.org/digital/collection.
Coolidge, Sharon. "Rhinegeist Steps Up to Help with Streetcar Funding." *Cincinnati Enquirer*, December 17, 2014.
Cronin, J.F. "Good Ole Days' Eclipsed by Breweries; Cincinnati Exceeds Pre-Dry-Era Output." *Cincinnati Enquirer*. August 4, 1947.
Dowdy, Rob. "Brewery Is On Tap for Former Heritage Restaurant." *Cincinnati Enquirer*, January 28, 2012.
Drug Policy Alliance (September 2018). Drug War Statistics. www.drugpolicy. org.
Duis, Perry R. *The Saloon: Public Drinking in Chicago and Boston, 1880–1920.* Champaign: Board of Trustees of the University of Illinois, 1983.
Egner, Foster. "Newspapers Barrier to 'Bone Dry' Nation: Starch from Paper Possible Source of Alcohol, Says Brewmaster, Discussing Possibilities." *Cincinnati Post*, October 9, 1931.
Ford, Henry A., and Kate B. Ford. *History of Cincinnati, Ohio, with Illustrations and Biographical Sketches*. Cincinnati, OH: L.A. Williams & Company, 1881.
Genealogy of the Shoemaker Family of Cheltenham, Pennsylvania. North America, Family Histories, 1500–2000, via Ancestry.com, 2016.
Goelz, Carle. "Beer and Taxes: City's Brewing Is Rapidly Regaining Place as Key Industry; One-Fourth of State Supply Is Produced Here." *Cincinnati Post*, August 1, 1934, 9.
Gridley, Richard L. "Lost Ground Is Regained by Business: Industry Is Furnished Tonic by Passage of 3.2 Per Cent Beer Bill." *Cincinnati Post*, April 1, 1933, 1.
Hartman, Margaret Strebel. Campbell County Courthouse Abstracts Vol. 2. (No publisher or publication date information available.) (Copies of

original Alexandria Court Records, Campbell County, KY, 1798—1831.) Volume contained within the collection of the Kenton County Public Library, Covington, KY.

Haydu, Jeffrey. *Citizen Employers: Business Communities and Labor in Cincinnati and San Francisco, 1870–1916.* Ithaca, NY: Cornell University Press, 2008.

Holian, Timothy J. *Over the Barrel: The Brewing History and Beer Culture of Cincinnati.* Vol. 2, *Prohibition—2001.* St. Joseph, MO: Sudhaus Press, 2001.

Holthaus, David. "Brewer Succeeds in Finding a Market: Rivertown's Still Small, but Beers Are in Demand." *Cincinnati Enquirer*, April 24, 2010.

———. "Little Kings Looking to Rule Again: Local Ale Aims for Younger Crowd." *Cincinnati Enquirer*, April 4, 2010.

———. "Moerlein Redeems 2 Dreams: Lager House Pours Life into Riverfront and Reclaims City's Brewing Heritage." *Cincinnati Enquirer*, February 19, 2012.

———. "New Brewpub Draws on Local Talent." *Cincinnati Enquirer*, August 13, 2001.

———. "OTR Plant to Brew Again: Moerlein to Bring Husman Building Back to Roots." *Cincinnati Enquirer*, April 17, 2010.

———. "A Renaissance Is Brewing for Local Brands: Business' Ambitions Are No Small Beer." *Cincinnati Enquirer*, August 29, 2010.

Mains, Brian. "Listermann Brewing Co. Celebrates a Decade of Craft Beer." September 5, 2018. www.WCPO.com.

———. "MadTree Brewing's Founder on Five Years in Business: 'It's Been Insane.'" February 12, 2018. www.WCPO.com.

Mertie, Scott R. *Nashville Brewing.* Charleston, SC: Arcadia Publishing, 2006.

Morgan, Michael D., in discussion with Bret Kollmann Baker of Urban Artifact Brewing Company, September 7, 2018.

———, in discussion with Dan Listermann and Jared Lewinski of Listermann Brewing Company, September 17, 2018.

———, in discussion with Kenny McNutt and Brady Duncan of Mad Tree Brewing Company, September 17, 2018.

———, in discussion with Mike Cromer, former owner of Barrel House Brewing Company, September 6, 2018.

———, in discussion with Randy Schiltz of Wooden Cask Brewing Company, June 7, 2018.

———, in discussion with Scotty Hunter of Urban Artifact Brewing Company, October 5, 2018.

Mosher, Randy. *Tasting Beer: An Insider's Guide to the World's Greatest Drink.* China: Dai Nippon, 2009.

Nelson, S.B., and J.M. Runk. *History of Cincinnati and Hamilton County....* Cincinnati, OH: S.B. Nelson & Company, Publishers, 1894.

New in Town. "New Brewery in Northside." May 3, 2015.

Nordsieck, Joseph. "The Prohibition Crusade in Cincinnati." M.A. thesis, University of Cincinnati, 1969.

Okrent, Daniel. *Last Call: The Rise and Fall of Prohibition.* New York: Scribner, 2010.

Oliver, Garrett. *The Oxford Companion to Beer.* New York: Oxford University Press, 2012.

Owsley, Cara. "Rivertown Brewery to Open Second Location in Monroe." *Cincinnati Enquirer*, November 14, 2015.

Pichler, Josh. "Brewing Up an Example for Startup Innovation: Braxton Plans to Open in Covington in the Fall." *Cincinnati Enquirer*, April 7, 2014.

———. "Rhinegeist Bringing History to Life." *Cincinnati Enquirer*, March 10, 2013

Sorcher, David. "Rivertown Brewing Company." Metromix, June 13–19, 2012.

Southwood, John. "First (Documented) Cincinnati Brewer." Cincinnati Brewing History, 2018. www.cincinnatibrewinghistory.com.

Steigerwald, Shauna. "Beer Collaborations on Tap at Oktoberfest." *Cincinnati Enquirer*, September 15, 2017.

———. "Big Brewery Built on Owner's Big Dreams." *Cincinnati Enquirer*, January 19, 2017.

———. "Blank Slate Brewery's Business More Filling with New Taproom." *Cincinnati Enquirer*, November 29, 2014.

———. "Blank Slate Brewing Co. Closes After 5 Years." *Cincinnati Enquirer*, August 9, 2017.

———. "Braxton Brewing Announces Opening Date." *Cincinnati Enquirer*, March 6, 2015.

———. "Braxton Brewing Announces Opening of Second Location." *Cincinnati Enquirer*, May 20, 2017.

———. "Check Out Rhinegeist Rooftop Deck." *Cincinnati Enquirer*, October 31, 2015.

———. "Drink Up: Rhinegeist Tripling Production." *Cincinnati Enquirer*, March 15, 2015.

———. "Meet the Brewer: Patrick Clark." *Cincinnati Enquirer*, March 8, 2014.

———. "New MadTree Brewery Breaks Ground." *Cincinnati Enquirer*, January 7, 2016. www.cincinnati.com.

———. "Rivertown Brewing Co. Plans to Open New Monroe Brewery Jan. 20." *Cincinnati Enquirer*, January 6, 2017.

———. "Rivertown Rebrands." *Cincinnati Enquirer*, April 26, 2015.

———. "Urban Artifact Brewery Moving Forward in Northside: Historic Church Complex to Include Event Space." *Cincinnati Enquirer*, February 15, 2015.

———. "Urban Artifact Brewing Sets Tentative Opening Date." *Cincinnati Enquirer*, April 10, 2015.

———. "West Side Brewery Aims to Open in May or June: 30 Taps to Start with Mostly Guest Beers, Followed by Up to a Dozen of Their Own." *Cincinnati Enquirer*, March 4, 2017.

———. "Wooden Cask Brewing Coming to Newport." *Cincinnati Enquirer*, February 13, 2016.

Swarthmore College, Swarthmore, Pennsylvania. Genealogy of Berks. Collection: Quaker Meeting Records, call no. MR-PH 170. U.S. Quaker Meeting Records, 1681–1935. Accessed via Ancestry.com.

Thausing, Julius E., Anton Schwarz and A.H. Bauer. *Theory and Practice of the Preparation of Malt and the Fabrication of Beer*. Philadelphia: Henry Carey Baird & Company, 1882.

Tolzmann, Don Heinrich. *Christian Moerlein: The Man and His Brewery*. Milford, OH: Little Miami Publishing Company, 2012.

———. *George Wiedemann: Northern Kentucky's Beer Baron*. Milford, OH: Little Miami Publishing Company, 2015.

Tremblay, Victor J., and Carl Horton Tremblay. *The U.S. Brewing Industry: Data and Economic Analysis*. Cambridge, MA: MIT Press, 2005.

Truong, Quan. "A Blow to OTR: Brewery Was Part of Push for Renewal." *Cincinnati Enquirer*, January 10, 2010.

Van Wieren, Dale P. *American Breweries II*. West Point, PA: East Coast Brewiana Association, 1995.

Wakeland, Lisa. "Brewery Eyes Site Near Airport." *Cincinnati Enquirer*, May 28, 2011.

Wallner, Jeff. "Brewery Forges Ahead: Mt. Carmel's Variety of Craft Beers Growing throughout the Region." *Cincinnati Enquirer*, March 18, 2012.

———. "Resident Opening Brewery Near Lunken." *Cincinnati Enquirer*, April 19, 2012.

Wimberg, Robert J. *Cincinnati Breweries*. Cincinnati, OH: Ohio Book Store, 1989.

ABOUT THE AUTHOR

Michael D. Morgan, JD, is president of Queen City History & Ed., a history-focused consultancy that creates tours and events and develops content for exhibits. Morgan teaches "Hops & History" at the University of Cincinnati and serves as curator of Cincinnati's Brewing Heritage Trail. Although a reformed attorney, he occasionally backslides. Morgan is a graduate of Manchester High School, Ohio University and the University of Toledo College of Law, none of which are likely to erect a statue in his honor. After more than a decade of dedicating his life to the preservation and redevelopment of Over-the-Rhine, advocating for common-sense reform in Cincinnati's municipal government and dedicating dozens of hours a week to nonprofit work—every act of which was severely punished—Morgan now lives in exile in the relative paradise of Newport, Kentucky. He currently belongs to zero clubs or organizations, except for the Maple Avenue Happy Hour Gang, whose selfless mission is to provide economic stimulus to Newport bars and breweries every Friday of the year.

Author photo by Bob Scott.

Visit us at
www.historypress.com